What They Say about Us

"One organization with a long record of success in helping people find jobs is The Five O'Clock Club."

FORTUNE

"Many managers left to fend for themselves are turning to the camaraderie offered by [The Five O'Clock Club]. Members share tips and advice, and hear experts."

The Wall Street Journal

"If you have been out of work for some time . . . consider The Five O'Clock Club."

The New York Times

"Wendleton has reinvented the historic gentlemen's fraternal oasis and built it into a chain of strategy clubs for job seekers."

The Philadelphia Inquirer

"Organizations such as The Five O'Clock Club are building . . . an extended professional family."

Jessica Lipnack, author, *Professional Teams*

"[The Five O'Clock Club] will ask not what you do, but 'What do you want to do?' . . . [And] don't expect to get any great happy hour drink specials at this joint. The seminars are all business."

The Washington Times

"The Five O'Clock Club's proven philosophy is that job hunting is a learned skill like any other. The Five O'Clock Club becomes the engine that drives [your] search."

Black Enterprise

"Job hunting is a science at The Five O'Clock Club. [Members] find the discipline, direction and much-needed support that keeps a job search on track."

Modern Maturity

"Wendleton tells you how to beat the odds—even in an economy where pink slips are more common than perks. Her savvy and practical guide[s] are chockablock with sample résumés, cover letters, worksheets, negotiating tips, networking suggestions and inspirational quotes from such far-flung achievers as Abraham Lincoln, Malcolm Forbes, and Lily Tomlin."

Working Woman

"On behalf of eight million New Yorkers, I commend and thank The Five O'Clock Club. Keep the faith and keep America working!"

David N. Dinkins, former mayor, City of New York

What Job Hunters Say

"During the time I was looking for a job I kept Kate's books by my bed. I read a little every night, a little every morning. Her common-sense advice, methodical approach, and hints for keeping the spirits up were extremely useful."

 Harold Levine, coordinator, Yale Alumni Career Resource Network

"I've just been going over the books with my daughter, who is 23 and finally starting to think she ought to have a career. She won't listen to anything I say, but you she believes."

 Newspaper columnist

"Thank you, Kate, for all your help. I ended up with four offers and at least 15 compliments in two months. Thanks!"

 President and CEO, large banking organization

"I have doubled my salary during the past five years by using The Five O'Clock Club techniques. Now I earn what I deserve. I think everyone needs The Five O'Clock Club."

 M. S., attorney, entertainment industry

"I dragged myself to my first meeting, totally demoralized. Ten weeks later, I chose from among job offers and started a new life. Bless You!

 Senior editor, not-for-profit

"I'm an artistic person, and I don't think about business. Kate provided the disciplined business approach so I could practice my art. After adopting her system, I landed a role on Broadway in Hamlet."

 Bruce Faulk, actor

"I've referred at least a dozen people to The Five O'Clock Club since I was there. The Club was a major factor in getting my dream job, which I am now in."

 B. R., research head

"My Five O'Clock Club coach was a God-Send!!! She is truly one of the most dynamic and qualified people I've ever met. Without her understanding and guidance, I wouldn't have made the steps I've made toward my goals."

 Operating room nurse

"The Five O'Clock Club has been a fantastic experience for my job search. I couldn't have done it without you. Keep up the good work."

 Former restaurant owner, who found his dream job with an organization that advises small businesses

What Human Resources Executives Say about The Five O'Clock Club Outplacement

*"**This thing works.** I saw a structured, yet nurturing, environment where individuals searching for jobs positioned themselves for success. I saw 'accountability' in a nonintimidating environment. I was struck by the support and willingness to encourage those who had just started the process by the group members who had been there for a while."*

Employee relations officer, financial services organization

*"**Wow! I was immediately struck by the electric atmosphere** and people's commitment to following the program. Job hunters reported on where they were in their searches and what they had accomplished the previous week. The overall environment fosters sharing and mutual learning."*

Head of human resources, major law firm

*"The Five O'Clock Club program is **far more effective** than conventional outplacement. Excellent materials, effective coaching and nanosecond responsiveness combine to get people focused on the central tasks of the job search. Selecting The Five O'Clock Outplacement Program was one of my best decisions this year."*

Sr. vice president, human resources, manufacturing company

*"**You have made me look like a real genius** in recommending The Five O'Clock Club [to our divisions around the country]!"*

Sr. vice president, human resources, major publishing firm

The Five O'Clock Club®

Advising Professionals, Managers, and Executives for Over 25 Years

NAVIGATING YOUR
CAREER

DEVELOP YOUR PLAN, MANAGE YOUR BOSS, GET ANOTHER JOB INSIDE

KATE WENDLETON

THOMSON

DELMAR LEARNING™

Australia Canada Mexico Singapore Spain United Kingdom United States

THOMSON
DELMAR LEARNING

Navigating Your Career: Develop Your Plan, Manage Your Boss, Get Another Job Inside
Kate Wendleton

Vice President, Career Education SBU:
Dawn Gerrain

Director of Editorial:
Sherry Gomoll

Acquisitions Editor:
Martine Edwards

Developmental Editor:
Kristen Shenfield

Editorial Assistant:
Jennifer Anderson

Director of Production:
Wendy A. Troeger

Production Manager:
J.P. Henkel

Production Editor:
Rebecca Goldthwaite

Director of Marketing:
Wendy E. Mapstone

Marketing Specialist:
Gerard McAvey

Marketing Coordinator:
Erica Conley

Cover Design:
TDB Publishing Services

Library of Congress Cataloging-in-Publication Data

Wendleton, Kate.
   Navigating your career: develop your plan, manage your boss, get another job inside / Kate Wendleton.
      p. cm.
   "The Five O'Clock Club."
   Includes index.
   ISBN 1-4180-1501-6
   1. Career development. 2. Managing your boss.
I. Five O'Clock Club (New York, N.Y.) II. Title.

HF5381.W4375 2005
650.1'3—dc22
                                        2005050697

NOTICE TO THE READER

Preface

Dear Reader:

Congratulations! Chances are, you're reading this book because you want to take care of your career. Moving ahead in your career is complex these days and you need all the help and encouragement you can get.

I remember the *good old days*—the days of one employer and one career. It used to be when you found a job, you found a home. You expected to get in there, do what the organization wanted, learn to play the game, rise through the ranks, and eventually retire. People had secure jobs with large, stable employers.

People may have had job security, but the downside was they were often stuck. Changing jobs was frowned upon. If you were an accountant in a certain industry, you stayed an accountant in that industry. For every satisfied person, there was someone stifled who knew he or she had made a dreadful mistake.

Today, many of us fear losing our jobs—even from week to week—but *no one— absolutely* no one—needs to feel stifled, deadened, or stuck in a career no longer satisfying. *Everyone has an opportunity to do something that is better.*

Many people today want to make a career change—almost impossible in the past. A career change means you want to change industries (e.g., from the film industry to the magazine industry), professions (from accounting to sales), or geographic areas (e.g., from Chicago to Denver). If an accountant in the film industry wants to move into the magazine industry or move to a different geographic area, he or she can do so.

One reason for this is that industries must make constant changes based on competitive conditions. They must respond as the market changes, creating flux—and opportunity. Making a career change requires more effort than a career continuation (staying in accounting in the same industry). To make a career change, you cannot depend on job postings or the help of human resources. You have to understand yourself better (Part One of this book) and your target market (Part Two). You have more responsibility for developing yourself professionally and managing your relationships (Part Three) and knowing how to reposition yourself and search internally (Part Four).

For example, business relationships are more complex these days. People no longer work with the same teams for 10 years. This is a time of revolving bosses, peers, and subordinates. It's up to you to figure out how to meet people in other areas of the organization, understand their areas, and convince them they should hire *you* rather than an outsider who has already worked in their industry. After all, they have to stay competitive and you have to show them you understand the industry enough to be more of a help than a hindrance.

It's complex, but we're here to help. There is a methodology you can follow based on more than 25 years of research. Make no mistake about it: *You cannot take the internal job-search process too casually.* The way you present yourself in your résumé, for example, will affect your ability to get interviews and even guide the interviewing process.

Whatever worked for you the last time you made an internal move (if you ever have) is unlikely to be the best technique for you this time around. The situation has changed. You have more (or at least different) experience to offer, the kind of job you want next may have changed, and the job market has certainly changed.

We suggest you take an organized, methodical, *research* approach to your own search. Observe what is working for you and what is not—and do more of whatever is working. We'll show you how.

Chances are, you have focused on published job *openings* rather than unpublished job *possibilities*. If you chase posted openings, you will automatically have competition for those openings. We suggest you develop more *possibilities*. This means contacting hiring managers who do not happen to have an opening right now, but would *love* to have someone like you on board. Then keep in touch with those managers (we'll tell you how) and develop 6 to 10 similar contacts. This may sound like a lot of work, but it's a lot less work than applying for openings and continually coming in second or third because there is a lot of competition.

In addition, when you are searching internally, you have to manage what people say about you: your reputation in the organization. It's not enough to simply do a good job; you have to make sure others know about the good job you are doing. We'll tell you how.

This book gives you career-development guidelines, but also offers you flexibility in deciding which approaches are right for you. When you understand what is happening and why, you will be in a better position to chart your own course and plow full steam ahead, relying less on chance or on what a specific expert tells you.

Career development is ongoing. Most of the approaches in this book are businesslike rather than intensely psychological. Thinking of career development in a business-type way allows you to use the problem-solving skills you might use at work to help you advance in your own career.

I feel duty-bound to address the issue of life planning. Most people interested in moving their careers ahead don't want to give much thought to what they should do with their *lives*. So be sure to complete the Seven Stories Exercise and Forty-Year Vision worksheets to make sure your career is in sync with your life goals. When you uncover what it is you want to do long term, you can gently and continually move your career in that direction.

This book is the result of years of research about how people move ahead. The Five O'Clock Club will stay with you throughout your career. As you grow in experience and education, you can work with Five O'Clock Club coaches and fellow members who are right for you. After all, no matter how young or old you are, this is the *beginning* for you. You don't want just any old job. This is the start of a *career-development process*. We'll be there with you every step of the way.

Cheers, God bless, and good luck!

Kate Wendleton
New York City, 2005
www.fiveoclockclub.com

Contents

PART THREE   Developing Yourself Professionally

(AND ADAPTING TO CHANGE)

PART FOUR   Managing Up, Down, and Across

(DEVELOPING YOUR INTERPERSONAL RELATIONSHIPS)

PART FIVE   Searching for a New Job within Your Present Firm

(BUILD YOUR RÉSUMÉ, CONTACT PEOPLE, FOLLOW UP)

PART SIX What is The Five O'Clock Club?
(AMERICA'S PREMIER CAREER-COACHING NETWORK)

The
Five
O'Clock
Club

PART ONE

Deciding What You Want

START BY UNDERSTANDING YOURSELF

The
Five
O'Clock
Club

You and Your Career: Playing the Career Game

*If you haven't the strength
to impose you own terms upon life,
then you must accept the terms it offers you.*

T. S. Eliot,
The Confidential Clerk

Career management is like every type of navigation—there are rules to follow. Someone may tell you the rules of navigation, but no one tells you career rules. You have to observe them for yourself—or read this book. For example:

- If you're hoping to get ahead by simply working hard and thinking someone will notice you and reward you, then you don't know the rules. Working hard is not enough. Those who get ahead make *sure* they are noticed. In this book, we'll tell you how they do it.

- If you find yourself complaining that your boss is holding you back, not giving you the right assignments, or not training you in a way that will help you grow in your career, you are back in the 1970s. Those were the days when a person had one boss for a decade and your fortunes rose or fell with your boss's career. Today, most people need to create those assignments and training programs for themselves.

- If you're relying on your boss to tell those up the ladder how good you are, you're taking the wrong approach. Today, *you* have to make sure it happens—in a way that doesn't threaten your boss. Our "Eight-Word Message" is the key.

- If you'd like to move into another area of your organization, you may think that talking to Human Resources and responding to job postings are the best approaches to use. But later you'll suspect that someone who had an inside track—who was already a favorite—is the one who got the job. You're probably right. She was navigating properly. You were not. *You* should become the one who's on the inside track and we'll tell you how.

- You may think your boss's opinion of you is the only one that matters. But if your peers don't like you, you are unlikely to get promoted. And the higher up you go, the more "buy in" you have to get from other people. In fact, if a person has problems getting ahead, it's most often because of peer disapproval rather than incompetence. In this book, we'll talk about how you can develop good relationships with your bosses, peers, and subordinates.

- You're doing the same old job you've been doing for years and doing it well. But the organization has changed around you and you're now out of sync. You may not even know it. Half of your job these days is to *change as the situation changes,* acquiring new skills and information.

Figuring out how to chart your career can be challenging, as well as rewarding. However, just *knowing* that it's like sailing can make you more lighthearted and more observant about what's going on.

And the first to reach port successfully is the person who . . .

- has more control over his or her career,
- has more satisfying assignments, and
- gets the desired experience and challenges.

This person can be you. So, let's set out and you'll see how it works. All of the examples in this book are true stories culled from more than 25 years of experience helping thousands of job hunters.

Resolving Problems in Your Present Job

Half the people attending The Five O'Clock Club are employed and looking for a new job. We tell them, "The best job hunts start at home"—by which we mean they might do better in their present organizations. Some were looking outside because they were working long hours in their present jobs, traveling too much, didn't like their bosses, or were not getting good assignments. Often, just thinking about *navigating your career* helps you gain the courage to discuss these problems with the appropriate person at work and resolve those problems rather than leave. The grass is not always greener. You may be trading one set of problems for another. In this book, we'll guide you in having a career discussion with your boss.

Security is mostly a superstition. It does not exist in nature, nor do the children of men as a whole experience it. Avoiding danger is no safer in the long run than outright exposure. Life is either a daring adventure or nothing.

Helen Keller

Finding a New Job Internally

Many people say they want a new job inside and have already tried to search internally, but *noth-ing's happened*. They don't realize much more is involved than simply being pointed in the direction of an opening with the help of Human Resources or a job posting. For example, did they craft a well-positioned résumé and well-thought-out cover letter? Did they get coaching on how to interview and follow up after the meeting? Perhaps they were granted the interview as a courtesy and *didn't realize all the work* they would have to do to really be considered for the job.

But an internal job search is just like an external job search. In the outside world, only 6 percent of all jobs are filled through search firms (the equivalent of human resources) and only an additional 6 percent of all jobs are filled through ads (the equivalent of job postings). We'll show you how to be effective at finding jobs internally and how to get ahead in your present organizations. We can tell you how to make sure you're the one the hiring team wants. But first, you have to go through all the steps successful Five O'Clock Clubbers go through:

- Complete the assessment to find out more about yourself and how to talk about yourself.
- Prepare your résumé and cover letter.
- Decide with whom you want to meet internally.
- Prepare a pitch about yourself.
- Develop a plan for the meeting.
- Meet with people in the department or divisions you are targeting. Find out if they would hire you if they had an opening.

So, the method is—contact those who actually do the hiring, that is, the department or division heads, and not only human resources. Meet with the department or division heads *who have no openings right now* but may keep you at the top of their lists if they do hire someday. Then *you'll* be the one who's on the inside track. And when they have an opening, they'll tell you, "Just sit tight. I have to post this job, but you're going to get it."

That's how the game works.

Continuous Improvement: The Key to Marketability

Although most employed people come to The Five O'Clock Club because they want jobs elsewhere, a surprising number end up becoming more valued by their present organizations. That's because these workers start exploring what is going on outside their organizations, pick up new skills that make them more marketable, and often take that information back to their present employers. Because they no longer feel dependent on one organization, they develop greater self-esteem and become more assertive in developing ideas and programs for their present employers. Their employers start to treat them differently.

In the next few pages, we're going to look at case studies of people who *stayed* with their present employers—by learning to chart their careers. We will point out some of the lessons learned.

CASE STUDY *Martin*
On His Way Out: Then Promoted

Martin is now the head of the direct-marketing arm of a major not-for-profit. Before he was promoted to this position in his current organization, he felt he was undervalued and perhaps was even being squeezed out. He wanted to get into the for-profit world. To learn more about this target area, The Five O'Clock Club suggested he read the trade journals, join associations having to do with direct marketing, and get to know people in the field. Martin learned so much in his intensive research that he went a few steps further: He *spoke* at the association meetings, began writing for the trade journals, and even appeared on the cover of one prestigious trade magazine.

This caught the attention of his current employer, who began to value him much more. Coincidentally, Martin's boss moved elsewhere in the organization. Martin was surprised when he was asked to take his boss's job. That promotion reduced Martin's desire and motivation to find a new job quickly. In addition, his résumé was looking better and better.

If Martin ever decides to look for a new job again, his new title and experience will help, as will his new visibility as a guru in the direct-marketing field. He continues to stay involved and improve his career—as well as his worth—at his present place of employment. And he continues to navigate his career to stay sharp in his field.

A New Way of Thinking about the Job Market

Any assignment (or job) you get is a temporary one. It doesn't matter what kind of work you do, you *don't have a permanent job*. Your situation today is much like that of an actor who lands a part. He or she does not really know how long it will last. Furthermore, actors tend to worry about whether or not a role will typecast them and potentially cause them to lose future roles. Or, they may intentionally decide to be typecast, hoping it will increase their chances of moving forward. Actors understand that they will have to land another role after the present one and they constantly think about how a certain role will position them for the future. And so must you. Your next job is only a temporary assignment.

This process of staying aware and marketable is what employees must do to keep their present jobs longer or to make career moves inside or outside of their present organizations.

Old Goal: Job Security
New Goal: Marketability

In the old days, if you simply did a good job, you would be okay. These days, navigating your career means you must think and act like a consultant:

- Keep up with what is happening in your industry: join professional associations, read trade journals, take courses, and network with people outside of your organization.

- Keep up with what is happening *outside* of your industry. This will prevent you from becoming insular and you may come up with ideas that will apply to your industry as well.

- Acquire new skills that are in demand in your industry—and in the workplace in general.

- Bring these new skills, and new information and ideas, back to your present employer—as a consultant would. You will do better in your present job and will get to keep it even longer—just as Martin did.

- Think of yourself as an *investigator* on behalf of your present employer. Meet people outside who do what you do and bring information back.

People are always blaming their circumstances for what they are. I don't believe in circumstances. The people who get on in this world are the people who get up and look for the circumstances they want, and if they can't find them, make them.

George Bernard Shaw

How to Find *Your* Place in the World: Change As Opportunity

Don't expect to hold on to the way things have worked for you in the past. Get on with the new way the world is operating. You cannot stop the changes, but you *can* choose the way you will respond. You can see change as a threat to resist—or as an opportunity to move forward.

Change represents danger to you when you choose to resist it. While your energy goes into trying to keep your situation the same, you will become more dissatisfied as you see others taking advantage of changes.

You can use change to your advantage if you decide to see it as a source of opportunity. Then it won't be so threatening. You will reduce your

chances of being run over. You will be running your own life.

To look at change as a source of opportunity, become more aware of the changes taking place around you—events that can affect you and your job. Decide which are best for you and how to take advantage of those that interest you. The pace of change in today's economy can be overwhelming unless you can assess changes more objectively. In doing so you will have more control *over the way you respond*. Later in this book we'll tell you how to respond to change.

No One Is Immune: Job Hunting for the First Time in 27 years

Even entrenched workers can feel the pressure to change and move on. Kevin, a senior-level manager, spent 27 years in publishing operations—the last 11 years in one division of a large media company. But because it had been so long since he had searched for a job, Kevin lacked confidence and job-search skills.

Through the assessment exercises in this book, Kevin learned that in addition to his operations and systems-management skills, he was excellent at building teams and creating relationships within all levels of the organization. This knowledge gave him the confidence he needed. Then he found out how to market himself internally and landed a job in another operations area of this large organization that was actively acquiring other companies.

This was the perfect job for him. It brought together all the important skills Kevin had acquired—in fact, he had once managed the operations side of another media acquisition. In addition, the position was very highly visible and served an important business need for his employer.

Kevin said, "*Navigating Your Career* taught me how to view the interview process through the eyes of the interviewer, sell my strengths, and talk about my weaknesses. I also saw the importance of doing research before the interview. I learned a lot about myself and I hope this process will be used by more managers throughout the organization."

Labor is the superior of capital, and deserves much the higher consideration.

Abraham Lincoln

Managing Your Career Rather Than Finding a Job

Moira was stuck. After being a customer-service representative for 13 months, she was going nowhere despite her manager's support. What's worse, she thought her lack of skills would keep her from moving elsewhere.

Although skeptical, she did The Five O'Clock Club assessment, which consisted of the Seven Stories Exercise and her Fifteen-Year and Forty-Year Visions (covered in Part Two of this book). She worked with her career coach and started working on her interviewing skills. Moira learned what she had to offer and found she could present herself very differently going forward. She now felt unstuck and could see that she was starting to attain some control over her future career direction.

Moira now knew that it would take research and planning to get ahead. She decided not to focus on job postings; she wanted to take her career more seriously and spend time developing it while in her present job. She learned how to network internally to find out more about what people do with their careers. She knew that meeting with people would help her develop a better career plan. What's more, she felt sure that she would develop relationships with people who would help her when she was ready to make a career move.

Moira does not yet have a clearly defined career plan, but she knows how to get one and is no longer in a rush to leave her present job. She has recommended the navigation approach to a lot of other people.

How to Relocate

In the back of his mind, Paul thought about moving from New York to California. His assessment exercise results and his session with his career coach confirmed this interest and he did some networking through his present financial services firm—with no immediate result. Frustrated, Paul thought his employer could do more to help him move to California. After all, he had been there for 14 years.

So Paul decided to steer his own career; he developed networking support, a better résumé, and a better plan for conducting a job search in California. A human resources representative in his organization also suggested informational sources such as organization charts, and job posting reports for the West Coast.

On Paul's behalf (and with Paul's permission), his human resources representative contacted the local staffing unit manager and another key business executive. They both agreed to meet with Paul while he was in California and he also met with other key players.

Paul received a job offer from one of his networking contacts in California who had left his employer to join another California-based company. However, Paul decided to stay with his present employer.

Paul continues to build his contact base, has kept in touch with a number of his important contacts in California, and feels more empowered in his career. He now knows he can get a job in California but wants to wait for the right one.

Don't Be Scared by the Headlines

Job hunters are starting to realize that a large number of people may be laid off in one part of an organization while different kinds of workers are hired in other parts of the same organization. You will hear about the layoffs in the news, but the organization doesn't publish the hirings—it would be deluged with résumés.

Get used to the headlines. Organizations must react quickly to changing world circumstances and don't have time to figure out where those laid off could fit within other areas of the same organization. Sometimes employees who have been laid off are allowed to job-hunt both inside and outside the organization. This can be an efficient way for the organization to change direction, and perhaps save 10 percent of these employees by incorporating them into the new direction.

*Fighting futility is a waste of energy, Samantha.
Either do something or quit fretting.*

Celebra Tueli

Getting Repositioned for the Future

Brian's once-successful career was becoming derailed. He had worked for a major financial institution for 17 years in a management position, and had spent the last few years working on one special project after another. His most recent job ended due to a change in business strategy. Brian was no longer in the mainstream. How could he get back on track?

Through The Five O'Clock Club assessment process, Brian realized he was eager to work on projects important to senior management. While he enjoyed working in a collaborative atmosphere and wanted to see his people grow, he also wanted to grow. He wanted to re-experience the successes of his earlier career.

In examining his past successes (through the Seven Stories Exercise, which you will use later), Brian found that his achievements were connected to his strong project management, presentation, public speaking, and relationship-building skills. His Career Buddy (someone he teamed up with to get support during his job search) thought he might want to capitalize on these skills once again.

Brian landed a job in another division: a global customer-service business that specialized in high technology. It was a high-profile job in which he could learn more about the high-tech business and position himself for future growth.

In addition, Brian would now have some bottom-line responsibility. He felt that new life had been breathed into his once-stagnant career.

Nobody owns a job, nobody owns a market, nobody owns a product. Somebody out there can always take it away from you.

Ronald E. Compton, president/chairman, Aetna, as quoted in *The New York Times,* March 1, 1992

A Changing Economy

Today, we know that doing a good job is not enough. Our career prospects can now change for reasons that have nothing to do with our personal job performance, but instead with the performance of our employers. It's a new economy—a world economy—and the changes are not going to slow down. Not only will things not return to the way they were but the amount of change will increase.

Government statistics show the impact of change on job hunters:

- **The average American has been in his or her job for only four years.**

- The average American graduating from college today can expect to have 5 careers during his or her lifetime—not 5 jobs, but 5 separate careers!

- This means *you* will probably have 12 to 15 jobs in the course of your 5 careers.

A few smart organizations have wisely embraced a process of helping employees take charge of their own careers. Most of us, however, will have to develop career plans on our own and this book can help you do that.

Continual Career Development: An Enlightened Approach

All of this fits in with what we teach at The Club: It is best for both the employee and the employer if *job hunting* is seen as a continual process—and not just something that happens when a person wants to change jobs. **Continual job search means always being aware of market conditions both inside and outside of your present organization and continually learning what you have to offer—to both markets**.

With this approach, workers are safer because they are more likely to keep their present jobs longer: They learn to change and grow as organizations and industries change. And if they go elsewhere, they will be more marketable. Organizations are better off because employees who know what is going on outside of their insular halls are smarter, more sophisticated, and more proactive, and make the organization more competitive.

The economy is changing too fast for the career-planning techniques and attitudes about job hunting that worked in recent decades.

Understanding How the Hiring System Works

Knowing why things work the way they do will give you flexibility and control over your career. Knowing how the hiring system works will help you understand why things go right and why they go wrong—why certain things work and why others don't. Then you can modify the system to fit your own needs and temperament and the workings of the job market in which you are interested.

It is overly simplistic to say that only one career-development or job-hunting system works. The job-selection process is more complicated than that. Employers can do what they want. You need to understand the process from their point of view. Then you can plan your own career in your own industry. You will learn how to compete in this market.

Always remember, **the best jobs don't necessarily go to the most qualified people but to the people who are the best job hunters**. You'll increase your chances of finding the job you want by using a methodical job-hunting approach.

The Only Port in This Storm: You

They cannot offer you job security or even a career direction. The rules have changed very quickly and they expect you to adapt very quickly.

If you don't plan your own path through all of this, you will continue to be thrown around by the turbulence. The better you understand yourself—your motivations, skills, and interests—the more solid your foundation will be.

If you complete the exercises in this book—especially the Seven Stories—you will understand your own value, and your self-esteem is more likely to remain intact. You will keep yourself on course and continue to follow your plan. Otherwise, in our world of revolving bosses, you will come across a shallow person who does not understand your value. If you don't understand your value, it's unlikely that others will either.

The better you are at plotting your own future, the more you will get out of each job or assignment. Each will fit in with your long-term vision and you will not get so ruffled by corporate politics and pettiness. You will be following your own vision.

The Benefits of Staying with Your Employer

Today, most people leave their employers involuntarily. The market changes, the employer changes, and people are asked to leave as the company cuts back or changes direction. It is a heart-wrenching experience.

Yet, during the dot.com era of the late 1990s, *employees* often chose to leave, hoping they would find a pot of gold. Many job hopped and ended up with cluttered résumés. But research shows that those who stay with one employer longer tend to earn more than those who leave for greener pastures. That's why it's best to see if you can fix the situation in your present place of employment.

I was lucky at one point early in my career. After three years of professional experience elsewhere, I stayed with one excellent company for nine years. I started out in computer programming for three years, moved into a training function in the technology area for three years, and then moved into the public relations area, learning a third field. Sometimes you can have the best of both worlds: the stability of working for one employer while learning new, growing areas.

While your basic emotional temperament may not change much during your lifetime, you can make significant day-to-day adjustments in the way you perceive events and respond to them. When you face an emotionally trying situation, guard against exaggerating or over-generalizing, and focus instead on your specific options for taking direct action. Avoid putting yourself down by doing something that will exercise your good traits. And seek the company of others, whether it's to gather more rational views on the situation or simply to change your mood.

Jack Maguire,
Care and Feeding of the Brain

The Career Buddy System

Career management can be a complex process. There's no reason to figure it out alone. Get a Career Buddy. It's vital to have someone to talk to—fairly often and informally—about the big picture and the little things, too. "Here's what I'm planning to do today in my career development. What are you planning to do? Let's talk two days from now to make sure we've done it." You and your buddy can keep each other positive and on track and encourage each other to do what you promised: making that call, sending out those letters, writing that follow-up proposal, focusing on the most important things to be done—rather than (for example) spending endless hours responding to job postings.

With your buddy, you can talk about your accomplishments, practice your Two-Minute Pitch (which will be covered in Part Five), get ready for interviews, and bounce ideas off each other. You may decide to talk with each other every few days or once a week—by phone or in person. The important thing is to make sure you talk on a regular basis. Time can slip away, and it is easy to get caught up in the normal pressures of everyday life. Unless you *make* time for your own career development, you can easily wind up not working at career development at all and making very little career progress.

Sometimes people match themselves up as buddies. Just pick someone you get along with *who is also career oriented*. Your buddy may be a coworker or someone outside of the organization with whom you can talk while playing the career game. Sometimes your human resources person can match you up. However you do it, *stay away from negative people* who talk about how bad things are; they will drag you down. Pick a Career Buddy who is positive, upbeat, and constructive. When working with a Career Buddy, keep the discussions focused on the exercises in this book, as well as your future careers. Talking every other day about football will not help either of you in your career.

You may have different Career Buddies over time: People get jobs; their schedules become overloaded. If you lose one buddy who got a job, get another.

Your buddy does not have to be in your field or industry. In fact, being in the same field or industry could keep you focused on the industry rather than on the process. But you do have to get along! The relationship may last only a month or two or go on for years. Some buddies become friends. In any case, you and your buddy can help each other become more successful in your careers.

If you opt to work alone, adopt measures to keep yourself honest! Practice the exercises by speaking into a tape recorder or talking in front of a mirror.

Alice said nothing: she had sat down with her face in her hands, wondering if anything would ever happen in a natural way again.

Lewis Carroll, *Alice in Wonderland*

Change Means New Opportunities

The world is changing. What's hot today is not tomorrow. Use these changes to your advantage. Choose to move your career in the direction that's right for you.

You can impose your own terms upon life. You don't have to accept the terms it offers you. Read on and see what others have done.

The Five O'Clock Club

Targeting the Jobs of the Future

The time is not far off when you will be answering your television set and watching your telephone.

Raymond Smith, chairman and chief executive of the Bell Atlantic Corporation, *The New York Times*, February 21, 1993

The Times Are Changing

Ten years from now, half the working population will be in jobs that do not exist today. Positions and industries could disappear almost completely—edged out by technological advances or new industries. When was the last time you saw a typewriter repairman? Or even a typewriter? There are few TV or radio repair jobs, either; they have been replaced by new jobs in new industries.

Some industries retrench—or downsize—slowly and trick us into thinking they are solid and dependable. At the turn of the last century, there were literally thousands of piano manufacturers. A few still remain, but that industry was affected by new industries: movies, TV, radio, and other forms of home entertainment—most recently, the Internet, CD-ROMs, and video game systems.

In 1900, most people probably thought: "But we'll *always* need pianos." People today think the same way about the industries they are in.

Experts say the traditional advertising industry has permanently retrenched. Those who want to stay in that industry often must go to small U.S. cities or abroad—or work for corporations rather than advertising agencies.

Peter Drucker said: "Network television advertising is in a severe crisis. . . . None of the mass advertisers—Procter & Gamble, Coca-Cola— . . . knows what to do about it."

All our lives we are engaged in the process of accommodating ourselves to our surroundings; living is nothing else than this process of accommodation. When we fail a little, we are stupid. When we flagrantly fail, we are mad. A life will be successful or not, according as the power of accommodation is equal to or unequal to the strain of fusing and adjusting internal and external chances.

Samuel Butler, *The Way of All Flesh*

Temporary Setbacks

Some industries and occupations ebb and flow with supply and demand. When there is a shortage in a well-paid field—such as nursing, engineering, or law—school enrollments increase, creating an excess. Then people stop entering these fields, creating a shortage. So, sometimes it's easy to get a job and sometimes it isn't.

The overall economy may also temporarily affect a field or industry. Real estate, for example, may suffer in a weak economy and pick up in a strong one.

Ahead of the Market

When the Berlin Wall came down in 1989, there was a rush of companies wanting to capitalize on the potential market in Eastern Europe. Given all they were reading in the papers, job hunters thought it would be a good market for them to explore as well. They were ahead of the market. It took a few years before the market caught up with the concept. Now many people are employed in Eastern Europe or in servicing that market.

The same may be true for the area you are in or are trying to get into: The market may not be there because it has not yet developed.

Another growth area is "new media." This is such a rapidly changing area that it is still hard to define. As of this writing, it can include cable stations, a number of which are devoted to home shopping; "imaging" of medical records and credit-card receipts; supermarket scanners and other devices that promote items or record what you buy; multimedia use of the computer (sound, motion, and color instead of just text, which you now take for granted); virtual reality; interactive TV; telephone and cable companies; cell phones; CD-ROMs (compact discs containing "read-only memory"), which hold materials such as games and encyclopedias; the increasingly important Internet; and gadgets such as personal data assistants, and DVD and MP3 players.

And let's not forget biotech, health care, and related areas (gyms, nutritionists, physical fitness instructors). Americans now take it as their right that they should have anything that makes them healthier. Such industries make up a significant part of the gross national product, and are projected to grow even more. Large corporations often have divisions or areas involved in these new media fields. You can determine your company's involvement by looking at its website, talking to human resources managers, looking through the company directory, and finding the appropriate people knowledgeable about the company's operations. This could be an excellent opportunity to use your skills in a growing area,

as well as to learn new skills or make an exciting career move.

If you succeed in judging yourself rightly, then you are indeed a man of true wisdom.
Antoine de Saint-Exupéry, *The Little Prince*

What about *Your* Industry or Profession?

Is your dream industry or field growing, permanently retrenching, or in a temporary decline because of supply and demand or other economic conditions? If you are lucky, your employer is ahead of the market and the industry will pick up later. Often, you can find out just by reading your organization's annual report and other information it gives out to the public.

Most people in permanently retrenching industries, including the leaders, incorrectly think the decline is temporary. You have to decide for yourself. You could perhaps gain insight and objectivity by researching what those outside your industry have to say.

Many experts predict that if things continue as they are going, there will soon be a great divide in America, with technologically and internationally aware workers making fine salaries, while unaware and unskilled workers earn dramatically lower wages. (Even high-level executives can be unaware and unskilled and may face reductions in their salaries as they become less useful.) If this does come to pass, the best a career coach can do is encourage people to try to be on the winning side of that divide.

Retrenching Markets Are All Alike

When an industry retrenches, the results are predictable. A retrenching market, by definition, has more job hunters than jobs. The more that market retrenches, the worse it gets.

Those who want to stay in the field have increasingly longer searches as more people chase fewer jobs. They will also tend to stay in their new jobs less time as companies in the retrenching industry continue to downsize or go out of business.

Profit margins get squeezed as companies compete for a slice of a shrinking pie. Those companies become less enjoyable places to work because there is less investment in training and development, research, internal communications, and the like. Of course, salaries are cut.

Many young people are enticed into glamour fields, regardless of the practicality, or into fields their parents or friends are in, regardless of the fit for them personally, despite the projections for those fields. Yes, you should pursue your dreams, but check them out a little first.

Most people target only their current industries, fields, or professions at the start of their search. They consider other targets only after they have difficulty getting another job in their present field. They would probably have found something faster if they had looked in other fields from the beginning.

Those in retrenching industries who also target new industries have a shorter search time.

**The new fields are new to everyone.
An outsider has a chance of
becoming an insider.**

One doesn't discover new lands without consenting to lose sight of the shore for a very long time.

André Gide

Expanding Your Search Geographically

If you have been ignoring the suburbs, think about them. Consider moving to one of your company's offices in the nearby suburbs or even in other cities. Jobs may also be available outside of the U.S. If you want to change locations, the first place to look is in your own *backyard*—other locations of your current employer.

Bull Market for Labor Likely to Continue into the Foreseeable Future

Richard Bayer, Ph.D., an economist and chief operating officer for The Five O'Clock Club, is optimistic. He notes that both the Bureau of Labor Statistics and the Conference Board project labor shortages over the next 10 years.

Predictions are of course uncertain, and there could easily be a recession or two in this time frame, but the overall employment trend line remains strongly positive.

He notes:

- The demand for labor will continue to grow. The supply of labor will barely be adequate to meet the demand.

- There will almost surely be pockets of *skills mismatch* in which some positions are very difficult to fill.

- Overall, the educational level required to function in this new economy will rise.

- Although workers will continue to be needed at all levels, the larger increases in employment are coming in the various managerial, professional, and skilled technical ranks. This goes against the myth that the new economy is producing mainly low-skill and low-wage jobs.

- The occupations with the greatest declines tend to be lower skilled and lower paid: garment workers, customer service (those who answer 800 telephone calls), farm workers, textile machine operators.

So, what might the implications of all this be for Five O'Clock Clubbers and others?

This is a great time to be alive and have a career! The efforts you put into your education, into career development, into salary negotiation, into networking, into targeting a meaningful job have never had such a strong chance of bearing good fruit!

There is guidance for each of us,
and by lowly listening,
we shall hear the right word.

Ralph Waldo Emerson

Getting More Sophisticated

Whether you are relatively new to the labor force or have been working awhile, think past the obvious and think more deeply about the changes that are occurring.

Listed below are a few of the industries that business experts project will grow in the near future. Try to discover other areas that could be affected by these or how your own job could be affected by growth in these areas. Each is huge and changing and can be better defined by your investigation through networking, as well as Internet and library research.

Here is the list of some of the industries expected to grow:

- Health care and biotech, or anything having to do with them. Health care is considered a sure bet because of the aging population and the advances being made in medical technology.

- Anything high-tech, or the high-tech aspect of whatever field or industry in which you are employed.

- The international aspect of the field/industry you are considering.

- The environmental area; waste management.

- Safety and security (especially since the September 11 attack on the United States).

- Telecommunications, the new media and global communications (movie studios, TV networks, cable companies, computer companies, consumer-electronics companies, and publishers).

- Education in the broadest sense (as opposed to the traditional classroom), including computer-assisted instruction. (Researchers have found that people who are illiterate learn to read better with computer-assisted instruction than they do in a classroom.)

Because all of us will have to keep up to date in more areas in order to do our jobs well, technology will play an important part in our continuing education. Further, with the United States lagging so far behind other countries educationally, the for-profit and not-for-profit sectors are both working hard to revamp our educational system.

- Alternative means of distributing goods. Instead of retail stores, think not only about direct mail, which may already be a bit out of date, but also about purchasing by TV—or the Internet.

- Anything serving the aging population, both products and services.

In studying the preceding list, think of how you can combine different industries to come up with areas to pursue. For example: Combine the aging population with education, or the aging population with telecommunications, or health care with education, and so on. The more you research, the more sophisticated your thoughts will get.

If you combine education with the new media, you will be thinking like many experts. Students in schools are learning from interactive multimedia presentations on computers—presentations that will be as exciting as computer games and MTV combined and almost as up to date as the morning news (most textbooks are years out of date). Teachers will do what computers cannot do: facilitate the groups, encourage, reinforce learning.

A computer-based approach can be used to train and update the knowledge of America's workers: Employees can learn when they have the time and at their own pace, rather than having large numbers of workers leave their jobs to learn in a classroom situation.

Think about the field in which you are interested, and how it is being affected by technology. Virtually every job and industry—whether it is publishing, entertainment, manufacturing, or financial services—is being impacted by technology and by the global marketplace. If you are not aware, you will be blindsided.

Some Areas Are Safer Bets

The rate of change is so fast that technologies you read about may never reach the mainstream or may be replaced with new developments. However, some areas are safer bets than others. *Hard skills* are more marketable than *soft skills*. For example, a person who wants to get a job as a general writer will have more difficulty than someone who can bring more to the party—such as some specialization or computer skills.

When there is no vision, the people perish.
Old Testament, Proverbs 29:18

Figure It Out

It's your job to figure out how your dream industry or field is being significantly affected by technology, global competition, and the market in general. Think where you fit into the future. Do research.

We are now on the ground floor of many industries and at an exciting time for those who choose to take advantage of the revolutionary changes taking place.

So, once again, remember the definition of job hunting developed by The Five O'Clock Club:

Job hunting in a changing economy means continuously becoming aware of market conditions inside, as well as outside, your present organization, and learning more about what you have to offer.

A New Way of Thinking

Remember—any job or assignment is only temporary. Do not lose sight of your long-term goals.

The
Five
O'Clock
Club

Targeting *Your* Future

The factory of the future will have only two employees, a man and a dog. The man will be there to feed the dog.

The dog will be there to keep the man from touching the equipment.

Warren Bennis

Learning to Track Trends and Move into a New Market

You are not stuck in your present field or industry just because it's where you have your experience. You do not have to take a pay cut or start at the bottom to get into a new field. Trade off what you already know. Learn the new area. Become an insider. In this volatile market, where jobs are disappearing every day, new jobs are appearing. Select a field that will position you for the long run. The people in our stories are picking up skills and experience that will be transferable to other jobs—and they will be extremely marketable.

Virtually every industry is in turmoil. Read what experts write about the industries that interest you. Then think about—or research—the industry you are in now. What are the trends? What outside forces are affecting *your* industry? How might you be affected? How can you prepare for the future?

If you are targeting other industries, research them to see how you fit in with their new directions. This research and planning will keep you more prepared—and more stable—in this unstable world.

The Attributes of a Growth Industry

By definition, growth industries must hire from outside: They don't have enough people inside the industry. The new industry attracts new competitors—many of whom will fail—and there will be a shakeout. But if the industry is still growing, those who get in early are the most knowledgeable and valuable and can command larger salaries. If the industry does *not* continue to grow, new entrants create a surplus of labor and salaries decrease.

Are you more likely to find stability in the old, retrenching industries, or in the uncertain industries of the future?

Within the next decades education will change more than it has changed since the modern school was created by the printed book over three hundred years ago. An economy in which knowledge is becoming the true capital and the premier wealth-producing resource makes new and stringent demands on the schools for education performance and educational responsibility. . . . How we learn and how we teach are changing drastically and fast—the result, in part, of new theoretical understanding of the learning process, in part of new technology.

Peter Drucker, *The New Realities*

The Growth of the Web

A few years ago, the pace of technological change started to pick up: There was a confluence of technological work in various arenas that began to bear fruit.

You may know that the Internet itself was envisioned in 1945—more than 60 years ago—by Vannevar Bush, an electrical engineer. Hypertext, the basis for interactivity on the Internet, was developed in 1965! The World Wide Web was created in 1989 using hypertext. HTML, the "hypertext markup language," was developed in 1990. Yet, interactive business applications on desktop computers were in relatively wide commercial use by 1980.

Here's one way to look at it:
Radio → TV → Computers → Internet

The long-accepted concept of computer-based interactivity, combined relatively recently with HTML and URLs, laid the groundwork for the surge we are experiencing today.

In the mid-1990s, we told concerned Five O'Clock Clubbers who were targeting Internet-related companies that even if the Internet didn't make it, their new skills would be transferable to whatever interactive technologies took its place.

Clearly, *interactive* was here to stay: Computer interactivity has been popular in business applications for more than 20 years! But the Internet was not just another interactive medium, such as ATMs, interactive kiosks, telephones, or even CD-ROMs. The Internet was an international infrastructure for commerce and ideas, an intelligent medium that made people smarter and proactive. It was a core medium that would change everything.

The Same Development Pattern in Other Industries

The development of the Internet—a long gestation period followed by a "sudden" appearance on the market—was paralleled by developments in a number of unrelated industries, and the results added to the cataclysm. Probably half the jobs that exist today did not exist 10 years ago:

- HMOs and alternative medicine have changed the face of health care. Ask any physician.

- Telecom, with cellular phones that can take photographs and access the Internet with an international reach, looks nothing like it did only a few years ago.

- Education will be permanently changed by for-profit schools, the erosion of tenure, and the technological advances impacting the industry —with or without the approval of powerful unions.

- "Retail" no longer necessarily means going into a store or even talking to a person. Alternative distribution methods have been in the works for decades—through direct mail and other means—and now through the Internet. People don't need stores to buy computers, travel agents to arrange travel, or stockbrokers to purchase stocks. Automobiles are sold over the Internet, a new direct-marketing approach; showrooms are there so you can kick the tires.

- The entertainment industry has morphed in unpredictable ways and media growth is being driven by technology, not programming. For example, 20 years ago, there were 3 broadcast networks and 20 cable channels. DVDs did not exist. Today, there are 6 broadcast networks, 300 cable channels (perhaps going to a 600+ channel universe), PCs in virtually every home, as well as DVD players and VCRs. A large number of families have installed video game consoles. Cell phones, PDAs, and MP3 players are all part of the entertainment arena. Traditional marketing approaches are becoming less efficient. And, as of this writing, content is the entertainment king, allowing companies to exploit it over multiple mediums.

Who could have dreamed of today's situation just five years ago? But these changes opened windows in new areas while traditional fields retrenched and revamped.

Cato learned Greek at eighty; Sophocles
Wrote his grand Oedipus, and Simonides
Bore off the prize of verse from his compeers,
When each had numbered more than
four-score years. . . .
Chaucer, at Woodstock with the nightingales,
At sixty wrote the Chaucer Tales;
Goethe at Weimar, toiling to the last,
Completed Faust when eighty years were past.

Henry Wadsworth Longfellow,
Morituri Salutamus

Professions Also Get Outmoded Overnight

It used to be a person's profession was a source of stability. That is absolutely no longer the case: Professions change overnight. Ask physicians or attorneys about their early visions of those professions and you will quickly hear how their fields have dramatically changed. Physicians in their 50s and 60s say they are lucky to have been part of the "golden age" of medicine—when doctors could see whomever they wanted, recommend whatever they felt was in their patients' best interests, get referrals from other physicians, and earn good money. Now, nothing is the same.

Ten years ago, we rarely saw an attorney at The Five O'Clock Club and until a year ago, we had no physicians. Now, we have plenty of both—and computer programmers as well. Their professions have changed—quickly.

In this high-risk society, each person's main asset will
be his or her willingness and ability to take intelligent
risks. Those people best able to cope with
uncertainty . . . will fare better in the long run than
those who cling to security.

Michael Mandel, *The High-Risk Society*

The High-Risk Society

In 1996, Michael Mandel wrote in *The High-Risk Society* that times are good but prosperity has come at a high price: more intense and pervasive economic uncertainty than Americans have suffered at any time in the past 50 years.

Mandel pointed out that prosperity and security no longer go hand in hand. "Today, the very forces behind economic turbulence are also the world's greatest engines of growth. As a result, success hinges on your willingness to embrace risk—rather than flee from it."

Those who keep up and see where the future is heading—in both their professions and their industries—can benefit from the changes that are going to take place anyway.

Now, we all expect new developments and we expect uncertainty. We expect our fields and industries to change. This time, we're ready.

Our eyes are open now. We keep up to date. We stay in touch. We're thinking about our next move even before we start a new position. We know we have to take charge of our careers and that doesn't seem so bad anymore. We've got perspective.

God bless you as you face the uncertain future. It's better than trying to stay in the nonexistent past.

The essence of the high-risk society is choice:
the choice between embracing uncertainty
and running from it.

Michael Mandel, *The High-Risk Society*

What about Your Field, Industry, or Geographic Area?

A job target is *a clearly selected geographic area, an industry or organization size, and a function or position within that industry.* An accountant, for example, may target a certain industry (such as telecommunications or hospitals) or may see himself in the accounting function and may not care in which industry but prefer instead to focus on *organization size*. This means he wants to target a small, medium, or large organization, regardless of industry.

Examine your targets to see how each is doing. Perhaps, for example, your industry is okay, but large organizations are not doing well, while smaller organizations are hiring. In this case, target smaller organizations.

What changes are taking place in your industry or function? If you think your industry or function will continue to retrench, find a *new horse to ride:* an industry or function that is on a growth curve or one where you will gain transferable skills.

The person who fears to try is thus enslaved.
Leonard E. Read

It's Time to Take Control of Your Own Career

Get in the habit of reading the papers and noticing what news may affect your industry or field. Learn about the industries of the future.

Even if all you want right now is a job, instead of a career, complete the exercises in the next section. Be sure to include at least the Seven Stories Exercise, Interests, Values, and Forty-Year Vision. They won't take long, and they will shorten the length of your search.

Retraining Is for Everybody —Even Executives

When people talk about retraining in the U.S., they are usually talking about lower-level workers who don't have computer skills. Retraining is necessary at all levels. Do research to learn the terminology of the industry you want to enter so you can be an insider, not an outsider.

By definition, new industries must hire people from outside. If a job hunter studies the field and develops a sincere interest in it, he or she has a good chance of being hired.

Careful research is a critical component and a central part of every sophisticated person's job search.

If you just think off the top of your head about the areas you should be targeting, your ideas will probably be superficial—and outdated.

Achieving Stability in a Changing World

How can you keep yourself stable in a constantly changing economy? If the world is being battered, and organizations are being battered, and many CEOs cannot keep their jobs, what are you going to do?

The following exercises will give you confidence and a sense of stability in a changing world. You will learn to know yourself and become sure of exactly what you can take with you wherever you go.

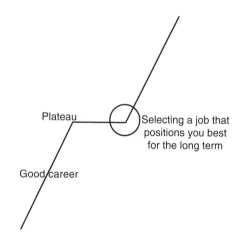

Plateau

Selecting a job that positions you best for the long term

Good career

The Result of Assessment Is Job Targets

If you go through an assessment with a career coach or vocational testing center and do not wind up with tentative job targets, the assessment has not helped you very much. You must go one more step and decide what to *do* with this information.

The Result of Assessment Is Power

The more you know about yourself, the more power you have to envision a suitable job for you. The exercises give you power.

People find it hard to believe that I went through a period of about 30 years when I was painfully shy. In graduate school, I was afraid when they took attendance because I obsessed over whether I should answer "here" or "present." When I gave a presentation, the best I could do was read the key words from my index cards. (Today, my throat is actually hoarse from all the public speaking I do.) I will be forever grateful for the kindness of strangers who told me I did well when I knew I was awful.

The only thing that ultimately saved me was doing the Seven Stories Exercise. When I was little, I led groups of kids in the neighborhood and I did it well. It gave me strength to know I was inherently a group leader regardless of how I was behaving now. (I was in my 30s at the time.)

The Seven Stories Exercise grounds you and the Forty-Year Vision guides you. When people said, "Would you like to lead groups?" I said to myself, "Well, I led groups when I was 10. Maybe I can do it again." The transition was painful and took many years, but my Seven Stories exercise kept me going. And my Forty-Year Vision let me know there was plenty of time in which to do it.

How to Decide What You Want

Let me listen to me and not to them.

Gertrude Stein

Looking Ahead—A Career Instead of a Job

If you don't decide where you want to go, you may wind up drifting from one organization to another whenever you're dissatisfied with pretty much the same job each time. Even deciding to continue what you're doing right now is a goal in itself and may be difficult to achieve.

The first step in career management is goal setting. There are a lot of processes involved in the goal-setting area. But the one considered most central is examining your past accomplishments, looking at your strongest and most enjoyable skills.

This process is not only the one favored by coaches, it is also the one most often used by successful people. In reading the biographies of such people, I see again and again how they established their goals by identifying those things they enjoy doing and also do well. This process of identifying your "enjoyable accomplishments" is the most important one you can go through.

It has long been an axiom of mine that the little things are infinitely the most important.

A. Conan Doyle, *A Case of Identity*

What Successful People Do

When Steven Jobs, the founder of Apple Computers, was fired by John Sculley, the man he brought in to run the company, he felt as though he had lost everything. Apple had been his life. Now he had lost not only his job but his company. People no longer felt the need to return his phone calls. He did what a lot of us would do. He got depressed. But then he took action.

Confused about what to do next . . . he [Jobs] put himself through an exercise that management psychologists employ with clients unsure about their life goals. It was a little thing, really. It was just a list. A list of all the things that mattered most to Jobs during his ten years at Apple. "Three things jumped off that piece of paper, three things that were really important to me," says Jobs.

Michael Meyer, *The Alexander Complex*

The exercise Steve Jobs went through is essentially what you will do in the Seven Stories exercise. The threads that ran through his stories formed the impetus for his next great drive: the formation of NeXT computers. If the Seven Stories exercise is good enough for Steve Jobs, maybe it's good enough for you.

"Successful managers," says Charles Garfield, head of Performance Services, Inc. in Berkeley, California, "go with their preferences." They search for work important to them and when they find it they pursue it with a passion.

Lester Korn, chairman of Korn, Ferry, notes in his book *The Success Profile:* "Few executives know, or can know, exactly what they aspire to until they have been in the work force for a couple of years. It takes that long to learn enough about yourself to know what you can do well and what will make you happy. The trick is to merge the two into a goal, then set off in pursuit of it."

I was going to buy a copy of The Power of Positive Thinking, *and then I thought:
What the hell good would that do?*

Ronnie Shakes

This book will help you decide what you want to do in your next job as well as in the long run. You will become clearer about the experiences you have enjoyed most and may like to repeat. You will also examine your interests and values and look at past positions to analyze what satisfied you and what did not. In addition, you will look further ahead (through your Forty-Year Vision) to see if some driving dream may influence what you will want to do in the short term. I did my Forty-Year Vision many years ago, and the vision I had of my future still drives me today.

Knowing where you would like to wind up broadens the kinds of jobs you might be interested in today.

Look at it this way:

A B   **C**

The line represents your life. Right now, you are at A. Your next job is B. If you look only at your past to decide what to do next, your next job

is limited by what you have already done. For example, if you have been in finance and accounting for the past 15 years and you base your next move on your past, your next job is likely to be in finance or accounting.

If you know at C you would like to wind up as vice president of finance and administration, new possibilities open up. Think of all the areas you would manage:

Finance	Operations
Administration	Personnel
Accounting	Computers

Experience in any one of these would advance your career in the right direction. For example, you may decide to get some computer experience.

Without the benefit of a Fifteen- or Forty-Year Vision, a move to computers might look like the start of a career in computers, but *you* know it's just one more assignment leading to your long-term goal. You'll keep your vision in mind and take jobs and assignments that will continually position you for the long run. For example, in the computer area, you may focus on personnel or administrative systems, two areas that fit your goal. Then your computer job will be more than a job. You will work hard for your employer, but you will also know why you are there—you are using your job as a stepping stone to something bigger and better.

To have a great purpose to work for, a purpose larger than ourselves, is one of the secrets of making life significant; for then the meaning and worth of the individual overflow his personal borders, and survive his death.

Will Durant

Deciding What You Want:
Selecting Your Job Targets

*It may sound surprising when I say, on the basis of
my own clinical experience as well as that of my
psychological and psychiatric colleagues,"that the
chief problem of people in the middle decade of the
twentieth century is emptiness."*

*By that I mean not only that many people do not
know what they want; they often do not have any
clear idea of what they feel.*

Rollo May, *Man's Search for Himself*

Studies have shown that up to 85 percent of all
American workers are unhappy in their jobs.
After going through an evaluation process
(assessment), some find that a small change is
all they need. On the other hand, some want to
make a major career change.

The exercises in this book will help you
assess yourself in an organized way so you can
better understand the situations in which you
perform your best and are happiest.

*What seems different in yourself; that's the rare thing
you possess. The one thing that gives each of us his
worth, and that's just what we try to suppress.
And we claim to love life.*

André Gide

Getting Started

You may do certain exercises in this book and skip
others. But don't skip the Seven Stories Exercise,
and try to do the Forty-Year Vision. If you have

had problems with bosses, analyze those situations. Examining your values may also be an issue
at this time. Your insights about yourself from the
Seven Stories Exercise will serve as a template for
selecting the right job.

After you do the exercises, brainstorm a
number of possible job targets inside and outside
your present organization. Then research each
target to find out what the job possibilities are for
someone like you. This book will guide you
through the entire process.

Consider Your History

If you have enjoyed certain jobs, attempt to
understand exactly what about them you enjoyed.
This will increase your chances of replicating the
enjoyable aspects.

For example, an accounting assistant will
probably not be happy in just any accounting job.
If what he really enjoyed was *helping* the business
manager make the business profitable and if this
thread of helping reappears in his enjoyable experiences (Seven Stories Exercise), then he would be
unhappy in a job where he was *not* helping.

If, however, his enjoyment primarily came
from reconciling numbers and resolving messes
while working alone, he needs a job with
accounting messes to be resolved and the
promise of more messes to come.

Furthermore, if he wants to replicate those
things he enjoyed, he can state them in the summary on his résumé.

For instance:

Accounting assistant
Serve as right hand to business manager,
improving organization's profitability.
or
Accounting assistant
Reconcile accounts and resolve problem situations

The Results of Assessment: Job Targets—*then* a Résumé

A job target contains three elements:

- industry or organization size (small, medium, or large organization)
- position or function and
- geographic location.

Industry or Organization Size

If someone is a lawyer, it makes a great deal of difference whether that person works for a corporation, a law firm, or a not-for-profit organization. Your environment affects your satisfaction level.

By the same token, some people are better suited to working in a large organization and others are better suited to a small one. Those who are unhappy may simply need to work in an organization of a different size.

. . . [A]nd then I decided that to turn your life around you had to start from the inside.

Ethan Canin, *Emperor of the Air*

Position or Function

Some people are urged to go into finance or work the family farm, when those fields may not be at all appropriate for them. When you do the Seven Stories Exercise, you will notice whether there is any self-support for the fields others have chosen for you.

If you already have experience in one field, you may be reluctant to find something else. Even

very young people feel it is *too late to start over*. But you owe it to yourself to find your rightful place in the world. It may be you have to take a job in one field while you get experience in your dream field on the side. In general, it is relatively easy to get experience in the new field if you really want it.

Geographic Location

Is one geographic area the same as another to you? Probably not. Assess your feelings about this, because nothing will affect your lifestyle more than the geographic area you choose. On the other hand, you may accept living in an otherwise unacceptable location so you can get the experience you need.

A man is what he thinks about all day long.

Ralph Waldo Emerson

Looking Ahead—A Career Instead of a Job

Assessment will help you decide what you want to do in your next job as well as in the long run. Through your Forty-Year Vision, you may uncover a hidden dream that will dramatically influence what you want to do in both the short and the long run. I did my own Forty-Year Vision many years ago and the idea I had then about my future still drives me today, even though that vision was actually rather vague at the time. Knowing where you would like to wind up in 10, 20, 30, or 40 years can broaden your ideas about the kinds of jobs in which you may be interested today. The Forty-Year Vision is powerful.

The Seven Stories Exercise is equally powerful. Without it, many job hunters develop stilted descriptions of what they have accomplished. The exercise frees you up to brag a little and express things very differently. The results will add life to your résumé and your interviews and also dramatically increase your self-confidence.

No Easy Way

It would be nice if you could simply take a test to tell you what you should be. Unfortunately, there is no such sure-fire test. But fortunately in today's rapidly changing world you are allowed to be many things: You can be a doctor *and* a concert violinist. You have an abundance of choices.

A Clear Direction

People are happy when they are working toward their goals. When they get diverted from their goals, they are unhappy. Life has a way of sneaking up and distracting you. Many people are unhappy in their jobs because they don't know where they are going.

People without goals are more irked by petty problems on their jobs. Those with goals are less bothered because they have bigger plans. To control your life, you have to know where you are going and be ready for your next move—in case the ax falls on you.

Even after you take that next job, continue to manage your career. Organizations rarely build straight-line career paths for their employees anymore. Many progressive moves are actually lateral and broaden your experience base. Make your own way inside your organization.

Exercises to Analyze Your Past and Present: The Seven Stories Exercise

The direction of change to seek is not in our four dimensions: it is getting deeper into what you are, where you are, like turning up the volume on the amplifier.

Thaddeus Golas, *Lazy Man's Guide to Enlightenment*

In this exercise, you will examine your accomplishments, looking at your strongest and most enjoyable skills. The core of most coaching exercises is some version of the Seven Stories Exercise. A coach may give you a lot of tests and exercises, but this one requires *work* on your part and will yield the most important results. An interest or personality test is not enough. There is no easy way. Remember, busy executives take the time to complete this exercise—if it's good enough for them, it's good enough for you.

Do not skip the Seven Stories Exercise. It will provide you with information for your career direction, résumé, and interviews. After you do the exercise, brainstorm about a number of possible job targets. Then research each target to find out what the job possibilities are for someone like you.

If you're like most people, you have never taken the time to sort out the things at which you're good and also are motivated to accomplish. As a result, you probably don't use these talents as completely or as effectively as you could. Too often, we do things to please someone else or to survive in a job. Then we get stuck in a rut—that is, we're *always* trying to please someone else or *always* trying to survive in a job. We lose sight of what could satisfy us and work

becomes drudgery rather than fun. When we become so enmeshed in survival or in trying to please others, it may be difficult to figure out what we would rather be doing.

When you uncover your motivated skills, you'll be better able to identify jobs that allow you to use them and recognize other jobs that don't quite fit the bill. "Motivated skills" are patterns that run through our lives. Since they are skills from which we get satisfaction, we'll find ways to do them even if we don't get to do them at work. We still might not know what these skills are—for us, they're just something we do and we take them for granted.

Tracking down these patterns takes some thought. The payoff: Our motivated skills do not change. They run throughout our lives and indicate what will keep us motivated for the rest of our lives.

One's prime is elusive. . . . You must be on the alert to recognize your prime at whatever time of life it may occur.

Muriel Spark, *The Prime of Miss Jean Brodie*

The Seven Stories: An Exercise for Developing Self-Awareness

In addition to becoming aware of the outside world, you need to become more *self*-aware. You need to figure out the things you enjoy doing and also do well, and the best way to do this is the Seven Stories Exercise.

You will start by analyzing your accomplishments. Think about the answer to this: "Tell me an accomplishment in your life you enjoyed doing and also did well." Be as specific as possible. "Writing" is not good enough."Writing some text for the company's annual report" is an accomplishment you can analyze. After you name a few accomplishments, rank them in the order of the ones you enjoyed the most and did the best.

Examine those episodes that gave you a sense of accomplishment. Episodes from your childhood are important, too, because they took place when you were less likely to be trying to "get ahead."

You are asked to name 10 accomplishments so you will not be too judgmental—just list anything that occurs to you. Expect this exercise to take you 4 or 5 days. Most people carry around a piece of paper so they can jot down things as they occur to them. When you have 25, select the 7 that are most important to *you* by however you define important. Then rank them with the most important first and so on.

Starting with your first story, write a paragraph about each accomplishment. Then find out what your accomplishments have in common. If you are having trouble doing the exercises, ask a friend to help you talk them through. Friends tend to be more objective and will probably point out strengths you never recognized.

You will probably be surprised. For example, you may be especially good at interacting with people, but it's something you've always done and therefore take for granted. This may be a thread that runs through your life and may be one of your motivated skills. It *may* be you'll be unhappy in a job that doesn't allow you to deal with people.

Your *motivated abilities* (the things you enjoy doing and also do well) may or may not change over time. However, self-knowledge is a worthwhile skill to develop. The more aware you are about yourself, the better you will be at selecting appropriate careers. You are simply trying to understand yourself better.

Let's look at Suzanne, who described a dramatic accomplishment: "When I was nine years old, I was living with my three sisters. There was a fire in our house and our cat had hidden under the bed. We were all outside, but I decided to run back in and save the cat. And I did it."

No matter what the story is, delve in a little by asking yourself these two questions: What gave you the sense of accomplishment? and What about it made you proud? These questions give you a quick fix on yourself. You can also ask the questions listed earlier.

I asked Suzanne these questions. At first she said: "I was proud because I did what I thought was right." When I probed a little, she added: "I had a sense of accomplishment because I was able to make an instant decision under pressure. I was proud because I overcame my fear."

I asked Suzanne for another story to see what patterns might emerge when we put the two together. In both stories, Suzanne showed she was good at making decisions in tense situations. She showed a good intuitive sense. She's decisive and likes fast-paced, energetic situations. She likes to overcome her own fears, as well as the objections of others.

We needed more than two stories to see if these patterns ran throughout Suzanne's life and to see what other patterns might emerge. After the full exercise, Suzanne felt she definitely wanted excitement in her jobs, a sense of urgency—that she wanted to be in a position where she had a chance to be decisive and operate intuitively. Those are the conditions she enjoys and under which she operates at her best. Suzanne can confidently say she thrives on excitement, high pressure, and quick decision making. She'll probably do better in jobs with those elements since they match her skills, interests, and values.

Illness strikes men when they are exposed to change.

Herodotus, Greek historian

Your Anchor in a Changing World

Your motivated skills are your anchor in a world of uncertainty. The world will change, but your motivated skills remain constant.

Write them down. Save the list. Over the years, refer to them to make sure you are still on target—doing things you do well and are motivated to do. As you refer to them, they will influence your life. Five years from now, an opportunity may present itself. In reviewing your list, you will have every confidence that this opportunity is right for you. After all, you have been doing these things since you were a child, you know you enjoy them, and you do them well!

Knowing our patterns gives us a sense of stability and helps us understand what we have done so far. It also gives us the freedom to try new things regardless of risk or what others may say, because we can be absolutely sure this is the way we are. Knowing your patterns gives you both security and flexibility—and you need both to cope in this changing world.

Now think about your own stories. Write down everything that occurs to you.

We are challenged on every hand to work untiringly to achieve excellence in our lifework. . . . If a man is called to be a street sweeper, he should sweep streets even as Michelangelo painted, or Beethoven composed music, or Shakespeare wrote poetry. He should sweep streets so well that all the hosts of heaven and earth will pause to say, "Here lives a great street sweeper who did his job well."

Rev. Martin Luther King, Jr.

Our deepest fear is not that we are inadequate. Our deepest fear is that we are powerful beyond measure. It is our light, not our darkness, that most frightens us. We ask ourselves, "Who am I to be brilliant, gorgeous, talented and fabulous?" Actually, who are you not to be? You are a child of God. Your playing small doesn't serve the world. There's nothing enlightened about shrinking so that other people won't feel insecure around you. We were born to make manifest the glory of God that is within us. It's not just in some of us; it's in everyone. And as we let our own light shine, we unconsciously give other people permission to do the same. As we are liberated from our own fear, our presence automatically liberates others.

Nelson Mandela
1994 Inaugural Speech

The Ugly Duckling was so happy and in some way he was glad that he had experienced so much hardship and misery; for now he could fully appreciate his tremendous luck and the great beauty that greeted him. . . . And he rustled his feathers, held his long neck high, and with deep emotion he said: "I never dreamt of so much happiness, when I was the Ugly Duckling!"

Hans Christian Anderson, *The Ugly Duckling*

The Seven Stories Exercise® Worksheet

Here is an opportunity to examine the most satisfying activities of your life and discover those skills you will want to use as you grow older. You will be looking at the times when you feel you did something very well that you also enjoyed doing. It doesn't matter what other people thought, or when in your life the experiences took place. **All that matters is you felt happy about doing whatever it was and thought you did it well.** Think about when you were younger. When I did my own Seven Stories Exercise, I remembered the time when I was 10 years old and led a group of kids in the neighborhood, enjoyed it, and did it well. It make take you a few days to think of things to put on your list. Carry around a piece of paper to jot down ideas as you think of them.

Section I

List below all the activities that meet the above definition. Come up with at least 10. We ask for 10 stories so you won't be too selective. Just write down anything that occurs to you, no matter how trivial it may seem. Try to **think of concrete examples**, situations, and tasks, not generalized skills or abilities. It may be helpful if you say to yourself, **"There was the time when I . . ."** Here are a few examples:

RIGHT	WRONG
• Got extensive media coverage for a new product launch	• Writing press releases
• Delivered speech to get German business	• Delivering speeches
• Coordinated blood drive for division	• Coordinating
• Came in third in County bike race	• Cycling

1. _____
2. _____
3. _____
4. _____
5. _____
6. _____
7. _____
8. _____
9. _____
10. _____

Section II

For each accomplishment, describe what you did. Write the specifics, noting each step in detail. Notice the role you played and your relationship with others (member of team, working alone, leader, etc.), the subject matter, the skills used, and so on. Notice the threads that run through the stories so you can discover things you do well and that also give you satisfaction. What did you enjoy the most in each story? Do the best?

Analyzing Your Seven Stories

Now it is time to analyze your stories. You are trying to look for the threads that run through them so you will know the things you do well that also give you satisfaction. Some of the questions below sound similar. That's okay. They are a catalyst to make you think more deeply about the experience. The questions don't have any hidden psychological significance.

If your accomplishments happen to be mostly work related, this exercise will form the basis for your "positioning" or summary statement in your résumé and also for your Two-Minute Pitch.

If these accomplishments are mostly not work related, they will still give you some idea of how you may want to slant your résumé, and they may give you an idea of how you will want your career to go in the long run.

For now, simply go through each story without trying to force it to come out any particular way. Just think hard about yourself. And be as honest as you can. When you have completed this analysis, the words in the next exercise may help you think of additional things.

What did you **do best**? _____

What was your **key motivator**? _____

What **led up to your getting involved**? (e.g., assigned to do it, thought it up myself, etc.)_____

_____

What was your **relationship with others**? (e.g., leader, worked alone, inspired others, team member,

etc.) _____

Describe the **environment** in which you performed. _____

What was the **subject matter**? (e.g., music, mechanics, trees, budgets, etc.) _____

Story #2_____
Main accomplishment? _____
Enjoyed most?_____
Did best? _____
Key motivator? _____
What led up to it? _____
My role?_____
Environment? _____
Subject matter? _____

Story #3_____
Main accomplishment? _____
Enjoyed most?_____
Did best? _____
Key motivator? _____
What led up to it? _____
My role?_____
Environment? _____
Subject matter? _____

(continues)

Analyzing Your Seven Stories *(continued)*

Story #4_____
Main accomplishment? _____
Enjoyed most?_____
Did best? _____
Key motivator? _____
What led up to it? _____
My role?_____
Environment? _____
Subject matter? _____

Story #5_____
Main accomplishment? _____
Enjoyed most?_____
Did best? _____
Key motivator? _____
What led up to it? _____
My role?_____
Environment? _____
Subject matter? _____

Story #6_____
Main accomplishment? _____
Enjoyed most?_____
Did best? _____
Key motivator? _____
What led up to it? _____
My role?_____
Environment? _____
Subject matter? _____

Story #7_____
Main accomplishment? _____
Enjoyed most?_____
Did best? _____
Key motivator? _____
What led up to it? _____
My role?_____
Environment? _____
Subject matter? _____

We are here to be excited from youth to old age, to have an insatiable curiosity about the world. . . .
We are also here to help others by practicing a friendly attitude. And every person is born for a purpose.
Everyone has a God-given potential, in essence, built into them. And if we are to live life to its fullest, we
must realize that potential.

Norman Vincent Peale

Skills from Your Seven Stories

The numbers across the top represent each of your seven stories. Start with story #1 and check off all of your specialized skills that appear in it. When you've checked off the skills for all seven stories, total them.

Story #	1	2	3	4	5	6	7	Total
Administration								
Advising/consulting								
Analytical								
Artistic								
Budgetary								
Client relations								
Control								
Coordination								
Creativity								
Decisiveness								
Design								
Development								
Financial								
Foresight								
Frugality								
Fund-raising								
Human relations								
Information mgmt.								
Imagination								
Individualism								
Initiative								
Inventiveness								
Leadership								
Liaison								
Logic								
Management								
Marketing								
Mathematical								
Mechanical								
Motivational								
Negotiation								
Observation								
Organization								
Other talents:								

Story #	1	2	3	4	5	6	7	Total
Operations mgmt.								
Org. design/devel.								
Ownership								
Perceptiveness								
Perseverance								
Persuasiveness								
Planning								
Policy making								
Practicality								
Presentation								
Problem solving								
Procedures design								
Production								
Program concept								
Program design								
Project management								
Promotion								
Public relations								
Public speaking								
Quality assessment								
Research								
Resourcefulness								
Sales								
Service								
Showmanship								
Speaking								
Staff dev./mgmt.								
Strategic planning								
Stress tolerance								
Systems								
Teamwork								
Tenacity								
Training								
Travel								
Troubleshooting								
Writing								
Other talents:								

Note: Job hunters enjoy exercises like this because they are simple. But **your experiences are more complex than the words on this page**. These words alone do not reflect the richness of what you have to offer. So **pay more attention to the more in-depth answers you came up with on the preceding page** and continue to analyze your stories throughout your life. You will find deeper and deeper answers about yourself.

Top six or seven specialized skills according to which had the most checkmarks:

1. _____
2. _____
3. _____
4. _____
5. _____
6. _____
7. _____

Your Current Work-Related Values

What is important to you? Your values change as you grow and change, so they need to be reassessed periodically. At various stages in your career, you may value money or leisure time or independence on the job or working for something in which you believe. See what is important to you *now*. This will help you not to be upset if, for instance, a job provides you with the freedom you wanted but not the kind of money your friends are making.

Sometimes we are not aware of our own values. At one stage of our lives, time with our family may be most important to us. For some people, money or power is most important, but they may be reluctant to admit it—even to themselves.

Values are the driving force behind what we do. It is important to truthfully understand what you value to increase your chances of getting what you want.

Look at the list of values below. Think of each in terms of your overall career objectives. Rate the degree of importance you would assign to each for yourself using this scale:

1—Not at all important in my choice of job   3—Reasonably important
2—Not very but somewhat important   4—Very important

Add other values that don't appear on the list or substitute wording with which you are more comfortable.

___ chance to advance	___ artistic or other creativity
___ work on frontiers of knowledge	___ learning
___ having authority (responsibility)	___ workplace location
___ helping society	___ tranquility
___ helping others	___ money earned
___ meeting challenges	___ change and variety
___ working for something I believe in	___ having time for personal life
___ public contact	___ fast pace
___ enjoyable colleagues	___ power
___ competition	___ adventure/risk taking
___ ease (freedom from worry)	___ prestige
___ influencing people	___ moral fulfillment
___ enjoyable work tasks	___ recognition from superiors, society, peers
___ working alone	___ security (stability)
___ being an expert	___ physical work environment
___ personal growth and development	___ chance to make an impact
___ independence	___ clear expectations and procedures

Of those you marked "4," circle the five **most** important to you today:

- If forced to compromise on any of these, which one(s) would you give up? _____

- Which one(s) would you be most reluctant to give up? _____

Describe in 10 or 20 words what you want most in your life and/or career.

Other Exercises: Interests, Satisfiers, and Bosses

Interests Exercise

For many people, interests should stay as interests—things they do on the side. Others' interests may be a clue to the kinds of jobs they should do next or in the long run. Only you can decide whether your interests should become part of your work life.

List all the things you really like to do—anything that makes you feel good and gives you satisfaction. List those areas in which you have developed a relatively in-depth knowledge or expertise. For ideas, think of your day, your week, the seasons of the year, places, people, work, courses, roles, leisure time, friends, family, etc. Think of how you spend your discretionary time.

- Think about the books you read, the magazines to which you subscribe, the section of the newspaper to which you turn first.

- Think about knowledge you've built up simply because you're interested in something.

- Think about volunteer work you do—what are the recurring assignments you tend to get and enjoy?

- Think about your hobbies—are there one or two with which you have become so involved that you have acquired a lot of expertise/information in those areas?

- What are the things you find yourself doing all the time and enjoying even though you don't have to do them?

Your interests may be a clue to what you would like in a job. Rob worked at a law firm, but loved everything about wine. He left the law firm to become a lawyer in a wine company. Most people's interests should stay as interests, but you never know until you think about it.

Satisfiers and Dissatisfiers Exercise

List every job you have ever had. List what was satisfying and dissatisfying about each job. Some people are surprised to find they were sometimes most satisfied by the vacation, pay, title, and other perks, but were not satisfied with the job itself.

Job	Satisfiers	Dissatisfiers

Bosses Exercise

Make a list of all the bosses you have ever had in work situations, using a very broad definition of the word *boss*. If you are very young, they don't have to have been bosses in the strictest sense of the word. Include bosses from part-time jobs, summer jobs, and even professors with whom you worked closely as a student.

Examine those bosses you had a good relationship with and those with whom you did not and determine what you need in your future relationship with bosses. If you have had a lot of problems with bosses, discuss this with your coach.

Boss	Good Relationship	Poor Relationship

The
Five
O'Clock
Club

PART TWO

Designing Your Career

LOOKING INTO YOUR FUTURE

The
Five
O'Clock
Club

Job Hunting versus Career Planning

*Most people say their main fault is a
lack of discipline. On deeper thought,
I believe that is not the case.
The basic problem is that their priorities have not
become deeply planted in their hearts and minds.*

Stephen R. Covey,
The Seven Habits of Highly Effective People

Making career improvements is a continual process. To make smoother transitions, learn to plan ahead.

If you have a vision and keep it in mind, you can constantly "position" yourself for your long-range goal by taking jobs and assignments that lead you there. Then your next job will be more than just a job. It will be a stepping stone on the way to something bigger and better.

When faced with a choice, **select the job that fits best with your Fifteen- or Forty-Year Vision—the job that positions you best for the long term**.

The Forty-Year Vision is presented in this section of the book. Completing this exercise will help you establish your long-term goals. The Vision is perhaps the single most important criterion for selecting jobs. The case studies that follow will show how this Vision helped people make key career decisions. As in the rest of this book, all of the people described are real people and their case histories are true.

Selecting the Right Offer

Doing the exercises will give you some perspective when choosing among job offers. I hope you will attempt to get many job possibilities in the works. Then, choose the one that positions you best for the long run.

Thinking Big; Thinking Small

A Forty-Year Vision gives you perspective. Without one, you may think too small or too big. Writing it down makes you more reasonable, more thoughtful, and more serious. **Having a vision also makes you less concerned about others' progress because you know where *you* are going**.

Consider Objective and Subjective Information

If you tend to pay too much attention to subjective information, balance it by asking: "What is the logical thing for me to do regardless of how I feel?"

If you tend to be too objective, ask: "I know the logical thing to do, but how do I really feel about it?"

Life Skills, Not Just Job-Hunting Skills

A vision helps people see ahead and realize they can not only advance in their careers, but also change their life circumstances—such as who their friends are and where they live.

Your career is not separate from your life. If you dream of living in a better place, you have to earn more money. If you would like to be with better types of people, you need to **become a better person yourself**.

The Forty-Year Vision cannot be done in a vacuum. **Research is the key to *achieving* your vision. Without research, it is difficult to imagine what might be out there, or to imagine dream situations**.

The assessment exercises are important for another reason. Someday in your career, you will come across a shallow, rough person who does not understand your value. But if you have done the exercises in this book—especially the Seven Stories and the Fifteen- or Forty-Year Visions—you will understand your own value and your self-esteem is more likely to remain intact. You will keep yourself on course and continue to follow your vision.

The better you are at plotting out your own future, the more each job will fit in with your long-term vision, and you will not get so ruffled by corporate politics and pettiness.

America has entered the age of the contingent or temporary worker, of the consultant or subcontractor, of the just-in-time work force— fluid, flexible, disposable. This is the future. Its message is this: You are on your own.

For good (sometimes) and ill (often), the workers of the future will constantly have to sell their skills, invent new relationships with employers who must, themselves, change and adapt constantly in order to survive in a ruthless global market.

Lance Morrow, "The Temping of America," *Time*, March 29, 1993

Changes Mean New Opportunities

The world is changing. What's hot today is not tomorrow. You can use these changes to your advantage. You can choose to head your career in the direction that's right for you.

You can impose your own terms upon life. You don't have to accept the terms it offers you. Read on and see what others have done.

Why Use a Career Coach?

In this changing marketplace, we all have to be out there selling ourselves. This is causing people a great deal of understandable stress. Most of us would rather just do our jobs and trust we will be treated fairly. Since we cannot depend on this, some people have made a career coach a normal part of their lives—as normal as having a regular tune-up on their car or an annual physical. They go to their coach not just when they are conducting a job search or when they have problems, but perhaps once or twice a year for a checkup.

Clients working with a career coach learn what works for them personally and what does not, come to better understand the kinds of environments in which they should be working (bosses, corporate cultures, pace, and so on), learn how to be more effective in their work relationships (bosses, peers, subordinates, clients), learn how to balance their lives more effectively, and also lay the groundwork for the next career move they may have to make. They talk about their long-term career goals and the steps they need to take to reach them—or perhaps simply to stay even. They make sure they are doing what they must to develop their careers as the economy changes, such as getting specific experience, taking courses, or joining professional or industry organizations.

Over time, your coach gets to know you, just as your family doctor gets to know you, and can warn you against things that may cause you problems, or advise you about things you could be doing next. Just as a family doctor gives you a complete physical when you become his or her patient, so, too, your coach would want to give you an assessment to find out as much as possible about you.

If you decide to use a private coach, use someone who charges by the hour. Do not pay a huge up-front fee. After you have worked with the coach a number of times, assess your relationship with him or her. Make sure there's a good personality fit between you and your coach. For example, some coaches are very intense, while others have a softer approach. If the relationship is not good, or if the meetings damage your sense of self-worth, go to someone else.

For your part, make sure you are willing to make the necessary commitment. If you go only for one hour to have the coach handle an emergency you are facing, do not expect that coach to come to know very much about you. If you decide to use a coach, you are likely to learn more about the wonderful person you are, so you can figure out how you fit into this changing world. You will increase both your self-esteem and your effectiveness.

For most of us, it is easier to think about how to get what we want than to know what exactly we should want.

Robert N. Bellah et al., *Habits of the Heart*

Develop a Vision; Make a Commitment

Take a stand. Decide where you want to head, and go for it. You'll be happier because you'll have a goal and you'll work toward it. Work will no longer be *work,* but an activity that brings pleasure, pride, and a sense of accomplishment and that carries out your vision.

When you know yourself and make a commitment, things become clearer. You act more decisively, have less stress, and cope better with the progress of your career and the changes

around you. Negative things will not bother you as much. The direction will not be coming from someone else, but from inside you.

Without commitment, we are wanderers without roots in a rapidly changing world. We feel a lack of meaning in our lives.

Commitment means accepting your responsibility for your own career direction. It means *choosing* what you want to do in this changing society without losing your inner bearings.

A man may not achieve everything he has dreamed, but he will never achieve anything great without having dreamed it first.

William James

Looking for Where You Fit In

We each fit in. What you're looking for is *where* you fit in. Don't be *too* specific about what you want. If you are open to new opportunities, surprising things can happen. A large number of jobs are created with a certain person in mind. A job created with you in mind would probably be more satisfying than one in which you would have to mold yourself to fit a rigid job description. You would enjoy your job more and do better because you would be doing what you want.

What are the chances of having a job created to suit you? If you don't know what would suit you, the chances are slim. Having definite ideas increases your chances of finding such a job or even of changing your present job to better suit your goals. Opportunities come along all the time. You won't recognize them unless you know what you are seeking.

We change the world and the world changes us. As we grow, we are developing ourselves—in relation to the world. We are each trying to know what we want and how to get it, while we are also trying to understand and fit into a changing world. It is a lifelong process, but a happy one. It is a process of seeing change as an opportunity while accepting the limitations of the world.

CASE STUDY *Henry*
Aiming Too Low

Henry, an executive of about 45, had just been fired and I was asked to be his coach. Henry said he already had a clear idea of what he wanted to do next—something quite in demand, loan workouts (when loans go bad, he would try to salvage them). Henry could certainly have gotten such a job, and quickly, but I felt as though I didn't know him at all, so I asked if we could do a few exercises. If I understood him better, I would be in a better position to coach him.

In his Seven Stories, Henry stated he was proud he had grown up in a tiny Midwestern town (there were only 60 people in his entire high school), had gotten into Harvard, and graduated very high in his class.

Where was that little boy now? What had caused him to settle for a loan workout position that would have been right for lots of *other* people? I told Henry I thought he could do better. I asked him to aim at finding a job that would make him so proud it would wind up on his *future* Seven Stories list.

Within two-and-a-half months, Henry had landed a job that was better than anything he had ever dreamed possible. At an excellent salary, he became one of the top 10 executives in a major insurance company. Henry was so proud, he beamed. He's still there now and doing very well.

CASE STUDY *Alicia*
Knowing Where She Wants to End Up

Alicia has been in corporate marketing for eight years. Through the Seven Stories exercise and her Forty-Year Vision, she developed a long-term view of herself: head of a 500-person public-sector-related agency or organization such as the World Wildlife Fund.

Now that she knows where she wants to end up, she can work backward to figure out how she could get there. To head up such a large organization, she has two choices: She can start it from scratch or she can take over an existing organization. Alicia decided that five years from now, she would prefer to become the head of an existing 50-person organization and expand it to a 500-person organization.

But how can she go from where she is now to becoming the head of a 50-person organization? What she has to offer is her corporate marketing background. Therefore, her next logical step is to try to get a marketing job in a not-for-profit organization similar to the one she would eventually like to lead. That way, her next job will position her well for the next moves and increase her chance of getting where she wants to go.

The Benefits of Knowing What You Want

You are responsible for your own career development. Decide what you want, rather than hoping someone will think about it for you. Now is the time to get started.

The psychic task which a person can and must set for himself is not to feel secure, but to be able to tolerate insecurity, without panic and undue fear.

Erich Fromm, *The Sane Society*

Optimism Emerges as Best Predictor to Success in Life

"Hope has proven a powerful predictor of outcome in every study we've done so far," said Dr. Charles R. Snyder, a psychologist at the University of Kansas. . . . "Having hope means believing you have both the will and the way to accomplish your goals, whatever they may be. . . . It's not enough to just have the wish for something. You need the means, too. On the other hand, all the skills to solve a problem won't help if you don't have the willpower to do it."

Dr. Snyder found that people with high levels of hope share several attributes:

- Unlike people who are low in hope, they turn to friends for advice on how to achieve their goals.

- They tell themselves they can succeed at what they need to do.

- Even in a tight spot, they tell themselves things will get better as time goes on.

- They are flexible enough to find different ways to get to their goals.

- If hope for one goal fades, they aim for another. Those low on hope tend to become fixated on one goal and persist even when they find themselves blocked. They just stay at it and get frustrated.

- They show an ability to break a formidable task into specific, achievable chunks. People low in hope see only the large goal and not the small steps to it along the way.

People who get a high score on the hope scale have had as many hard times as those with low scores, but have learned to think about it in a hopeful way, seeing a setback as a challenge, not a failure.

Daniel Goleman,
The New York Times,
December 24, 1991

Whatever your level, to get ahead you need:

- **exposure** to other possibilities and other dreams
- **hard facts** about those possibilities and dreams (through networking and research)
- the **skills** required in today's job market
- **job-search training** to help you get the work for which you are qualified.

Looking into Your Future

*Every now and then I think about my own death,
and I think about my own funeral. . . . I ask myself,
"What is it that I would want said?"
Say I was a drum major for justice; say that I was
a drum major for peace; say that I was a drum
major for righteousness. All of the other shallow
things will not matter. . . . I just want to leave a
committed life behind.*

Rev. Martin Luther King, Jr.

Your motivated abilities tell you the *elements* you need to make you happy, the Values exercise tells you the values important to you right now, and the Interests exercise may give you a clue to other fields or industries to explore. But none of them gives you a feel for the *scope* of what may lie ahead.

Dreams and goals can be great driving forces in our lives. We feel satisfied when we are working toward them—even if we never reach them. People who have dreams or goals do better than people who don't.

Setting goals will make a difference in your life and this makes sense. Every day we make dozens of choices. People with dreams make choices that advance them in the right direction. People without dreams also make choices—but their choices are strictly present oriented with little thought of the future. When you are aware of your current situation and you also know where you want to go, a natural tension leads you forward faster.

When you find a believable dream that excites you, don't forget it. In the heat of our day-to-day living, our dreams slip out of our minds.

Happy people keep an eye on the future, as well as the present.

Freeing-Up Exercises

Here are a few exercises to inspire you and move you forward, add meaning to your everyday life, and give it some long-term purpose.

It's okay if you never reach your dreams. In fact, it can be better to have some dreams you will probably never reach, as long as you enjoy the *process* of trying to reach them. For example, a real estate developer may dream of owning all the real estate in Phoenix. He may wind up owning much more than if he did not have that dream. If he enjoys the *process* of acquiring real estate, that's all that matters.

Exercise #1—Write Your Obituary

Rev. Martin Luther King, Jr. knew how he wanted to be remembered. He had a dream, and it drove his life. Write out what you would want the newspapers to say about *you* when you die. Alfred Nobel had a chance to *rewrite* his obituary. The story goes like this: His cousin, who was also named Alfred, died. The newspapers, hearing of the death of Alfred Nobel, printed the prepared obituary—for the wrong man. Alfred read it the day after his cousin's death. He was upset by what the obituary said because it starkly showed him how he would be remembered: as the well-known inventor of a cheap explosive called dynamite.

Alfred resolved to change his life. Today, he's remembered as the Swedish chemist and inventor who provided for the Nobel Prizes.

Write your obituary as you want to be remembered after your death. Include parts *not* related to your job. If you don't like the way your life seems to be headed, change it—just as Alfred Nobel did. Write your own obituary, and *then make a list of the things you need to do to get there.*

Exercise #2—Invent a Job

If you could have any job in the world, what would it be? Don't worry about the possibility of ever finding that job—make it up! Invent it. Write it out. It may spark you to think of how to create that job in real life.

Exercise #3—If You Had a Million

If you had a million dollars (or maybe 10 million) but still had to work, what would you do?

When I asked myself this question some time ago, I decided I'd like to continue doing what I was doing at work, but would like to write a book on job hunting because I felt I had something to say. I did write that book—and I've gone on to write others!

People often erroneously see a lack of money as a stumbling block to their goals. Think about it: Is there some way you could do what you want without a million dollars? Then do it!

Exercise #4—Your Fifteen-Year and Forty-Year Visions

Take a look at this very important exercise, which starts on the next page.

The Five O'Clock Club

Your Fifteen-Year Vision®
and Your Forty-Year Vision®

In my practice as a psychiatrist, I have found that helping people to develop personal goals has proved to be the most effective way to help them cope with problems.

Ari Kiev, M.D., *A Strategy for Daily Living*

If you could imagine your ideal life five years from now, what would it be like? How would it be different from the way it is now? If you made new friends during the next five years, what would they be like? Where would you be living? What would your hobbies and interests be? How about 10 years from now? 20? 30? 40? Think about it!

Some people feel locked in by their present circumstances. Many say it is too late for them. But a lot can happen in 5, 10, 20, 30, or 40 years. Reverend King had a dream. His dream helped all of us, but his dream helped him too. He was living according to a vision (which he thought was God's plan for him). *It gave him a purpose in life.* Most successful people have a vision.

A lot can happen to you over the next few decades—and most of what happens is up to you. If you see the rest of your life as boring, I'm sure you will be right. Some people pick the *sensible* route or the one that fits in with how others see them, rather than the one that is best for them.

On the other hand, you can come up with a few different scenarios of how your life could unfold. In that case, you will have to do a lot of thinking and research to figure out which path makes the most sense for you and will make you happiest.

When a person finds the right vision, the most common reaction is fear. It is often safer to *wish* a better life than to actually go after it.

I know what that's like. It took me two years of thinking and research to figure out the right path for myself—one that included my motivated abilities (Seven Stories Exercise), as well as the sketchy vision I had for myself. Then it took *10 more years* to finally take the plunge and commit to that path—running The Five O'Clock Club. I was 40 years old when I finally took a baby step in the right direction and I was terrified.

You may be lucky and find it easy to write out your vision of your future. Or you may be more like me: It may take a while and a lot of hard work. You can speed up the process by reviewing your assessment results with a Five O'Clock Club career coach. He or she will guide you along. Remember, when I was struggling, the country didn't *have* Five O'Clock Club coaches or even these exercises to guide us.

Test your vision and see if that path seems right for you. Plunge in by researching it and meeting with people in the field. If it is what you want, chances are you will find some way to make it happen. If it is not exactly right, you can modify it later—after you have gathered more information and perhaps gotten more experience.

Start with the Present

Write down, in the present tense, the way your life is right now and the way you see yourself at each of the time intervals listed. **This exercise should take no more than one hour.** Allow your unconscious to tell you what you will be doing in the future. Just quickly comment on each of the questions listed on the following page, and then move on to the next. If you kill yourself off too early (say, at age 60), push it 10 more years to see what would have happened if you had lived. Then push it another 10, just for fun.

When you have finished the exercise, ask yourself how you feel about your entire life as you laid it out in your vision. Some people feel depressed when they see on paper how their lives are going and they cannot think of a way out. But they feel better when a good friend or a Five O'Clock Club coach helps them think of a better future toward which they can work. If you don't like your vision, you are allowed to change it—it's your life. Do what you want with it. Pick the kind of life you want.

Start the exercise with the way things are now so you will be realistic about your future. Now, relax and have a good time going through the years. Don't think too hard. See where you wind up. You have plenty of time to get things done.

> **The 15-year mark proves to be the most important for most people. It's far enough away from the present to allow you to dream.**

There are more things in heaven and earth, Horatio, than are dreamt of in your philosophy.

William Shakespeare, *Hamlet*

Your Fifteen- and Forty-Year Vision Worksheet

The most fundamental application of "begin with the end in mind" is to begin today with the image, picture, or paradigm of the end of your life as your frame of reference or the criterion by which everything else is examined.

Stephen R. Covey, *The Seven Habits of Highly Effective People*

1. The year is **xxxx** (current year).
   You are _____ years old right now.

- Tell me what your life is like right now. (Say anything you want about your life as it is now.)
- Who are your friends? What do they do for a living?
- What is your relationship with your family, however you define "family"?
- Are you married? Single? Children? (List ages.)
- Where are you living? What does it look like?
- What are your hobbies and interests?
- What do you do for exercise?
- How is your health?
- How do you take care of your spiritual needs?
- What kind of work are you doing?
- What else would you like to note about your life right now?

Year: _____   Your Age _____

_____

Don't worry if you don't like everything about your life right now. Most people do this exercise because they want to improve themselves. They want to *change* something. What do *you* want to change? **Please continue.**

2. The year is **xxxx** (current year + **5**).
   You are _____ years old.
   (Add 5 to present age.)
   Things are going well for you.

- What is your life like now at this age? (Say anything you want about your life as it is now.)
- Who are your friends? What do they do for a living?
- What is your relationship with your "family"?
- Married? Single? Children? (List their ages now.)
- Where are you living? What does it look like?
- What are your hobbies and interests?
- What do you do for exercise?
- How is your health?
- How do you take care of your spiritual needs?
- What kind of work are you doing?
- What else would you like to note about your life right now?

Year: _____   Your Age _____

_____

48

3. The year is **xxxx** (current year + **15**).
   You are _____ years old.
   (Current age plus 15.)

- What is your life like now at this age? (Say anything you want about your life as it is now.)
- Who are your friends? What do they do for a living?
- What is your relationship with your "family"?
- Married? Single? Children? (List their ages now.)
- Where are you living? What does it look like?
- What are your hobbies and interests?
- What do you do for exercise?
- How is your health?
- How do you take care of your spiritual needs?
- What kind of work are you doing?
- What else would you like to note about your life right now?

Year: _____   Your Age _____
_____
_____
_____
_____
_____
_____
_____
_____
_____
_____
_____
_____
_____

The 15-year mark is an especially important one. This age is far enough away from the present that people often loosen up a bit. It's so far away that it's not threatening. Imagine _your_ ideal life. What is it like? Why were you put here on this earth? What were you meant to do here? What kind of life were you meant to live? Give it a try and see what you come up with. If you can't think of anything now, try it again in a week or so. On the other hand, if you got to the 15-year mark, why not keep going?

4. The year is **xxxx** (current year + **25**).
   You are _____ years old!
   (Current age plus 25.)

Year: _____   Your Age _____
Using a blank piece of paper, answer all of the questions for this stage of your life.

5. The year is **xxxx** (current year + **35**).
   You are _____ years old!
   (Current age plus 35.)

Repeat.

6. The year is **xxxx** (current year + **45**).
   You are _____ years old!
   (Current age plus 45.)

Repeat.

7. The year is **xxxx** (current year + **55**).
   You are _____ years old!
   (Current age plus 55.)

   (Keep going—don't die until you are past 80!)

Keep going. How do you feel about your life? You are allowed to change the parts you don't like.

You have plenty of time to get done everything you want to do. Imagine wonderful things for yourself. You have plenty of time. Get rid of any "negative programming." For example, if you imagine yourself having poor health because your parents suffered from poor health, see what you can do about that. If you imagine yourself dying early because that runs in your family, see what would have happened had you lived longer. It's your life—your only one. As they say, "This is the real thing. It's not a dress rehearsal."

Case Study: Howard

The
Five
O'Clock
Club

Developing a Vision

We live in an age when art and the things of the spirit come last. The truth still holds, however, that through dedication and devotion one achieves another kind of victory. I mean the ability to overcome one's problems and meet them head on.
"Serve life and you will be sustained." That is a truth which reveals itself at every turn in the road.
I speak with inner conviction because I have been through the struggle. What I am trying to emphasize is that, whatever the nature of the problem, it can only be tackled creatively. There is no book of "openings," as in chess lore, to be studied. To find an opening one has to make a breach in the wall—and the wall is almost always in one's own mind. If you have the vision and the urge to undertake great tasks, then you will discover in yourself the virtues and the capabilities required for their accomplishment.
When everything fails, pray! Perhaps only when you have come to the end of your resources will the light dawn. It is only when we admit our limitations that we find there are no limitations.

Henry Miller,
Big Sur and the Oranges of Hieronymous Bosch

Howard attended a Five O'Clock Club group specializing in helping people who are not yet in professional-level jobs. He had done the Seven Stories and other exercises and had tried to do the Forty-Year Vision. Like most people, he had left out important parts, such as what he would be doing for a living. That's okay. I asked him if he would mind doing it in the small-group discussion.

At the time, Howard was 35 years old and worked in a lower-level job in the advertising industry. He wanted to advance in his career by getting another job in advertising. Based on our research into the jobs of the future showing his current industry was a shaky choice, we asked him to postpone selecting an industry while we helped him complete his Forty-Year Vision.

Howard was just getting started on his career even though he was 35. You're just getting started too. Regardless of your age, take pen to paper and force yourself to write something. You can always change it later.

In the thick of active life, there is more need to stimulate fancy than to control it.

George Santayana, *The Life of Reason*

A human being certainly would not grow to be seventy or eighty years old if his longevity had no meaning for the species.

C. G. Jung

Filling in His Forty-Year Vision

Kate: "Howard, you're 35 years old right now. Tell me: Who are your friends and what do they do for a living?"

Howard: "John is a messenger; Keith minds the kids while his wife works; and Greg delivers food."

Kate: "What do you do for a living?"

Howard: "I work in the media department of an advertising agency."

Kate: "Okay. Now, let's go out a few years. You're 40 years old and you've made a number of new friends in the past five years. Who are these people? What are they doing for a living?"

Howard: "One friend is a medical doctor; another works in finance or for the stock exchange; and a third is in a management position in the advertising industry."

Kate: "That's fine. Now, let's go out further. You're 50 years old and you have made a lot of new friends. What are they doing for a living?"

Howard: "One is an executive managing 100–200 people in a corporation and is very well respected; a second one is in education—he's the principal or administrator of an experimental high school and gets written up in the newspapers all the time; a third is a vice president in finance or banking."

Kate: "Those are important-sounding friends you have, Howard. But who are you and what are you doing that these people are associating with you?"

Howard: "I'm not sure."

Kate: "Well, how much money are you making at age 50 in today's dollars?"

Howard: "I'm making $150,000 a year."

Kate: "I'm impressed. What are you doing to earn that kind of money, Howard? What kind of place are you working in? Remember, you don't *have* to be specific about the industry or field you're in. For example, how do you dress for work?"

Howard: "I wear a suit and tie every day. I have a staff of 60 people working for me: 6 departments, with 10 people in each department."

Kate: "And what are those people doing all day?"

Howard: "They're doing paperwork or computer work."

Kate: "That's great, Howard. We now have a pretty good idea of what you'll be doing in the future. We just need to fill in some details."

I said to the group: "Perhaps Howard won't be making $150,000, but he'll certainly be making a lot by his own standards. And maybe it won't be 60 people, but it will certainly be a good-sized staff. What Howard is talking about here is a concept. The details may be wrong, but the concept is correct."

Howard said: "But I'm not sure if that's what I really want to do."

Kate: "It may not be exactly what you want to do, Howard, but it's in the right direction and contains the elements you really want. What you just said fits in with your Seven Stories exercise (one story was about your work with computers; another was about an administrative accomplishment). Think about it for next week, but I'll tell you this: You won't decide you want to be a dress designer, like Roxanne here. Nor will you say you want to sell insurance, like Barry. What you will do will be very close to what you just described.

"If you come back next week and say you've decided to sell ice cream, for example, I'll tell you that you simply became afraid. Fear often keeps people from pursuing their dreams. Over the week, read about the jobs of the future and let me know the industries you may want to investigate for your future career. It's usually better to pick growth industries rather than declining ones. You stand a better chance of rising with the tide."

The Next Week

When it was Howard's turn in the group the next week, he announced that he had selected health care as the industry he wanted to investigate. That sounded good because it is a growth field and because there will be plenty of need for someone to manage a group of people working on computers.

We brainstormed areas within health care for Howard to research. He could work in a hospital, an HMO, a health-care association, and so on.

He could learn about the field by reading the trade magazines having to do with health-care administration and he could start networking by meeting with someone else in the group who had already worked in a hospital.

Week #3

Howard met with another person in the group and got a feel for what it was like to work in a hospital. He also got a few names of people with whom he could talk—people at his level who could give him basic information. He spent some time in a library reading trade magazines related to health-care administration.

Howard needed to do a lot more research before he would be ready to meet with higher-level people—those in a position to hire him.

Week #4

Howard announced to the group that he had done more research, which helped him figure out that he should start in the purchasing area of a hospital as opposed to the financial area, for example. In previous jobs, he had worked as both a buyer and a salesman, so he knew both sides of the picture. He would spend some time researching the purchasing aspect of health care. That could be his entry point and he could make other moves after he got into the field.

Week #5

Today Howard is ready to meet with higher-level people in the health-care field. As he networks around, he will learn even more about the field, and select the job and the organization that will position him best for the long run—the situation that fits in best with his Forty-Year Vision.

After Howard gets his next job, he will occasionally come to the group to ask the others to help him think about his career and make moves within the organization. He will be successful in

living his vision if he continues to do what needs to be done, never taking his eye off the ball.

If Howard sticks with his vision, he will make good money and live in the kind of place in which he wants to live. Like many people who develop written plans, Howard has the opportunity to have his dream come true.

If I see what I want real good in my mind, I don't notice any pain in getting it.

George Foreman, former heavyweight boxing champion of the world

You Can Do It Too

As I mentioned earlier, the group Howard attended was a special Five O'Clock Club program that works mostly with adults who are not yet in the professional or managerial ranks and helps them get into professional-track jobs. For example:

Emlyn, a 35-year-old former babysitter, embarked on and completed a program to become a nurse's aide. This is her first step toward becoming an R.N., her ultimate career goal.

Calvin, who suffers from severe rheumatoid arthritis, hadn't worked in 10 years. Within five weeks of starting with us, he got a job as a consumer advocate with a center for the disabled and has a full caseload. We are continuing to work with him.

These ambitious, hard-working people did it and so can you. It's not easy, but what else are you doing with your 24 hours a day? The people who did it followed this motto: "Have a dream. Make a plan. Take a step. Keep on climbing."

You can complain you haven't gotten any lucky breaks, but Howard, Emlyn, and Calvin didn't get any either.

They made their own breaks, attended a branch of The Five O'Clock Club, and kept plugging ahead despite difficulties. If they can do it, you can do it too.

The
Five
O'Clock
Club

Case Study: Dinah

Developing a Detailed Plan

You can either say the universe is totally random and it's just molecules colliding all the time and it's totally chaos and our job is to make sense of that chaos, or you can say sometimes things happen for a reason and your job is to discover the reason. But either way, I do see it meaning an opportunity and that has made all the difference.

Christopher Reeve, former star of *Superman,* in an interview with Barbara Walters. Reeve became a quadriplegic after a horseback-riding accident.

This is a real test of the wedding vows. He's my partner. He's my other half, literally. It's not within the realm of my imagination to do anything less than what I'm doing.

Mrs. Christopher Reeve (Dana) in that same interview

As important as it is to have a vision of your future, it's not enough. You need to test it realistically and have a plan for getting there. You may want to hedge your bets and come up with a few scenarios for your future. Then you can explore each one to see which is the most fun for you, as well as the most doable. For example, you may consider developing a plan for one or two of the following options:

- staying where you are and rising through the ranks to reach a certain position,
- starting or buying a specific kind of business,
- becoming a consultant in your field,
- changing careers and becoming an expert in another field, or

- attaining a certain position in a small company, such as that of controller.

Think as big and as long term as you can. You may even imagine yourself having "a job and a dream"—a day job to earn money while you pursue your dream on the side.

Whatever your vision, you are more likely to achieve it if it is backed by a plan. Plans, however, are not rigid. As you start to investigate and implement your plan, you will learn things you could not have known before. Then you will adjust your plan going forward.

If you still don't have a goal—a vision for your future—do the exercises in this book to the extent that you can and then take the results to a career coach. Together, you can come up with a vision and a plan for getting there.

Think as big and as long term as you can.

Planned All the Way

Dinah had already completed her Seven Stories Exercise and her Forty-Year Vision, as well as all of the other exercises. She had put off doing the Forty-Year Vision for a long time; it seemed so intimidating. Once she finally put pen to paper, it took her only an hour or so to complete it and she felt relieved. In retrospect, she wondered why it had taken her so long to start writing it.

Dinah's vision of herself is someday to be the head of a community-based national not-for-profit. Well-educated, dignified, and artic-ulate, Dinah volunteered to help with one organi-zation's Harlem program.

Whatever your vision, you will need to learn new things, form helpful relationships, and start acting in a way that suits the position to which you aspire.

Dinah's Huge Vision

Dinah's vision is to head up an educational pro-gram in Harlem and get it to the point where it runs smoothly. Later, she wants to move the program to other cities, such as Detroit.

Implementing her vision will take a huge effort and can last her entire lifetime. Dinah *can* make this vision happen and it is up to her. Now she needs to flesh it out. She needs a very *concrete plan* about how she will get there.

In this section, you will see one planning method. It does not matter what kind of approach you use. If you are comfortable with any other planning tool, use it. If your planning method uses different definitions for words we use here, such as "goals" or "objectives," do not get hung In this section, you will see one planning method. It does not matter what kind of approach you use. If you are comfortable with any other planning tool, use it. If your planning method uses different definitions for words we use here, such as "goals" or "objectives," do not get hung up on the differ-ences. Just use your own definitions and your own method. What is important is that you actu-ally plan and that you write down your plan.

Think of yourself as a business. Just as any business needs a plan to get where it wants to go, so do you.

Many people go through life looking for favorable "breaks." Perhaps the biggest break anyone could ever receive is to decide exactly what it is he or she wants and then become obsessed with obtaining it.

Dennis Kimbro, *Think and Grow Rich: A Black Choice*

Identifying the Most Important Goals

At a Five O'Clock Club program, the group brain-stormed the most important steps Dinah would need to take to head this not-for-profit and lead it to the national level. We came up with the following:

Goal 1. Learn how to run a not-for-profit, especially in the area of fund-raising.

Goal 2. Learn about Harlem and form strong bonds in the Harlem community. Work closely with other not-for-profits there.

Goal 3. Recruit and retain the best: volun-teers, staff, and members of the board.

Goal 4. Create a program based on the needs and best interests of the community.

Goal 5. Develop processes, an operations manual, and computer and other systems to allow this program to be exported to other geographic areas.

Goal 6. Learn about career development and related areas, including the mentoring process, job development, and so on.

Goal 7. Observe and emulate, where appro-priate, the professional behavior of someone who is already the head of a national not-for-profit or similar organization.

The Same Applies to You

Whatever *your* vision, you will need to learn new things, form helpful relationships, and start to act in a way that fits the position to which you aspire.

For example, if you want to rise to a higher level in corporate life, you need:

- appropriate technical and interpersonal skills,
- in-depth knowledge about specific topics,
- a network of contacts, and
- a certain demeanor, vocabulary, and dress.

The Multiplier Effect: Select Strategies That Satisfy More Than One of Your Goals

Next, you need to come up with strategies for reaching each goal. If Dinah needed to learn how not-for-profits work, she could, for example:

- take classes,
- talk to people who are already involved in the not-for-profit world, and/or
- work for a not-for-profit and get some on-the-job training.

If Dinah actually decides to work for a not-for-profit, she needs to think this through. She could choose to work for a hospital, an association, a university, or the government. But would these be relevant to what she wants to do?

If Dinah could work for a not-for-profit and—at the same time—learn about the Harlem community or the area of education, she should choose that not-for-profit. The more goals a strategy supports, the more multiplier effect it will have.

Her strategy could be refined even more. Dinah needed to be in a position where she would actually learn *how to run* a not-for-profit herself. Therefore, if she could find a job in a staff function, such as administration or finance, in a not-for-profit that dealt with Harlem or with education, she would achieve a "multiplier effect": one of her strategies would satisfy more than one of her goals.

On her plan, Dinah would write this strategy—"Work in a staff function in a not-for-profit dealing with Harlem or with education"—under Goals 1, 2, and 6. As she conducted her research, Dinah would decide whether she would get more mileage out of working for an organization related to Harlem, to education, or to both. Achieving a multiplier effect—even in two goals—will save her years of effort to reach her vision.

In your career, you will always do better if you can achieve a multiplier effect: *develop strategies that satisfy more than one of your goals.*

It may take you three or four weeks to come up with a plan with multiplier strategies, but that plan could guide you for the next 20 years or so.

> **In your career, you will always do better when you achieve a multiplier effect: develop strategies that satisfy more than one of your goals.**

Goals Are Achieved through Strategies; Strategies Are Achieved through Action Plans

Develop your career plan as if you were planning someone else's business. Don't shortchange yourself. Be sure your personal plan is as well thought out as if you were handing in a business plan for a company. If you are serious about reaching your goals, nothing less is good enough. It will affect your whole life.

Even if your goals are not as lofty as Dinah's, a plan will help you get there. And those who have written plans are more likely to get there than those who don't write their plans down.

So, **for each goal, develop the strategies** you need to get there. See how often you can come up with strategies that serve more than one goal. **Within each strategy, develop action plans**. For example, if one strategy for learning about not-for-profits is to take classes, Dinah would need action steps to support this strategy. These could include researching various organizations that teach what she needs, deciding which classes would be best, and so on.

There are two kinds of people, those who finish what they start and so on . . .

Robert Byrne

Review Your Plan and Set Dates

Now step back and take a look at your plan. Set dates for completing those steps over which you have some control. In my own planning, for example, I can very easily set a date by which I should have a book written. Writing a book is completely under my control. There is a good possibility I will be able to meet the goal if it is what I really want to do.

But if my plan said, for example, "Get a book published by a major publishing house by a certain date," less is under my control. I cannot guess how long the action steps would take—regardless of how long and how hard I work at it. The steps could be: find an agent, write a book proposal, develop a book-marketing plan, wait for the agent to sell the book to a publishing house.

I cannot tell how long it would take me to find an agent. And if I attach a deadline to it, either I will be inclined to work with an agent who is inappropriate for me or I will become discouraged that I did not meet the arbitrary date. However, I could set dates for writing a book proposal and a book-marketing plan, because those two areas are completely under my control.

So if I don't have dates on items beyond my control, what can I do to make sure I do not ignore those uncontrollable areas? How can I make sure I am constantly making progress on my plan?

One technique is to devote a certain amount of *time* to achieving the plan. The second technique is to develop *stages* for the plan.

Work at Least 15 Hours a Week toward Your Goals

Make sure you spend a certain number of hours a week working toward your goals. If you spend no time implementing your plan, or just a few hours, you will make no progress at all. A rule of thumb is to spend 15 hours a week at it—assuming you are working full-time at a job. Then you have to make sure you are doing the right things during those 15 hours so you are getting the most from the time you are spending.

Develop the Stages of Your Plan

After you have developed goals, strategies, and action steps, the plan usually seems very daunting—even if you are working 15 hours a week on it. So it's usually helpful to implement your plan in stages. After all, you can only do so much at one time. You may still be working in your present job. You just want to bite off a chunk of this plan and stay headed in the right direction.

The stages you lay out for yourself are hypothetical: When you start to implement them, you will change things. However, looking at the plan in stages helps you see where you intended to go.

Then, because you are bright and energetic, life will present you with other options that could take you off track. If you have laid out a plan, you can reject those that do not fit in with it, and accept those that fit with the stage you are at right now.

Stage 1—What can Dinah do right now?

Dinah has to keep her day job. But there are certain things she can do right away to advance toward her long-term goal. She could:

- take on assignments in her day job to develop skills she will need for the future;

- better develop the plan for Harlem, improve the program somewhat, and think of what she should eventually do to make the program stable and self-supporting; and

- think about how she could eventually move into a job with more of a multiplier effect.

For most people, it is advisable to have a day job that somehow supports their other career-related goals—rather than one completely at odds with their long-term vision.

If your job requires so much energy and brainpower that it will take away from your dream, you are unlikely to achieve your dream.

Stage 2—Free up time to devote to this vision.

We each have the same amount of time. How can we find the time to do what we need to do to reach our goals? No matter how energetic you may be, there is still a limit to your energy. It's better to think through how you want to spend your time and energy.

What are some of the things that Dinah should consider so she is not spending her time and energy on the wrong things?

Certainly she could continue to run the Harlem program. However, she should hold off on growing it. If she increases its size a great deal in Stage 2, she won't have time to learn all the other things needed to eventually reach her long-term goal.

To conserve her time and energy, she could spend some of her time gathering information and other time recruiting people to take over some parts of the program. This would free her up for reaching her long-term goals.

Stage 3—Grow the Harlem program.

Dinah could find out how to raise funds, develop a stronger program, and build the infrastructure she would need to export the program to other areas, such as the manual for running the operation.

Stage 4—Work on the program full-time.

By this time, the program should be large enough to support Dinah. In addition, it would need its own full-time space for classrooms because it is slated to be a six-day-a-week operation.

Stage 5—Make it into a regional organization.

Dinah could plant the seeds for other locations in the region. Getting herself on prestigious boards would help her even more with fund-raising and with running the organization.

Stage 6—Be a national organization.

Take the organization to other geographic areas.

Stage 7—Influence national policy.

Dinah could sit on national boards and work with those at the highest levels of government. The work she would be doing affects the U.S. and can help narrow the growing gap between the haves and have-nots. She wants to have some say in national policy.

Deadlines

There are no dates on the "Stages" plan. When Dinah develops a plan for herself (as opposed to the one the group came up with), she will implement it as quickly as she can. In real life, the stages overlap. An element from Stage 7 may start when she is only in Stage 4. The timing of the plan depends on her dedication—and her ability to plan and keep on moving the plan along despite other demands in her life.

I never put deadlines on my plan stages. I know I would never meet them, which would discourage me. Or, I would meet them at the expense of quality. The dates are arbitrary. I am proceeding as quickly and sensibly as I can. Putting a date on a stage would not make it happen any sooner in my case. I just keep working toward my plan.

What If I Don't Achieve My Complete Vision?

If your vision is big enough, you may never fully achieve it, but you won't care. You will be doing what you want, your plan will keep you on track, and you will be having a lot of fun. You will get further with a plan than you ever would have without one.

Some people come up with *plans* beyond their abilities. This is less likely when a person actually writes out the details of what it would take to achieve a plan. For example, a person can easily say: "My plan is to have my own business and earn $100,000 a year."

That's not a plan. That's a dream. When a person actually writes down how he or she will get there, then it becomes more realistic. Either they wind up changing their vision or they develop the steps they need to get there. They stand a better chance of succeeding.

The secret of success is constancy of purpose

Benjamin Disraeli

My Own Plan—Dealing with Failure

I wrote my plan for The Five O'Clock Club in 1986. Some of the details turned out differently, but the strategies stayed the same. For example, to get credibility in this field, I had imagined myself teaching at New York University and Columbia. In fact, I wound up at the New School for Social Research, which fit in with my plan very well.

After a stage is completed, I write down the month and year—just for the record. Stage 3 of my plan failed completely. Many years ago, I had been running The Five O'Clock Club in my apartment and Stage 3 called for me to move it out of my apartment. I took out ads in local magazines, rented space for a meeting, and otherwise promoted the program. Only 12 people registered. It wiped me out financially and emotionally.

I thanked God for this clear failure. There was no doubt that this effort had failed. It would have been worse if the results had been ambiguous. Then perhaps I would have kept at it.

I rewrote Stage 3. I realized that I needed more credibility before I *went public* with this

program. So, I decided to write a book. After the book was written, I moved the program out of my apartment—but more cautiously this time. I moved into a very low-rent location. Everything else in the plan stayed exactly the way it was.

In fact, The Five O'Clock Club failed three times in those early years. Each time, it was a clear failure. Each time, I had to stop the program to recover financially and emotionally. Each time, I thanked God for the clear failure. Each time, I decided that this was still a good vision (to make the highest-quality career coaching available to people at all levels) and that it was what I wanted to do with my life. As the saying goes, I picked myself up, brushed myself off, and started all over again.

Most successful people fail, I told myself, and in my failures I collected more quotations that inspired me. And now I pass them on to you.

It is a time for men and women of courage to assert themselves, to try to find a way to bring together people whose ignorance of one another is profound and whose hatreds are intensifying.

Bob Herbert, *The New York Times*, October 6, 1995

Running a company is easy when you don't know how, but very difficult when you do.

Price Pritchett

When we begin to take our failures non-seriously, it means we are ceasing to be afraid of them. It is of immense importance to learn to laugh at ourselves.

Katherine Mansfield

The
Five
O'Clock
Club

My Ideal Job

*Human . . . life is a succession of choices, which every
conscious human being has to make every moment. At
times these choices are of decisive importance; and the
very quality of these choices will often reveal that
person's character and decide his fate. But that fate is
by no means prescribed: for he may go beyond his
inclinations, inherited as well as acquired ones.
The decision and the responsibility is his: for he is
a free moral agent, responsible for his actions.*

John Lukacs, *A History of the Cold War*

Throughout *Navigating Your Career*, you have
been actively planning, identifying action steps,
determining good-fit work environments, and
analyzing the appropriateness of career decisions.
Your ultimate goal is to develop a career plan on
which you can begin taking action immediately. Right
now, you will do a simple exercise to help you picture
yourself in your Ideal Job. Then you will be able to
identify some of the strategies you can use to get
there.

*Choose a job you love, and you will never
have to work a day in your life.*

Confucius

Describing Your Ideal Job

A visualization exercise will help you define your
ideal job in specific detail. It only requires your
thinking and visualizing skills to complete.

This can be your current job in its ideal state,
another ideal job in the organization, or any other
job that would be ideal for you. At this point you

should not be concerned about whether or not
this job appears to be realistic or feasible.

Creative visualization is a technique many
people use to visualize clearly and specifically the
results they want. Research has shown that the
more clarity you have about what you are trying
to achieve, the more likely you are to achieve it.

Many star athletes have used this technique
with great success. Before and during the match,
a tennis player pictures himself or herself successfully executing each stroke. Before the race, a
slalom skier pictures every twist and turn in the
course and exactly how he or she will negotiate
each one. Previewing the action in detail, like
running a movie in their minds, helps these athletes achieve far better results than they would be
able to achieve otherwise.

But sports is only one area where this technique is effective. You can use it in any context to
set yourself up for success.

For example, what if you will soon be attending a meeting and you feel a little uncomfortable
about it? You can preview the meeting in your
mind. Imagine the room in which the meeting
will be held. Think of the people who will be
sitting around the table. Who will be there? What
are they likely to say? What do you think their key
issues will be that have anything to do with you?
What is your opinion of those issues?

How are you dressed for this meeting? How
do you sit? Perhaps someone brings up a project
you have been working on. What would you say
about your project in this meeting? Imagine yourself talking about your project.

If you didn't like the way you spoke about your project in your own mind, replay it and try again. Perhaps you need to informally meet with some of the attendees ahead of time to get a better feel for what may happen in the meeting and then you can visualize the meeting again—but with more information.

You can use visualization for everything that may come up. You can visualize the next step you plan to take in your project and the informal meetings you may have. If you have been reluctant to tackle a certain problem, such as working at a computer, you can visualize yourself using certain computer software.

You can use visualization now to start imagining your own future. There are a couple of ways you can go about this:

You can work with your Career Buddy. Your Career Buddy can slowly read the questions to you while you imagine your Ideal Job and then you can do the same for your Career Buddy.

Or you can imagine your future all by yourself. You can't rush this exercise. Instead, arrange a time when you will not be distracted. Set aside about half an hour. Relax for a while. First, you'll want to sit comfortably by yourself and eliminate distractions. Take out a pad of paper.

You'll think about a series of questions. Let the answers come to you and picture the results silently as opposed to giving your responses aloud. At the end of the exercise, you can jot down your answers in this manual. When you are ready, start by getting very comfortable. Now imagine the following:

You see yourself one or two years from now—or further ahead if you like. Some people find it more comfortable to imagine themselves 5 or even 15 years from now because they may want to imagine something very different from what they are doing now. Making big changes takes time and you want to give yourself the time it really takes to make progress in your career. Very little of significance happens quickly.

So here you are—1, 2, 5, 10 or even 15 years from now. You are in your ideal job. Everything is going very well. You've managed your career in ways that have brought you personal and professional satisfaction in terms of what you are doing, with whom, where, and how.

Take a long time to imagine your ideal job, and take a long time to answer the questions below. Do not rush. Make the image as realistic as possible for yourself.

- What do you see?
- How do you feel?
- What are you saying?
- How do you talk about yourself in this ideal job?
- What has happened in your career?
- What are the signs that you are successful?
- In achieving this, what was the first thing you did?
- Who did you use as resources in achieving your goal?
- When did you contact them?
- What was the hardest lesson you learned?
- What was the best lesson you learned?

Now, without speaking to anyone, fill in Describing Your Ideal Job below. Jot down your answers to the questions asked above in as much detail as you can remember. Use extra paper if you need to. The greater the detail of your description, the more firmly the scene can remain implanted in your mind.

Describing Your Ideal Job Worksheet

Thinking back over what you just visualized, answer the following questions as specifically as possible in order to describe your ideal work outcomes. Your answers will help you determine how you will know when you have achieved your goals.

What has happened in your career?

_____

_____

_____

What are the signs that you are successful?

_____

_____

Looking around you, what do you see?

_____

_____

_____

What are you saying?

_____

_____

_____

How do you feel?

_____

_____

_____

How do you talk about yourself?

_____

_____

_____

What was the first step you took?

_____

_____

_____

Who did you use as resources in achieving this goal?

_____

_____

_____

When did you contact them?

_____

_____

_____

What was the hardest lesson you learned in achieving your outcome?

_____

_____

_____

What was the best lesson you learned?

_____

_____

Even if you did not work with your Career Buddy on this, the two of you may want to discuss these results. Spend some time describing your ideal job and how you got there.

If you are not satisfied right now with your description of your ideal job, that's okay. Some people feel locked in by their present circumstances. Others simply have a hard time using visualization. Try it again in a few days, and see what you come up with. Or ask your Career Buddy to help you. If that still doesn't work, you may have to meet with a career coach.

Visualization can be a highly effective technique for creating a picture of what you want in your career. Once you have begun to see it in your mind's eye, a goal becomes much easier to realize. Knowing what you want sets the stage for achieving it.

"Apparently, Smith's desk just couldn't withstand the weight of the paperwork we piled on his desk."

Life can only be understood backwards; but it must be lived forwards.

Kierkegaard

The
Five
O'Clock
Club

My Ideal Work Environment

Life is an end in itself, and the only question
as to whether it is worth living is whether
you have had enough of it.

Oliver Wendell Holmes

Most of us occasionally think about what would be ideal for us in terms of lifestyle and work environment. The problem is, we may dream about that environment and do nothing to create it!

A motivating work environment can contribute greatly to career effectiveness and job satisfaction. So your next step will be to focus on identifying the work environment where you will be most productive and satisfied. That means getting even more specific about the ideal situation for you. Below are some elements you need to consider in creating your ideal work environment. You will be asked to consider these elements as you complete the worksheet that starts on page 64.

Physical surroundings/location—What does this environment look and feel like? Are you in an office or moving from place to place? Is it busy or quiet? Are you working primarily alone or surrounded by people?

People—What kinds of people are you working with? Are they energetic, quiet, creative, highly structured? Do you interact with many people or a few?

Activities—What kinds of activities are you engaged in? Are you working primarily with other people, equipment, or information? Are you a manager or an individual contributor?

Style—What type of work, communications, and management styles are prevalent? Are people formal or informal? How do they communicate with each other? How do they dress?

Recognition and rewards—What types of recognition do you receive? Do you get frequent recognition/acknowledgment from peers/superiors? How are you rewarded for good performance?

A little while ago, you pictured yourself in your ideal job. Now, once again, imagine yourself in your ideal job some time in the future. See how many specifics you can come up with about the environment of that job. Complete the Work Environment worksheet on the following pages, which looks at the five elements presented above.

Then talk to your Career Buddy. Take five minutes apiece to describe your ideal work environments to each other. Use the notes you took in this workbook, but elaborate even further. Your objective is to make your description as real as possible for your Buddy. Your Buddy, when listening to you, should ask you questions to help you make the picture clear for yourself. And you should do the same for your partner. When working with your Buddy, make sure each of you is focusing on your ideal and not your current environments. You should each be as specific as you can.

Assess what is needed to change your present work environment to make it an ideal work environment. If this change is within your control, what can you do about it? If the change is not within your control, remember: Your response to the situation is always within your control.

Don't forget what we said earlier about visualizing the results you want to create. The more specific you are about the results you want, the more you are setting yourself up to achieve them.

Additional Ideas

Below is a list of words employees have used to describe their ideal work environments. You may want to add one or two of these to your list.

- Friendly coworkers around me (they say, "Good morning")
- Geographic location—near stores
- Painted offices (they care about their environment)
- Large desk space
- My own desk
- Windows
- Resources, such as training materials

- Short commute
- Separation of work time and personal time
- Smart people
- If open space, conference space is private
- Good lighting
- Phone system that meets people's needs
- Personalized space
- Quiet so I can think

---

*Dear sir, be patient toward all that is unsolved in your heart and try to love the **questions themselves** like locked rooms and like books that are written in a very foreign tongue. Do not now seek the answers, which cannot be given you because you would not be able to live them. And the point is, to live everything.*

__Live__ the questions now. Perhaps you will then gradually, without noticing it, live along some distant day into the answer. Perhaps you do carry within yourself the possibility of shaping and forming as a particularly happy and pure way of living; train yourself to it—but take whatever comes with trust, and if only it comes out of your own will, out of some need of your inmost being, take it upon yourself and hate nothing.

Rainer Maria Rilke

My Ideal Work Environment
Worksheet

You have identified your ideal job; the next step is to think about the specific elements that make up your ideal work environment. Review the list of questions in each category and jot down your thoughts in the spaces provided.

Physical surroundings/location:

- Are you in an office or are you moving from one place to another?

- If you are in an office, describe its appearance. How is it furnished?

- Is it a formal or informal environment?

- Are there distractions or is it quiet?

- Do you have a place you can go to relax, do necessary paperwork, talk with your coworkers?

- Are the processes computerized for control?

- Are you isolated or surrounded by people?

- How do you get to work—bus, train, car, bicycle, car pool, walk?

People:

- What kind of people do you work with (e.g., creative, energetic, technical, or mechanical)?

- Do you prefer to work with many people or a few?

- Do you socialize with your colleagues outside the work environment?

Activities:

- Are you working with other people, equipment, or information?

- Are you managing or directing people?

- Are you reading reports?

  _____

- Do you attend meetings regularly?

  _____

- Are you communicating with others?

  _____

- Are you responsible for complete tasks? Or are you responsible for a piece of a task?

  _____

- What kinds of activities are most rewarding? Least rewarding?

  _____

- Do you attend meetings of external professional organizations?

  _____

- How much do you travel?

  _____

- Are you a decision maker?

  _____

- How much freedom do you have to carry out your responsibilities?

  _____

Style:

- Are people formal or informal in how they relate to each other?

  _____

- What type of management style is typical?

  Do people prefer to communicate mainly through talking or in writing?

  _____

- What are people wearing?

  _____

Recognition/rewards:

- What types of recognition do you receive?

  _____

- How are you rewarded?

  _____

- Are monetary rewards based on individual or team performance?

  _____

- What are your work hours?

  _____

- Do you have flexible work hours?

  _____

The
Five
O'Clock
Club

What I Want Most in My Career

We all have personal issues or preferences of importance in making career choices. These preferences can be things we want in our careers, or they can be boundaries we set defining what we do not want in our careers.

Personal Considerations

In addition to what you absolutely want in your career, there is one other aspect of your ideal work environment on which we need to focus. These are certain personal considerations that can have a major impact on your career satisfaction.

When you have career discussions with your manager and others, you will need to start off these discussions with a simple, clear, easy-to-understand statement of what you want in your career. It is important for your statement to take into account all facets of who you are, including personal as well as professional requirements.

Harry liked his job and how it fit with his family-oriented lifestyle, but he really wanted to be a manager. So he set up a career discussion with his manager and said, "I want to be a manager."

Now Harry's out in Nebraska managing 10 people, working the night shift, surviving winter blizzards, and preparing a more careful and complete statement of what's important to him for his next career discussion. Unfortunately, he overemphasized one aspect of his ideal job and left out some other key elements.

What Do You NOT Want in Your Career?

When making career decisions, you need to be aware of preferences and limitations that may influence your choices. These may be family considerations, educational plans, willingness to relocate, and so on.

Most people know what they do not want. For example, a person may say, "I don't want to work in the city," or "I don't want to work with numbers," or "I don't want to work 70 hours a week."

Sometimes a negative statement can be reframed as a positive. For example, "I don't want to be isolated," might translate as, "I want to work more closely with other people."

Others, such as "I don't want to travel or relocate," are usually best stated in the negative.

Think about what these considerations may be for you.

You probably have some preferences and limitations on your career related to issues concerning mobility, family, education, and the like. If certain choices come up, these preferences show what you would choose: no travel, no relocation to California, no management responsibility, no weekend work, etc.

So list these preferences now. After you have listed all of them, assign a ranking indicating relative importance. Rank your most important #1, the next in importance #2, and so on.

What I Don't Want   **Ranking**

_____

_____

_____

_____

_____

Personal Considerations Exercise

In creating your vision of your ideal work environment, you also need to take into account any personal issues or preferences important in making choices regarding your career. These include issues such as family considerations, educational plans, willingness to relocate, desire to travel, work schedules, etc.

In the space below, list the personal considerations or preferences critical to you.

_____

_____

_____

_____

_____

Describing Your Current Work Environment

Take a look at your current work environment and then think about what you can do to make it better.

1. **What are some of the characteristics that describe the physical surroundings of your current work environment?**

   _____

   _____

   _____

2. **What kinds of rewards are you currently receiving?**

   _____

   _____

   _____

3. **What kinds of behaviors do you currently demonstrate?**

   _____

   _____

   _____

4. **In what types of professional activities are you presently engaged on the job?**

   _____

   _____

   _____

5. **With what kinds of people do you presently work?**

   _____

   _____

   _____

6. **What would you like to change or improve about your current work environment?**

   _____

   _____

   _____

If It's Right, You'll Know It

In choosing the best strategy for your career planning, a good place to begin is to imagine your most satisfying and rewarding work environment. Essential in this consideration is determining the ideal working conditions where you are "at your best." This was covered in the previous section. Remember, your environment is much more than walls and what your *cube* looks like. It's who you work with, how you are managed, what your hours and commute are, plus many other factors. Use the following summary and the next section on enriching your environment, assess what your environment is now, what you want ideally, and how you can change your current environment to make it more like your ideal.

Summary Questions

1. **Looking at your work environment, what do you want in your career?**

   _____

   _____

   _____

2. **In terms of your work environment, what do you already have but want more of?**

   _____

   _____

   _____

3. **In terms of your work environment, what would you like to have less of or to change?**

   _____

   _____

   _____

4. **What action will you take to move toward any of the above?**

   _____

   _____

   _____

Enriching Your Current Work Environment

To create an ideal work environment, you need to compare it with your current work environment. By doing this, you may discover a number of aspects of your current environment that already match up with your ideal.

At the same time, you may also identify gaps between your current environment and your ideal. These gaps represent opportunities to enhance your current job.

The following questions will help you do some action planning around enriching your current job based on your ideal work environment.

1. **What exists in your current work environment that matches up with your ideal?**

   _____

   _____

   _____

2. **Where are the gaps between your current and your ideal work environment?**

   _____

   _____

3. **Which of these gaps represent elements you have control over or have the opportunity to change?**

   _____

   _____

4. **What action will you take to make these changes occur?**

   _____

   _____

Identifying Your Goals

You have gathered a lot of information about yourself and what you want in your career. It is time to begin some planning based on this information.

Using your self-assessment results and the activities you completed on your ideal job and your ideal work environment, identify short- and long-term goals. These goals may include exploring options to enhance your current job, pursuing training or educational opportunities, or investigating specific job functions within your division or other areas of your organization. You will refer back to these goals when you create your Career Development Plan. If you need help in identifying your goals, talk to a career coach.

List your short-term (six months to a year) goals with milestones and a desired timetable. These should be planned so they are steps in realizing your ideal job.

Goal	By When

List your long-term goals (one year and beyond) with milestones and a desired timetable. As with your short-term goals, these goals should be planned so they are steps in realizing your ideal job.

Goal	By When

Who would not say that it is the essence of folly to do lazily and rebelliously what has to be done, to impel the body one way and the soul another, to be split between the most conflicting motions?

Seneca

All in All, What Do I Want in My Career?

A clear and simple statement of your career vision is the foundation of career management. If you know exactly what you want in your career, your chances of getting it are better.

What do I want in my career? That's the trick question, isn't it? If you only knew what you wanted, you'd be off and running in that direction. But the development of your career vision is a process and we're taking it one step at a time, defining pieces of it.

Furthermore, we'll have to link your vision with objective criteria for achieving it. When you tell others about your career vision, you will need some objective, practical ways of knowing if you are making progress and when you have arrived.

Sometimes, it's easier to identify what you *don't* want rather than what you *do* want. Look again at the *don't wants* you put on the first page of this section.

And the end of all our exploring is to arrive where we started and see it for the first time.

T. S. Eliot

What I Do Want in My Career

This section includes only what you *do* want, which could be just about anything: doing certain kinds of work, working in certain environments or with certain management styles, salary levels, learning new fields of work, and so on.

These are all things you are willing to work toward over time. Some may be easily attainable in a short time. Others may take a lot of work over the long haul.

For now, don't ask yourself whether or not these things you want are realistic or how you might obtain them. We will cover these issues later. For now, simply define what you want.

You may want to refer back to the results of your assessment exercises (Seven Stories,

Forty-Year Vision, and so on). Those may give you some ideas for a more complete list.

What I Do Want	Rating

Summary Questions

1. **All in all, what do you want in your career? Why is this important to you?**

   _____

   _____

   _____

   _____

   _____

2. **List limitations and boundaries affecting your career plans.**

   _____

   _____

   _____

   _____

3. **List your short-term (less than one-year) goals with milestones and a desired time-table. Goals should be planned so they are steps in realizing your career vision. By when?**

   _____

   _____

   _____

4. **List your long-term goals (more than one year) with milestones and desired time-table. Goals should be planned so they are steps in realizing your career vision. By when?**

   _____

   _____

   _____

Taking Advantage of Support Systems

Part of effective career management is using support systems and overcoming potential barriers to achieve your goals. To identify your own support systems and potential barriers, it can be helpful to break them down into four categories:

- Personal life—family and close friends
- Social life—business associates, peers, and acquaintances
- Professional life—jobs, peers, and the ways we make an income
- Organizational life—ways we interact with the organization

The elements, conditions, and people who comprise these dimensions can be viewed either as supports or barriers to career effectiveness and a satisfying and rewarding life.

Understanding how and why something or someone is a support or a barrier is critical to effective career management.

The following exercises will help you strategize how you can use your support systems effectively and overcome potential barriers.

Take a look at each of the four life areas: Personal, Social, Professional, and Organizational. For each item within those areas, ask yourself whether it is a strong, medium, or weak support. After you have completed this exercise, you will see where your support systems are most useful and where there is an absence of support.

Here are some ways your support systems can help:

- Family or friends can help you clarify your career goals or boost your confidence.
- A manager can give you useful feedback and provide developmental opportunities.
- A professional association can offer opportunities for networking.
- Your employer can foster an environment that encourages you to learn new skills.

Be courteous to all, but intimate with few; and let those few be well tried before you give them your confidence.

George Washington, 1721–1799
Letter to Bushrod Washington
January 15, 1783

Possible Supports

Reviewing the list below might trigger your thoughts about supports in your life.

- Marriage/relationship
- Religious beliefs
- Family
- Versatility
- Neighbors
- Manager
- Health
- Organization/business
- Training/education
- Membership in outside organizations
- Friends
- Children
- Values/ethics
- Experience
- Visibility
- Image/appearance
- Mentors
- Geographic location
- Financial situation
- Job

Right now, simply list your supports in each area, and **whether each is a strong, medium, or weak support**:

- **Personal supports—**
  family and close friends   Strong, medium, or weak support

  _____
  _____
  _____
  _____
  _____

- **Social supports—**
  business associates,
  peers, friends, and
  acquaintances   Strong, medium, or weak support

  _____
  _____
  _____
  _____
  _____

- **Professional**
  supports—jobs, peers,
  and the ways you
  make an income   Strong, medium, or weak support

  _____
  _____
  _____
  _____
  _____

- **Organizational**
  supports—ways you
  interact with the
  organization   Strong, medium, or weak support

  _____
  _____
  _____
  _____
  _____

Strengthening Your Support Systems

Now you know where you stand with your support systems. You can use your supports to further your effectiveness in your present job and in your future career. Look at the medium or weak supports. Could they or should they be stronger supports? If so, how can you strengthen them?

Everything in life boils down to action steps. List the specific actions you will take to strengthen your support systems and when you expect to take these actions. Focus on those most important to you and those that will help you the most in achieving your goals.

Support system action plan	Done by when

Overcoming Potential Barriers

Whether you realize it or not, the environment in which you live, the people with whom you live, your friends, your health—either support you in your efforts or serve as barriers for you. Support systems make it easier for people to get what they need and want, while barriers stand in their way. When you become aware of what is helping you or hindering you in reaching your goals, you may be able to make better use of support systems, and get around barriers.

In fact, every element some people consider a support may be viewed as a barrier by others. For example, a spouse may be supportive or unsupportive and the same may be said for an organization or an immediate manager.

The following are some categories of potential barriers:

- Industry conditions
- Political environments

- Financial conditions
- Professional peers
- Spouse/family

For example, *industry conditions* could refer to a number of organizations in your industry cutting back on your line of business. That would be good for you to know.

Experience has shown us that there are two ways to reduce the impact of a barrier. One is to enhance the strength of other supports. A second is to break down the barrier into smaller parts.

In the space below, list potential barriers and the strategies you could use to overcome them.

Barriers and Strategies to Convert Barriers to Supports

1. _____

2. _____

3. _____

4. _____

5. _____

6. _____

If you're having difficulty coming up with solutions, don't be concerned—you can get some help from your Career Buddy or your career coach. In any case, talk to your Career Buddy about the barriers each of you is facing. Then brainstorm potential solutions or ways to convert barriers into supports or to at least neutralize them. Add these to your list of strategies above.

It's important to recognize the potential impact supports and barriers can have on our lives and careers. To manage our careers effectively, we need to view barriers as opportunities and use our support systems to their fullest extent.

Next, we will move on to the purpose of all of these exercises: the preparation of your Career Development Plan. But first, past influences need to be considered.

Let your own discretion be your tutor:
Suit the action to the word, The word to the action.

William Shakespeare, *Hamlet*

73

Understanding Past Influences

In this final area of the assessment process, you'll look at how you got to where you are today. If you can identify important influences from your past, you can better understand why you made the decisions you've made.

You will review your life and career to date to learn more about the influences and beliefs that led you to your current position. This information can help you make more informed career decisions in the future.

To understand past influences, you will focus on your early learning experiences as well as your beliefs about work and career.

Influences in your past had an impact on the choices you made in your career and your beliefs about where you expect to go in your career. These influences may have included family, social, religious, political, or environmental considerations; a birth or death; or a life crisis.

If you don't understand your past influences, you may recreate the same situation again and again. On the other hand, you can learn from your past. When you understand what has influenced you in the past, you can make more informed decisions and change your career going forward if that's what you want to do.

Examining Past Forces and Influences

1. During the first 15 years of your life, how did the following influences impact how you viewed work and, in particular, authority figures?

A. Community influences

_____

_____

_____

B. School influences

_____

_____

_____

C. Religious influences

_____

_____

_____

D. Social influences

_____

_____

_____

E. Political influences

_____

_____

_____

F. Family influences

_____

_____

_____

2. When critical career decisions were being made, what (situations/persons) influenced you the most?

_____

_____

_____

Examining Past Forces and Influences—Summary

1. Consider what you learned in the Seven Stories Exercise and the Forty- or Fifteen-Year Vision you completed in the Assessment section. List below at least three things you want more of in your career. What could you do to get more of these?

_____

_____

_____

_____

2. Considering those Assessment results, list at least three things you want less of in your career. What could you do to have less of these?

_____

_____

_____

_____

_____

_____

_____

The
Five
O'Clock
Club

Preparing Your Career-Development Plan

Promises that you make to yourself are often like the Japanese plum tree—they bear no fruit.

Frances Marion

You can use what you have learned about yourself to complete your Career-Development Plan. Then you will be in a better position to address your personal needs as well as the needs of your organization.

It's good to know what your Career-Development Plan is even if no one else in your organization knows about it. It will give you direction and add more meaning to your everyday assignments.

In organizations where you are encouraged to develop a career plan, you may want to discuss it with your manager—especially if your goals mesh with the goals of the organization. If you work in a bank and your career plan is to become a ballerina, it may not help you or your manager much to have a discussion about this. But if you are in one division that is cutting back and are interested in another division, a discussion with your manager or someone in human resources may be in order. These individuals can sometimes be strong allies in your career management if your employer is interested in helping people move from one area of the organization to another.

The Benefits of Career-Development Planning

Your Career-Development Plan can be a guide and provide focus and direction. It is a kind of map that specifies in writing the goal you want to achieve and the steps you will take to do so.

Career-development planning is vital to achieving your goals. All successful businesses devote considerable time to the planning process. Yet, strangely, relatively few individuals take the time to do it for themselves, despite the overwhelming evidence that success favors those men and women who actually plan for it.

Career-development planning enables you to identify strategies and action steps to ensure you will achieve your goal. Your Career-Development Plan can be a useful tool in conducting career discussions with your manager and/or a career coach or human resources professional.

You can use career-development planning in various stages of the career-management process. Typically, this process evolves over time and you will continually review and adjust your plan to reflect your current objectives.

The person who fears to try is thus enslaved.

Leonard E. Read

Potential Outcomes

If you have a Career-Development Plan, you can potentially:

- enrich your current job through skill development or enhancement of responsibilities,
- pursue a new position,

- make a change in your career field,

- take advantage of formal training opportunities,

- pursue a developmental experience such as a job rotation or special project assignment,

- volunteer for a task force or committee

- remain in your current position and get more out of it, and/or

- engage in external professional-development activities

A career discussion with your manager is often a good way to establish your professional image. It's a proactive method to inform others of your goals. And it is an opportunity for you to add value to the organization.

The more thorough you are in developing each component of your Plan, the higher your chances of success.

Think of your Plan as a living document. The information you gather along the way will enable you to refine your Plan by recasting objectives and adding new career-development steps to continually enhance your career growth.

Use the Career-Development Plan on the following pages for your initial thoughts. You may want to make extra copies—just in case you want to revise it before you discuss it with your manager.

What If Your Fifteen- or Forty-Year Vision Does Not Fit with Your Current Employment Situation?

You need a career plan of what *you* want to do—to guide you. But if you're working in a financial services firm, for example, and you really want to work in arts research, think of skills you could acquire in your present firm to help you with your long-term goals. For example, maybe it has an area that funds the arts or one that lends to arts organizations. Or, if it would help if you improved your writing skills, perhaps you could aim for a job to help you do just that.

Perhaps you could find a job in your present organization that satisfies you while you pursue your art research on the side. Later, you may find that the arts research did not work as a career path, but at least you have improved your skills and not burned any bridges. We all have a finite amount of time and energy. Usually it's better if what you do during the day meshes with your long-term goals. So think more about how your day job can fit in with your long-term vision.

It may not be in your best interests to reveal everything in your heart. Take care of your career at your present place of employment, do right by your employer, but keep your long-term vision in mind.

Your Career-Development Plan

Name: _____

Date: _____

At each phase, career-development planning can be your best guide. The more thorough you are in developing each component of the Plan, the higher your chances of success. The information you gather along the way will enable you to refine the plan (recast objectives and new development steps) and eventually reach your desired goal.

1. **Skills**

   Refer back to your *Skills from Your Seven Stories*. List your top five motivated skills (the ones that are your strongest and you enjoy using). List skills you want to develop to meet your goals.

   My Strongest Skills

   _____

   _____

   _____

   _____

   _____

   Where I Have Demonstrated Those Skills

   _____

   _____

   _____

   _____

   _____

   Skills I Need to Develop

   _____

   _____

   _____

   _____

   Why I Need to Develop Them

   _____

   _____

   _____

   _____

2. **Personal traits/characteristics**

   List some of the personal traits and characteristics that make you a valuable worker (for example, being ambitious and honest, showing initiative, accountable, creativity, team player).

   _____

   _____

   _____

   _____

78

3. **Ideal work environment**

   Describe your preferences in terms of the kinds of activities you prefer; the type of people with whom you would like to work and how you would interact together, the roles and functions you would be carrying out, and the work values you would be expressing. Refer to the exercise you completed earlier in this book.

   A work environment would probably be a good fit for me if it had some or all of these characteristics:

   _____

   _____

   _____

   _____

4. **Where do gaps between your ideal work environment and your current work environment exist?**

   Example: You are looking for an evolving environment offering a variety of challenges. Yet you are currently in a stable and predictable work environment. Therefore, the gap is in the area of variety and challenge.

   _____

   _____

   _____

   _____

5. **Based on your assessment results, and your ideal work environment, what career goals have you identified?**

   _____

   _____

   _____

   _____

6. **How do these goals match up with your understanding of the current needs at your present place of employment?**

   _____

   _____

   _____

(continues)

Your Career-Development Plan *(continued)*

7. **What challenges do you face in achieving your career goals?**

_____

_____

_____

_____

_____

_____

8. **Based on your assessment results and the gaps and challenges you identified, what specific development activities do you want to explore?**

Job Enrichment

❏ New responsibilities   ❏ Task team   ❏ Mentoring

❏ Career discussions   ❏ Project assignment   ❏ Other

Training and Development

❏ Internal training program(s)   ❏ Career-development discussions   ❏ On-the-job training

❏ Job rotation   ❏ External educational activities   ❏ Other

Job Search

❏ Networking   ❏ Career discussions with manager   ❏ Researching divisions

❏ Career Buddies   ❏ Direct contact   ❏ Career forums

❏ Résumé writing   ❏ Interviewing   ❏ Other

❏ Information gathering   ❏ Job posting

9. **Based on the above development activities, list the specific action steps you need to take to implement your development plan.**

    Your action steps can be small ones (e.g., reading organization materials to understand the business or reviewing the training catalogs for courses that interest you) or large ones (e.g., setting a goal of meeting with five individuals every month, or developing a proposal to enhance your job).

Action Steps   **Completion Date**

_____   _____

_____   _____

_____   _____

_____   _____

10. **What resources (people, data, money, time, etc.) will you need to implement your action steps?**

_____

_____

_____

_____

Keep away from people who belittle your ambitions.
Small people always do that,
but the really great make you feel that you, too, can become great.

Mark Twain

11. **List networking contacts.**

Name	Position/phone/E-mail	Department	Completion Date
_____	_____	_____	_____
_____	_____	_____	_____
_____	_____	_____	_____
_____	_____	_____	_____
_____	_____	_____	_____

Remember: Your Career-Development Plan will evolve over time as you take these action steps. So over time you'll want to update your Plan.

Here are the steps you may follow:
- Prepare your Career-Development Plan.
- Practice your Career-Development Discussion with your Career Buddy.
- Prepare your agenda for the meeting with your manager.
- Schedule the meeting with your manager.

The
Five
O'Clock
Club

Preparing for a Career Discussion with Your Manager

You need a Career-Development Plan and a Career Vision for yourself—to guide you in your career. In many progressive organizations, you may actually be encouraged to have a Career-Development Discussion with your manager. That's because things are changing fast. When circumstances change in an organization, it's better for them to be able to keep valued employees, perhaps in other areas of the organization.

Not so long ago, a discussion with a manager about performance or development might have been an uncomfortable prospect. Often, both employees and managers felt anxious about the meeting, because they didn't have the tools and resources they needed to ensure that the results would be positive and productive.

But times have changed and the culture at many companies has changed. Now, a Career-Development Discussion can be a time for openness. It can be an opportunity for you and your manager to work together to identify ways to enrich your job and your career. And it is a time when you may want to explore other parts of your organization—perhaps simply to learn more about how the place operates or perhaps to help you think of other options for the long run.

Preparing your Career-Development Plan is the first step in getting ready to conduct a Career Discussion with your manager. However, since your Plan is a working document, it is not absolutely necessary to complete every item. You may want to review it with your Career Buddy

and/or human resources professional first to get his or her input.

Once your plan is ready, the next step is to prepare an agenda to help you conduct an effective discussion. (See suggested discussion guidelines below.) Think about questions you want to ask and requests you want to make.

Then set up the meeting with your manager. It would be helpful to send the agenda to your manager in advance (we recommend forwarding your Career-Development Plan as well). In any case, be sure to take a copy of your Career-Development Plan with you to the meeting along with your agenda.

The people you want to reach, whether they're your coworkers, your boss or an organizational president, should be viewed as distinct target audiences that require different approaches and strategies.

Jeffrey P. Davidson, marketing consultant,
Management World

Discussion Guidelines

1. **Set the stage for the discussion.**
   Thank your manager for taking the time to meet with you. Open the discussion by reviewing the purpose of the meeting and your agenda.

2. **Present an overview of your ideal work environment and your goals.**

Refer to your Career-Development Plan to provide details. You may also want to share things you learned about yourself in the exercises.

3. **Discuss your strongest skills.**

Expand on this information, telling exactly why you believe you have the skills you claim and how they contribute to meeting customer needs. Accomplishments, experience, training, and feedback are all good evidence. Here, as in all discussions, specific examples are important.

4. **Propose development activities.**

Discuss your development needs and the activities you are proposing to increase your effectiveness. In discussing your proposed development activities, you are seeking to elicit your manager's support and explore additional suggestions he or she may make.

5. **Ask for questions.**

You have just completed your overview. Even though you may have invited questions along the way, check again now to see if anything needs clarification.

6. **Ask for feedback.**

Then ask for feedback, starting with a general question like, "I would like to have your feedback on what I have said so far." This is a critical step in the discussion. Your success will depend on your ability to listen to your manager's feedback and consider his or her point of view.

Since your manager is an important ally in making your career work, you should not come into this meeting with fixed ideas on its outcome. You need a consensus—a win-win. So listen carefully. He or she may have ideas even better than yours.

As you receive feedback, ask whatever questions you need to make sure you understand. Repeating a summary of the feedback is an excellent technique to ensure clear communication (e.g., "You're saying I . . . Is that

right?" You may wish to ask for specific feedback on the practicality of your plan or some other issue. You may also ask for ideas or suggestions on how to get where you want to go even faster.

7. **Come to agreement.**

After you have obtained feedback, you and your manager can come to agreement on your goals and next steps. You may wish to make requests for some specific support in attaining your goals.

If you and your manager find you need more information or you cannot come to agreement at this time, you may wish to schedule another meeting to continue your discussion at a later point.

8. **Conclude the meeting.**

At the conclusion of the meeting, be clear on what will happen next. Based on agreements reached, decide who needs to do what and by when. Thank your manager for his or her feedback and support.

Practice

Before you have your Career-Development Discussion with your manager, you can practice what you are planning to say and see how it sounds. You can practice talking about parts of your Plan with your Career Buddy.

With your Career Buddy taking the role of your manager, cover as many steps of the Career Discussion agenda as you can. It's okay if you only cover a few steps, but you may wish to cover them all.

Following your practice discussion, ask your Career Buddy to give you feedback on how you're coming across.

Then think about the following:

- What worked well for you in your practice discussions?
- What do you still need to work on?

- How do you feel about going back and having this discussion with your manager?

You now have a Career-Development Plan that identifies your career-development goals based on your self-assessment results and your ideal job and work environment and includes action plans for moving forward toward your goals. You have had an opportunity to practice key segments of the discussion you will have with your manager about your Plan.

When you are ready, schedule a Career-Development Discussion with your manager.

Congratulations on Completing This Section!

You have just taken an important step toward achieving greater career satisfaction and success. Through your efforts, you have gained increased understanding of yourself and your goals, which can lead to more effective career decisions.

This has been a very intensive process that has enabled you to take some time out to think about you—what's important to you, what you want to achieve, and how you might do that within the context of your employer's needs and goals. You were introduced to some information, tools, and techniques to help you take personal responsibility for managing your career more effectively and to help you meet the challenges of a changing business environment.

Next Steps

What happens next depends on the goals you have set for yourself.

- Based on your Career Discussion with your manager, you may want to refine your Career-Development Plan.

- You may also wish to take advantage of other programs and services offered by your employer.

- If you are interested in pursuing additional activities that will enhance your career effectiveness, read on.

What You Can Do in Your Present Situation

What has changed most fundamentally is the greater responsibility being given to workers to take charge of ensuring higher quality and to take a proactive role in organizing their own work—responsibilities that in the past management jealously kept for itself.

Hedrick Smith, *Rethinking America*

Now you have a vision of your future and a plan for what you should do to achieve that vision. You will need new skills and new relationships. To advance, you may feel as though you must get out of the job you are in right now. However, you may be able to add skills, experience, and a knowledge base without leaving your current position. Look at the following list of ideas. You may want to add some of these to your Career-Development Plan.

- Talk to colleagues about your present company's needs. Make plans to fill those needs.
- Expand the network of people with whom you interact internally and externally.
- Join an association that fits in with your long-term goals; get on a committee.
- Find out what people in your function do outside of your present company (or the function you are interested in long term).
- Learn a new technical skill.
- Manage a project.
- Volunteer for a task force.
- Train staff on new software.
- Select/determine software or equipment.
- Write a proposal to fill a need.
- Make a presentation.
- Take some classroom training.
- Substitute for your manager in a meeting.
- Run a meeting.

"Call me crazy, but I think my paperwork is actually following me."

- Assist with the budget process.
- Organize a community activity or do volunteer work to gain a new marketable skill.
- Train a new person.
- Research and write a report.
- Write and implement a *what-if* suggestion.
- Observe the demeanor of someone in a high-level position (even if only via video).
- Continue to develop your plan.
- Think of what may stop you from reaching your goals and overcome those barriers.

The first five items are generally considered to be the most important. These action steps will usually help you do better in your career—no matter what your career goals are. Consider adding them to your list if they are not already on it.

Items to add to my Career-Development Plan:

_____

_____

_____

_____

_____

_____

_____

Self-Assessment Summary

Summarize the results of all of the exercises. This information will help define the kind of environment that suits you best, and will also help you brainstorm some possible job targets. Finally, it can be used as a checklist against job possibilities. When you are about to receive a job offer, use this list to help you analyze it objectively.

1. **What I need in my relationship with bosses:** _____

2. **Job satisfiers/dissatisfiers:**

   Satisfiers: _____

   Dissatisfiers: _____

3. **Most important work-related values:** _____

4. **Special interests:** _____

5. **Threads running through the Seven Stories analysis:**
   Main accomplishments: _____
   Key motivators: _____
   Enjoyed most; did best: _____
   My role: _____
   Environment: _____
   Subject matter: _____

6. **Top six or seven Specialized Skills:**

   _____
   _____
   _____
   _____
   _____
   _____
   _____

7. **From Fifteen- or Forty-Year Vision:**

   Where I see myself in the long run: _____
   _____

   What I need to get there: _____
   _____
   _____

8. **My basic personality and the kinds of work cultures into which it will fit:**
   _____
   _____

The
Five
O'Clock
Club

PART THREE

Developing Yourself Professionally

AND ADAPTING TO CHANGE

The
Five
O'Clock
Club

Why Get Feedback from Others

"Jerkins and I worked it out. He can have the office with the window."

Open, honest feedback can help you:

- Determine whether or not there is consistency between your perceptions of yourself and the perceptions of others. You can find out if your self-assessment agrees with the way your colleagues see you.

- Develop realistic career goals. Once you have clearly defined your goals, you can do a "reality check" by getting feedback from your manager and others who know you well.

- Determine action steps toward your goals, including job enrichment, training and development activities, and identifying new job opportunities.

- Improve your performance in your current job. Receiving feedback on your strengths and development needs can help you identify ways to increase your effectiveness in carrying out your current responsibilities. By requesting feedback frequently from your manager and others on your team, you have an opportunity to improve and to confirm that improvements are recognized.

Obtaining candid and specific feedback is an important part of career management. Feedback provides information you can use to improve your professional and personal effectiveness.

Feedback does not define who you are, but it is an opportunity to communicate. Feedback can help you move from mind reading to reality.

The first criterion of success in any human activity, the necessary preliminary, whether to scientific discovery or to artistic vision, is intensity of attention or, less pompously, love.

W. H. Auden

Conducting an Effective Feedback Discussion

At times, you will want to solicit feedback from others with whom you work (your manager, peers, direct reports, customers). Here are a few tips for assuring that your discussion is successful:

- Identify those individuals from whom you are seeking feedback. Each person will be sharing a different perspective based on his or her relationship with you and each can be valuable.

- In approaching your manager or other individuals for feedback, state the purpose of your meeting and schedule sufficient time. Tell them you would find it helpful to obtain their insights and suggestions about what you are doing well and how you might be more effective.

- Prepare an agenda and identify the specific areas where you need feedback. These might include your current performance or future directions in your career.

- During the discussion, indicate through your verbal and nonverbal responses that you are truly interested in what the other person has to say. Paraphrase what you have just heard by repeating back, e.g., "What I hear you saying is . . . Is that correct?" Ask questions to clarify what you do not understand.

- Ask for specifics. Whether the feedback is positive or constructive, it is helpful to get examples of behavior so that you know what to continue doing, as well as what you need to change.

- Listen with an open mind. When you hear something with which you don't agree, it is important to hold off on justifying yourself or giving a knee-jerk response.

- It is not always easy to give feedback, particularly constructive feedback. It may make sense to reflect on what you have heard and respond at a later date. Thank the other person for the feedback, assuring him or her that you have found it helpful.

- Recognize that this discussion is just the beginning. The next step is to create a plan to become more effective based on the feedback you received.

Designing an Approach to Feedback

You can design your own feedback system by answering the following questions. Remember: If you want feedback, you need to ask for it. Discuss this with your manager/direct reports/peers and commit to giving and receiving constructive feedback. Be sure to set specific actions and time frames for feedback to happen. As you are answering the questions, think of a time when you received meaningful feedback that was useful to you.

- What specifically made the difference?
- Who should give me feedback?
- What specifically do I want them to give me feedback about?
- How often do I prefer to receive feedback?
- When was the last time I received feedback?
- How will I ask for feedback?
- How do I currently handle negative feedback? Are there any things I can do to handle it better in the future?

Your effectiveness in the organization and in your own career begins by developing a thorough and more accurate understanding of who you are and how you are representing yourself to others. Getting regular feedback from people you trust is one way to do this.

You will also find that the more regularly you ask for feedback, the more easily you will be able to stay on track.

You have had a chance to focus on ways to get information about how you are perceived in the organization. Now you will learn how you can continue to develop and enhance your professionalism going forward.

How to Think about Feedback

Important points to understand are:

- All organizational behavior—including feed-back—can be seen as empowering or disempowering.
- We have the power to choose our own behaviors and therefore create how others perceive us professionally.
- A supportive feedback system to help us understand ourselves is critical for career effectiveness.
- Certain methods for giving feedback are acceptable and not threatening.
- Your career effectiveness begins with a thorough understanding of who you are and how you are representing yourself to others.

Feedback is an important influence on how effectively we perform in our society. Feedback provides information to the individual as to how he or she contributes to the big picture of an organization, plus how the person is perceived by that organization. Well done, feedback is empowering. Poorly done, it can be disempowering.

Some important questions are: If feedback is so important and beneficial, why is it so difficult to ask for and receive? What can we do about that? What are empowering behaviors? And why is empowerment particularly important in feedback?

Safety—Moving Ahead: Two Responses to Change

There are two ways one can respond to change: Retreat to the apparent safety of the old ways or risk moving forward into unknown territory.

Safety

- Characterized by maintaining the familiar.
- Seeks to avoid change.
- Able to protect established methods.

Moving Ahead

- Characterized by moving beyond the familiar and confronting new situations.
- Seeks new opportunities.
- Able to confront new situations and manage change.

We often injure our cause by calling in that which is weak to support that which is strong.

Charles Caleb Colton, c. 1780–1832

Empowering and Disempowering Behavior

Empowering behavior helps you and others take constructive action. Disempowering behavior is an attempt to look good, sometimes by trying to make someone else look bad.

Empowering Behavior

Characterized as open, supportive, adding value, results oriented, energy oriented, and productive. Enables you and others to operate with maximum efficiency and effectiveness. These behaviors lend themselves to helping a person operate at a high level of personal responsibility. The choices enable the organization and the individuals who are part of it to operate with maximum efficiency and effectiveness.

Disempowering Behavior

Characterized as blaming, justifying, making excuses, withholding communication, gossiping, avoiding the inevitable, and acting out of general defensiveness or mean-spiritedness. Although these behaviors are common, they serve to increase the level of tension in an organization and can serve to disempower the organization's effectiveness.

Ways to Overcome Disempowering Behaviors and Move toward Being More Empowered

1. _____
   _____
   _____

2. _____
   _____
   _____

3. _____
   _____
   _____

4. _____
   _____
   _____

5. _____
   _____
   _____

Empowering and Disempowering Behavior as They Relate to Change

A matrix can be created by using the "Safety-Risk" criteria as column headings and the "Empowering-Disempowering Behavior" as row headings, resulting in a 2 × 2 matrix. Any behavior could fall within one of the four quadrants demonstrated in this arrangement. Below are some examples.

"SAFETY"

Empowering: Making comments that do not confront the issue. The end result: support of self, the organization, or another individual.

Disempowering: Making comments that do not confront the issue. The end result: disruption of self, the organization, or another individual.

"MOVING AHEAD"

Empowering: Making comments that force people to rethink their position. The end result: support of self, the organization, or another individual.

Disempowering: Making comments that force people to rethink their position. The end result: disruption of self, the organization, or another individual.

Feedback gives you information as to how you contribute to the organization and how you are perceived by the organization. Feedback is important and beneficial.

Feedback and Career Management

Getting honest feedback is an important part of career management. Honest, objective, negative feedback and specific, detailed, positive feedback are both of great value in career management. Both empower you to better take your career in the direction you want it to go. Both are prerequisites to getting what you want in your career. Unfortunately, both are also relatively rare.

The reason they are rare is simple. As a general rule, people do not ask for them. And when people do ask for them, they often react with strong emotion when they get what they asked for. This is particularly true of negative feedback; their reaction may be strongly negative at first. But if people mull it over, they sometimes have a more constructive reaction after some time has passed. The next section contains some typical first reactions to feedback.

The Value of Feedback

Feedback's value lies in the information it provides that you can use to improve yourself, both as a professional and as a person. Feedback has career-management value in two areas:

1. **Realizing your long-term vision**

   Feedback is key to getting what you want in your career. Once you have clearly defined your Fifteen- or Forty-Year Vision, you must "reality check" it.

   So, for example, if your career vision is to ultimately become team leader for your department, feedback from your peers on your leadership abilities would be valuable. Even more valuable would be honest feedback from someone further along on that "**fast track**" on how your record stacks up so far, where your strengths lie, and where you might need to work harder.

2. **Improving your performance appraisals**

People who receive weak performance appraisals sometimes complain that the manager didn't tell them sooner. More often than not, the reason the manager didn't tell them sooner is that they did not ask.

While a good manager will support you in managing your career, only *you* can manage it. People who ask for and get regular feedback from their managers usually know what their annual appraisal will say—they have been hearing it all year. This way, there is ample opportunity to improve and confirm that improvements are noticed.

How to Receive Feedback

1. **Ask for it.**

Feedback from peers, subordinates, and superiors all has value. As a rule, none of these people—except your manager—is required to give you feedback. So if you want it, ask.

A useful way to get feedback from your manager is to say, "I want to do a good job, but I can do so only if I have feedback on how I'm doing along the way. So please tell me what you expect, what you see I am doing well, and where you see I might improve."

2. **When and how to ask for it.**
   A. When
      - Performance appraisal
      - Planned follow-up to previous performance appraisal
      - Project or situation specific
      - General
      - Informal
   B. How
      1. *Performance appraisal*—Ask your manager how the meeting will be handled. "Would it be helpful if ahead of time I wrote a report on my current job, major

responsibilities, specific accomplishments and results, and future goals?"
      2. *Planned follow-up to previous performance appraisal*—"Can we meet to discuss how I am succeeding in meeting the objectives we agreed to in my performance review? I want your feedback, so I keep on track."
      3. *Project or situation specific*—"Can we plan a time to review my current project? I'd like to update you on my progress and get your feedback. It will help me meet your goals for this project."
      4. *General*—"Can we schedule a brief meeting? I'm interested in how you perceive me to be doing in this job, handling my staff, managing this client, etc."
      5. *Informal*—Stick your head in the door and say, "How satisfied are you with the way things are going in my group, with my project, etc. Anything you would want done differently? Anything I should know, be aware of? I want this to be successful and meet your goals."

3. **Promise to listen.**

Why should anyone give you feedback if you are going to argue, justify, and defend yourself rather than listen? Promise to listen carefully and coolly reflect on the information before responding to it at a later time.

4. **Listen—and ask for specifics.**

While listening, ask for specific behavioral examples. "What did I do to give you that impression?" is a very useful follow-up question after either positive or negative feedback.

Repeat the feedback back to make sure you heard what the person was really saying. Ask, "It sounds like you are saying . . . Is that right?"

It is not praise that does me good, but when men speak ill of me, then, with a noble assurance I say to myself, as I smile at them, "Let us be revenged by proving them to be liars."

Catherine II ("The Great"), 1729–1796, Empress of Russia, correspondence with the Baron F. M. Grimm

5. **Check with others.**

If several people tell you the same thing, it is either true or you are doing something that convinces people it is so. In asking for confirmation of negative feedback, be careful how you ask.

Asking, "My manager says I'm not good at meeting deadlines, but that's not true, is it?" is not likely to produce honest feedback. On the other hand, "What do you see as my three greatest strengths on the job and my three greatest weaknesses?" might be more effective. Another possibility is, "How would you rate me on decision making, deadlines, and handling details?" In both of these, ask for specific supporting examples.

Good judgment comes from experience; and experience, well, that comes from bad judgment.

Johnny Carson

How to Give Feedback

1. Start with "I"—rather than "You."

Especially in negative feedback, sentences starting with "You are . . ." tend to be inflammatory. "You are lousy about meeting deadlines" will probably be less effective than "I'm having trouble getting my reports done on time because I'm not getting the data from you on time."

2. Use positive language.

Language that blames people or "makes them wrong" is disempowering. Especially in negative feedback, positive language is important."You made the department miss three important deadlines last month" is blaming. On the other hand, "It looks to me like you might benefit by learning more about how to organize work in tight time frames so you could better meet deadlines" is more positive and empowering.

This is not simply *dressing up* the language. The first statement is a condemnation and probably not true. Could one inefficient person really stop a great department from meeting three deadlines? The second statement is an offer of support and assistance. The second also gives feedback about the underlying issue: organizing work.

3. Back up general statements with specific examples.

This is true for both positive and negative feedback. Let them know how you got your impression, positive or negative. What specific incidents or actions led you to your conclusion? Be open to the possibility that you read the incident incorrectly.

4. Examine—and possibly even voice—your motivation.

We have all probably received feedback at some time in our lives that left us feeling very disempowered and unsupported. So, when giving feedback, it's important to examine—and sometimes even voice—your motivation for maximum effectiveness. "Sam, I'd like to share an observation with you and my only reason for sharing it is I want to see you succeed . . ."

In the realm of ideas, everything depends on enthusiasm; in the real world, all rests on perseverance.

Goethe

My Personalized Feedback System

Having answered all the prior questions, finalize your feedback system by answering the following questions. Remember: If you want feedback, you need to ask for it. Discuss this with your manager/subordinates/peers and commit to giving and receiving constructive feedback. Be sure to set specific actions and time frames for feedback to happen, such as, "Let's meet next Wednesday in your office to review your feedback for me."

1. Who should give me feedback?

_____

_____

2. How often do I prefer receiving feedback?

_____

_____

3. When is the last time I received feedback?

_____

_____

4. How do I prefer receiving feedback?

_____

_____

5. How will I ask for feedback?

_____

_____

6. How do I currently handle negative feedback? Are there any things I can do to handle it better in the future?

_____

_____

_____

The
Five
O'Clock
Club

Getting Feedback from Others

*The most important finding my study yielded was:
The men who were introspective, who valued their
logic and intuition, were happier and more self-
confident than their less introspective counterparts
and better able to deal with the stresses of life.
However, those who appeared outwardly
successful, but ignored their inner life, were
often confused, empty, or discontented, which
resulted in their feeling overwhelmed or depressed
and caused them to run from their problems.*

Jan Halper, Ph.D.
Quiet Desperation—The Truth about Successful Men

Did you know that the highest-
performing executives are the most
self-aware and are most aware of the
impact they have on others? Yet 80 percent of
all managers *think* they are self-aware and think
they know how they come across. Statistically,
most of these managers are wrong. So even if
they are promoted, they will probably eventually
get derailed.

You cannot always expect direct, honest feedback from your bosses about how you are doing
on the job. It's a fact: "Five out of seven executives
and managers prefer to lie to an employee about
his or her performance rather than to give constructive criticism." (*Quiet Desperation—The Truth
about Successful Men* by Jan Halper, Ph.D.)

Even so, you can make yourself more like the
high-performers by increasing your personal self-
awareness.

One thing you can do immediately is **assess
all of your work-related relationships—**
**loosely defined as relationships with those
who affect your performance and livelihood**.
Make a list of:

- Your bosses—those above you. This certainly
includes your immediate supervisors and their
bosses. But "bosses" could also include those
in other departments, management in other
organizations that are customers of your organization, and those more senior to you who
can refer business to you.

- All of your peers. You may have to figure out
who your peers *really* are. They may be in
other geographic areas, other divisions, and
even other organizations. But you work with
them on a peer level.

- Your subordinates—those below you. This
means both direct and indirect reports. The
group can even include the person at the local
copy shop, the secretary of some of your
bosses, receptionists, and others with whom
you may (or may not) interact.

- Your *clients*. Again, these may be inside or outside of your organization. They are the people
using your service.

Most people wind up with a list of 8 or 10
bosses, 10 to 12 peers, and 4 to many more
subordinates. Assess your relationship with
each of these people. Decide which ones you
should do something about immediately. Then
develop a long-term plan for assessing and doing
something about your relationship with each
person.

You may need to develop methods and procedures for keeping your boss(es) better informed, building stronger ties with your peers, keeping your staff more up-to-date, and paying attention to your clients. If you think you can ignore your boss while doing a great job for your clients, you are wrong.

Ask yourself how aware you are of the way you come across to each of these people. To make yourself more objective, put yourself in your boss's shoes. What would your boss say about your performance and your relationship with *each* of your peers? If you are ignoring certain peers because you think they are stupid, think again. Ignoring them may not be your smartest response. What would your boss rather have you do about your stupid peers? Think about it and get rid of the ways you may be causing problems for your boss.

Why You Should Pay Attention to Your Work-Related Relationships

1. Getting work done in the new corporate environment now often depends more on influencing others (even your subordinates) than on formally directing them.

2. Corporations are changing so quickly that an employee can be blindsided if he or she is not plugged into what's happening. The organization could be heading in a new direction while the employee is following an old one. Often, these changes in direction are informal and unannounced—no one will officially say that things have changed. Or it will be said almost in passing. The employee is expected to catch on by osmosis. If not, he or she is labeled out of step.

3. You never know who can do you in—your bosses, peers, subordinates, or clients.

You're blind, not stupid. You've lost your sight, not your mind.

told to Ray Charles, blind since age six, by his mother

Increasing Your Self-Knowledge through Self-Assessment

You have already analyzed yourself through the Seven Stories, the Fifteen- and Forty-Year Visions, and other exercises. In a methodical way, you have learned what many already know about themselves but have not learned to articulate. These exercises helped you discover:

- Your skills, as seen through your life experiences; those things you did well and found especially satisfying. This helps increase your knowledge of situations you will be good at, or where there is a skill match or "fit."
- Interests/subject-matter knowledge.
- Job-related values.
- Job-related satisfiers/dissatisfiers.
- Relationships with bosses.

Attending The Five O'Clock Club or working privately with one of our career coaches can also provide you with valuable feedback. However, you must still increase your level of knowledge and awareness by gathering information directly from bosses, peers, and subordinates. Then you can take corrective action.

Getting Feedback from Others— the Exercise

This outside source of information is critical. The feedback is gathered from people selected by you. When you combine it with your self-assessment results, you wind up with a realistic and thorough picture of your skills, strengths, style, and areas for improvement.

1. Select five people who you think know you well in the work situation. These may be either inside or outside of the organization. It is best if you select a mix of bosses, peers, and subordinates so you can get feedback on your likely problems and issues.

2. Call each person and say something like: "I am participating in a career-development program

and I would like your feedback. I have selected five people who I think know me well from a work point of view and you are one of them. I hope you will be honest because the information I will be getting will help me in my career planning."

Then say either:

"I will send you a sheet with five questions I would appreciate your answering. You will also receive a stamped, self-addressed envelope so you can mail your responses back to me. But the questionnaire will not have your name on it so I will not be able to tell who said what."

Or, if you are having a career coach make calls on your behalf, you would say instead: "Please be open with the career coach who will be calling you."

The coach will call each participant and ask the same five questions:

1. Could you describe in general what you think of John/Jane from a work point of view?

2. What do you see as his or her most important strengths?

3. What do you see as his or her downsides or limitations or things that could hold him or her back, whether or not you think he or she would choose to change them?

4. If you could think of the ideal job for John/Jane, what would it be or what would it be like?

5. If you had one piece of career advice to give John/Jane, what would that be?

To keep the feedback even more confidential, the coach can combine all the responses before feeding them back to you.

If you decide to do it by sending a questionnaire to each person, simply use the form on the next page and sign your name. You will notice that there is more room for the person to answer question 3, which solicits opinions about your limitations. Don't be alarmed: Suggestions for improvement usually take longer to describe than simply stating your positives.

Selecting the Participants

You want a balanced assessment of how you come across to people. Therefore, if your present work situation is unhappy and everyone dislikes you and this is unusual for you, do not select those people.

Instead, select five people who you feel know you well from a work point of view. This means you have worked closely with each of them over a number of years. Make sure you include in the mix at least one boss, one peer, and one subordinate. Then select two others.

Typical First Reactions to Feedback

- My respondents didn't really know me that well.
- The wrong people filled out the surveys.
- My job makes me act this way. I'm not really like that.
- Some of my respondents had it in for me.
- My respondents don't understand the situation I'm in.
- My coach/the computer must have gotten this wrong.
- All of my strengths are right, but my limitations are not.
- I used to be this way, but I've changed recently.
- Nobody really understands me.
- This must be someone else's report.
- They just don't like me.
- This was just a bad time to do this.
- My respondents didn't understand the questions.
- I wasn't like this in my last job.
- My respondents are just jealous of my success.
- I was shocked. It sounded so much like me.
- My friend said it described me perfectly.
- I didn't notice how much people noticed and appreciated my work habits.

- If I'm honest, I'd say most of the feedback was right on target.

The Result of Feedback

After doing this, you will have a good idea of your strengths and weaknesses and a clear picture of how you are viewed by others.

You may uncover problems you need to address. You may do this alone or with the help of a career coach.

A state without the means of some change is without the means of its conservation.

Edmund Burke, *Reflections on the Revolution in France,* 1790

Optional: Working with a Career Coach

If you decide to work with a career coach, the process of making changes may take several months, depending on the issues you want to cover. After you have shown the coach the feedback you have received, the coaching may include the following:

1. Your regular reporting of what is going on at your job.

2. Development of a strategy for handling whatever problems exist.

3. Role-playing with the coach to prepare you for discussions you may have with bosses, peers, or subordinates.

4. Development of strategies for how you can better manage your job, work, time, communications—or whatever situations may arise.

5. Intermittent scheduled follow-up sessions to assess your continuing success with incorporating all you have learned.

Open, honest feedback can help you determine whether there is consistency between your perceptions of yourself and the perceptions of others. If there is a gap, you can close it and be more like the high-performing executives. Simply make five copies of the form on the next page. Good luck!

Career-Development Program

I appreciate your help in giving me feedback that will help me with my career. I have selected approximately five people who I think know me well from a work point of view. I sincerely value your feedback. Please fill out this form and return it to me in the enclosed stamped, self-addressed envelope. Since this form does not have your name on it, your responses will be confidential: I will not be able to tell who said what. To be even more sure of confidentiality, you may want to type this on a separate sheet.

Thank you for your time.

_____
(Signed)

1. Describe in general what you think of me from a work point of view.

_____
_____
_____
_____
_____
_____

2. What do you see as my most important strengths? _____
_____

3. What do you see as my downsides or limitations, or things that could hold me back, whether or not you think I would choose to change them? _____

_____
_____
_____
_____
_____
_____
_____

4. If you could think of the ideal job for me, what would it be or what would it be like? _____
_____

5. If you had one piece of career advice to give me, what would that be? _____
_____
_____

The Characteristics of Effective Professionals

When I was younger and working in a major organization, the chairman of our company issued a quarterly video-tape enabling all of us to listen to senior executives telling us how the company was doing. Many employees groaned and were bored, but I wasn't. In addition to listening to the content, I paid close attention to each executive's attitude, tone, demeanor, body language, gestures, facial expressions, dress, haircut, and any other clues I could get about the kind of people who got ahead.

It is important to *tune in*: Observe those who get ahead in *your* industry—both within your organization and outside of it. Ambitious young people can dress more professionally rather than looking like they are still in school. Older workers can spiff up rather than looking worn out. But remember, what is considered effective in one organization—or even one division within a large company—may not be considered effective or appropriate in another organization or division.

Visual cues are important. But even more important are the behavioral characteristics exhibited by the most effective people within an organization. Once you have identified those characteristics, you can decide which of your own behaviors you may want to change to become more effective.

So think of individuals whom you have considered to be highly effective in performing their jobs. Focus on professionals who have been successful in your own functional area or in those other areas you may be considering for future career steps. Or consider other high-achieving professionals you have known. What positive characteristics did they possess that created their effectiveness? What do you remember about those people in terms of their attitudes . . . knowledge . . . skills . . . behavior . . . style? List as many characteristics of these individuals as possible.

First list the person's name and then list the characteristics you've noticed. Refer to the list of characteristics below. Then add to your own list any characteristics particularly important to you.

Person	Characteristics

As you review your entire list below, look at yourself—which of these characteristics do you currently have, and which ones do you need to develop? Make a checkmark next to the ones you have. Circle the ones you would like to improve.

Articulate
Organized
Decisive
Gives feedback
Knowledgeable
Influencer
Prepared
Team oriented

Goal oriented
Fun!—has a sense of
   humor
Risk taker
Active listener
Empathetic
Clear thinker
Fair

Leader
Mature
Personable
Diplomatic
Disciplined
Coach
Smart
Mentor
Common sense
Balanced
Approachable
Apologizes
Committed
Shares credit
Focus on client
Proactive
Continued growth
Well read
Persistent

Enthusiastic
Has integrity
Open minded
Visionary
Flexible—rolls with the
    punches
Adaptable
Positive
Responsible
Ethical
Open
Creative
Solution oriented
Problem solver
Even tempered
Defender
Develops staff
Reliable
Highly intelligent

Are there more checkmarks than circles? If so, great—you are well on your way to being who you want to be and having what effective people in your profession have!

If you have more characteristics circled than checked, you may want to make some changes. Most of the changes are relatively easy to do—*but they do require determination*. To help you plan these changes, turn to the Action Planning Worksheet and assess your top priorities for change.

Now, I can look at you, Mr. Loomis, and see you a man who done forgot his song. Forgot how to sing it. A fellow forget that and he forget who he is. Forget how he's supposed to mark down life.

August Wilson, *Joe Turner's Come and Gone*

Developing a Plan for Becoming a More Effective Professional

You can increase your effectiveness and your potential for success by modeling behavior you have observed in other professionals whom you consider to be particularly outstanding. You've already noted the characteristics you would like to

develop further in yourself. Now, list up to five priorities for getting ahead and develop an action plan for each. For each, list your goal, the action steps you will take to get there, the time frame for completion, any potential barriers to completing that goal (and the potential strategies for overcoming them), and how you will know when you have reached your goal—that is, your objective criteria for success.

For example:

GOAL #1: Upgrade professional image/appearance.

- **Action Steps:**
  Develop more flexible, professional wardrobe.

- **Time Frame:**
  Do clothing budget by month end; revise business wardrobe within 12 months.

- **Potential Barriers:**
  Procrastination. Ask Sally to support me in keeping to budget and making useful purchases.

- **Objective Criteria for Success:**
  Eight outfits suitable for any business setting; three of them to travel well.

GOAL #2: Participate more in meetings; increase visibility.

- **Action Steps:**
  Meet with Mary to enlist her support as my manager.

- **Time Frame:**
  Schedule our meeting prior to next month's staff meeting.

- **Potential Barriers:**
  Feelings of intimidation by senior management. Work on self-confidence. Start taking risks and speaking up.

- **Objective Criteria for Success:**
  Participation in task-force groups; being asked to head important committees.

It is never too late to be what you might have been.

George Eliot

Action Planning

Identify the priorities you feel you can work on to improve your own effectiveness in your career objective position. Then create your action plan to accomplish these steps.

Use the following guidelines in creating your action plan:

1. Identify up to five priorities.
2. List the action steps needed to achieve the outcome.
3. Specify the time frames for completion of each step.
4. Identify factors that will influence the outcomes and ways to overcome barriers.
5. List your desired outcomes for each priority— How will you know when it is completed?

The Effective Professional
Action-Planning Worksheet

Life is just one damned thing after another.

Frank Ward O'Malley

Priority Items _____
Action Steps _____
Time Frames _____
Factors Influencing Outcomes _____
Outcomes _____

Priority Items _____
Action Steps _____
Time Frames _____
Factors Influencing Outcomes _____
Outcomes _____

Priority Items _____
Action Steps _____
Time Frames _____
Factors Influencing Outcomes _____
Outcomes _____

Priority Items _____
Action Steps _____
Time Frames _____
Factors Influencing Outcomes _____
Outcomes _____

In addition to the preceding, all of us must consider ways to keep up to date in our professional knowledge. List below the professional and industry organizations important to your industry and profession:

_____
_____
_____
_____

In summary, there are characteristics in all fields that distinguish truly excellent professionals from those who are mediocre. There are differences in the way people present themselves and in the ingredients of effective professionals. And there are actions you can take to enhance your professionalism.

The
Five
O'Clock
Club

PART FOUR

Managing Up, Down, and Across

DEVELOPING YOUR INTERPERSONAL RELATIONSHIPS

The Eight-Word Message

The Five O'Clock Club

Your security will come first and foremost from being an attractive prospect to employers, and that attractiveness involves having the abilities and attitudes that an employer needs at the moment.

William Bridges, *JobShift: How to Prosper in a Workplace without Jobs*

You can use an Eight-Word Message to make sure those more senior than you know what you want them to know about you. It will help you keep your career on track and improve your chances of getting ahead. Here are a few examples.

CASE STUDY *Judy*
Not Getting Credit

Judy, Jim, and Helen had worked 70 hours a week for the last three weeks to complete the Airbag Project. Judy was proud and relieved when it was done on time. Then she found out that Jim and Helen were getting all the credit. In fact, it seemed that no one even knew she had worked on the project. There had been a pattern for her of not getting recognition for her work. Once more, she was being overlooked. She thought about looking for a new job and working for a company that would be more fair—someplace that would appreciate her hard work. Or she could go to her boss and complain about not getting credit. Instead, she decided to start using a message of about eight words whenever she wanted people to know something about her—especially those higher up. And right now she had a strong message to get across. The message was: "I worked on the Airbag Project."

Most people miss everyday opportunities to get out information about themselves. For example, when Mr. Coyle, her boss's boss, is in the same elevator with Judy, he always greets her with his predictable "Good morning, Judy. How are you?" Judy, just as predictably, politely responds, "Fine, and how are you, Mr. Coyle?"

This time, however, Judy decided to say, "Great—now that we've completed the Airbag Project." He almost had to ask, "Oh, were you involved with that?" This gave her the opening she wanted. "Yes. Three of us worked 70 hours a week for the last three weeks. I was in charge of all the marketing literature. I think it's an award-winning package."

As she came into contact with other people whom she wanted to know about her work, Judy gave them the same message. Gradually people were showing their appreciation. Her self-esteem went way up. If she continues to do good work and makes sure the right people know about it, Judy's career will have a more promising future.

There is proper dignity and proportion to be observed in the performance of every act of life.

Marcus Aurelius Antoninus

Selecting the Targets for Your Message

It's not enough to do a good job. People—especially those more senior than you—have to know that you've done a good job. Managing the message they get about you is even more critical in these turbulent times when those over you come and go and you don't know who your immediate boss may be tomorrow. In the old days, you established long-term relationships and a long-term reputation. The management ranks changed more slowly. Now you have to make sure from time to time that people know your worth.

CASE STUDY *Ralph*
Overcoming Career Stereotypes

Ralph used to be the head of a marketing department before he joined Lavaloc. Now he is in charge of all advertising—a smaller position—and doing a good job. Management here forgets that he used to have much broader responsibilities and could contribute more than he currently does. For example, he could be on a task force to market a new Lavaloc product or have another area reporting to him, such as the direct-marketing department.

Over time, Ralph became so frustrated that he was thinking of writing a memo to personnel to let them know that he had come from a bigger job. Or, he thought about asking for a formal meeting with his boss and his boss's boss. Memos and formal meetings are often good techniques for getting ahead. This approach is discussed in another chapter. But an Eight-Word Message is usually a lot less risky. Ralph decided to try it. His message was: "I used to be head of marketing."

When Ms. Dolan, the division head, was in the proverbial elevator, she predictably said, "Hello, Ralph, how are you?" Ralph responded, "The energy in this place is just terrific. It reminds me of the energy at Galomar." She inevitably had to comment, "I forgot you had worked at Galo-

mar." This gave him the opportunity to say, "Yes. I was the head of marketing there." If appropriate, he could have elaborated.

Ralph's goal, at this point, is simply to remind people that he has a broad background. Later, he can change the message. And, at some point, he may even formally approach someone about being on a task force—once he has established a different image of himself.

Giving These Messages to Bosses

Part of the trick of managing your message is figuring out who your *bosses* are. You probably know who your immediate supervisor is (although in some companies it may be hard to tell), but who are the other people senior to you who can influence your career? Most people come up with a list of 6 to 10 people senior to them. The list could include your boss's boss, some of your boss's peers, or your boss's boss's peers. It could also include a few people outside your organization, such as the head of an important industry association, your boss's peer in another company, or someone considered a guru in your field. These are the people you want to consider when you have an important message to get across.

You can't constantly send out messages every time you run into someone and you'd look like an idiot if you kept saying the same thing. You may, for example, want to send a message that supports your boss or your group, such as "I think we have the best audit team in the industry."

Decide what message you want to send and to whom you want to send it. *Make sure your message is appropriate.* In the course of promoting yourself, make sure you do not undermine your boss or say anything negative about others. You are simply trying to manage your own career.

I don't want any yes-men around me.
I want everybody to tell me the truth even
if it costs them their job.

Samuel Goldwyn

Managing Relationships at Work: Bosses

Most people do not lose their jobs because of incompetence but because of poor relationships at work. By definition, work relationships can be divided into those with people who are at a higher level than you (bosses), at your level (peers), or at a lower level (subordinates). Of course, you must also have good relationships with clients, but we will not deal with that here. Your career can be completely derailed by a boss, a peer, or a subordinate—but in very different ways. On the other hand, your career can be greatly enhanced by learning how to communicate well with the people in each of these categories—again, in very different ways.

In this chapter, we'll take a look at the instructive examples of two people who totally ignored the importance of having good relationships up the line. And they each suffered the consequences.

CASE STUDY *Frank*
About to Be Fired

Frank's story is a common one: He forgot that it was his job to please his boss. Frank was the person in his company responsible for supporting computer departments all over the world and his work was excellent. He and his boss, Mr. Williams, received many letters of commendation from happy clients who appreciated the work Frank did. However, Frank thought his boss was stupid and nasty and deserved to be ignored. He would not tell his boss what he was going to say at meetings. What Frank said usually caught his boss by surprise, which gave Frank pleasure. When Mr. Williams gave him an assignment, Frank was sure his boss was wrong and did it his own way. Sometimes Frank's clients agreed with him and sent more letters praising him. This only encouraged him to ignore his boss further.

Frank was doing such a great job that he was ready to have his duties expanded. He wanted new assignments and a promotion. In fact, Frank thought he should report directly to his boss's boss. Because Frank served his clients well and did his job well, he thought that was enough. It wasn't. Frank was in trouble. He was about to be fired, but Mr. Williams thought Frank was worth saving and that some executive coaching could help change his attitude and behavior. Mr. Williams arranged for Frank to see me.

When I discussed the situation with Frank, he was adamant about not showing respect to his boss as a matter of principle. Why should he defer to someone he thought was inadequate and who treated everyone so horribly? It had become a point of honor with him.

To keep his job, Frank first had to accept the fact that he was in trouble: He had no chance of reporting to his boss's boss; he was not going to get new assignments, given the way he was acting; and I couldn't emphasize enough that he was actually going to lose his job if he didn't change. The turning point came when he saw it was possible to develop a good relationship with his boss *without* giving up his principles or his rapport with people in the field.

A subordinate cannot possibly know all the various pressures that affect his or her boss's decisions and therefore is not the best judge of whether a boss's requests are valid. If your boss says a certain assignment is the most important thing for you to do, you are in no position to second-guess him or her—in effect saying no. I told Frank I know from personal experience as a manager that I don't want to always have to explain to my employees why I want them to do something. At some point, I get tired of explaining. Sometimes when I say something is very important, I simply want them to do it.

As we continued our counseling sessions together, Frank came to see that his point of view was not always accurate and perhaps it made sense to pay attention to the boss. If Frank didn't learn to deal with this boss, he would probably have the same problem with the next one—who might simply fire him rather than *trying to help him* as this one was doing.

What could Frank do differently? He could find out his boss's priorities, let his boss know his agenda before he went into meetings, and send his boss a copy of all memos (or show him the content of sensitive memos before he sent them). But even if Frank kept making these little changes, how could Mr. Williams tell if Frank was simply trying to placate him or if he had seen the error of his ways and had a real change of heart? Over the course of time, Frank's boss would have to watch carefully for signs of Frank's true intentions: Was Frank still trying to undermine him or was Frank now supporting him? This situation would create a lot of pressure on both of them.

Making subtle changes at this point would not be enough. Frank's boss was too frustrated. Instead, Frank would have to do something more radical so his boss could see clearly that his attitude had indeed changed. Frank could make more dramatic and consistent changes in his approach, such as overtly deferring to his boss at meetings. An effective alternative would be actually to tell his boss that he had made a conscious decision to change and he was determined to become a new person. Then, even if his changes were not dramatic, Frank's boss would recognize the true significance of all those small changes: Frank is now a different person. Things *will* be better in the future.

To let Mr. Williams know that he'd had a change of heart, Frank needed to communicate a very simple message: "I was wrong. I've changed." So Frank said to his boss, "I can see now that I've been wrong. I'm sure you have plans I don't know about. I will make sure I do what you want and also let you know my agenda before we go into meetings." Now Frank was consistently asking his boss for feedback on things he planned to do and filling him in before they went into meetings. He developed a good relationship with Mr. Williams. After a few months, Frank got a number of new assignments. After a few more months, he got a promotion. Frank is still working for the same boss, but now he loves it, and Mr. Williams is as happy as can be.

According to the market paradigm, one's boss is really a major customer rather than an authority in the old sense.

William Bridges, *JobShift: How to Prosper in a Workplace without Jobs*

CASE STUDY *Melanie*
Getting Un-Fired

Melanie, an advertising manager, had already gotten fired. She came to me because she wanted help looking for a job. Her employer had offered her only a few weeks of severance pay and no outplacement help and she had not quite moved out of her old job. Because she would have no income except unemployment compensation, I asked her if she would like to try to stay with her present company. She reminded me that she had already been fired. I explained that it takes a lot more effort to change jobs than to attempt to stay where you are. If we put the new strategy into effect right away, before our next weekly session she would know whether or not it was working. It might not do the trick, but it would take relatively little effort. Would she like to try it? She said she would. After all, what did she have to lose?

I asked her to tell me about the situation in more detail. She was an account manager in an advertising agency. She and the creative director, slightly higher up than she was, disliked each other intensely. She admitted she had caused him a lot of problems. In fact, she had irritated a number of important people, including her boss and the president. Melanie first had to make a list of the people to whom she needed to make amends, decide what she should say to each person, and plan the sequence of this campaign to save her job. She also needed an overall theme to her campaign—a brief message that she could fall back on whenever things seemed to be going poorly in her discussions. Her pitch was: "I've loved working here. I want to stay." That's all there was to it—only 8 words.

You should be able to sum up the main idea you want to convey in about 8 to 10 words. Naturally, depending on the context and conversational opportunities, the way you express the message will vary and may call for a few more words. But your message has to be simple since you will repeat it like a mantra during these discussions. When things are going wrong and people are attacking you and saying things you didn't expect to hear, just keep going back to your pitch. If you don't have a main message, the conversation can go off in all directions. You can spend a lot of time defending yourself or rehashing old scenarios.

Melanie met with her boss. She said, "I know I've made mistakes and have irritated a lot of people. But I'm a changed person. I've loved working here and I want to keep my job." Her boss replied by naming lots of things she had done wrong. She agreed with him, said things would be different, and added, "I've loved working here. I want to stay." When she met with the creative director, she said she was sorry for any problems she had caused in the past, but promised she would support any creative ideas he had in the future. She said she now realized this was part of her job. She added, "I've loved working here. I want to stay." She did this with four more people and within two days found she was back in the fold. Not only did she get her job back but she was assigned to the company's most important account!

Melanie had bought herself some time until she could decide what to do. She had turned things around so she actually could stay if she wanted or she could leave when she was better prepared. She soon found another job and then resigned. But she resigned on very good terms with everyone in the company. They were all sorry to see her go.

This technique of telling someone you have changed—if indeed you have—is very powerful. The key to its power is not only in what you do afterwards, but in *saying* that you have changed. But there is no use in saying you have changed if you haven't. You will not be able to get away with it. They *are* looking for change. And it will only make the situation worse if you try to con them.

Stories about career crises are interesting and dramatic. However, it is better to manage your career to prevent the kind of crises you may bring on yourself. You don't have to wait until things get critical. You can make corrections at any stage. First, assess your situation. Make a chart of everyone in the organization with whom you have contact. Think through what your relationship is with each person and what it should be. If you are in danger of losing your job, make a plan. The most effective ways to buy time for yourself are to make a dramatic change that takes the pressure off you and to deliver a concise and consistent message.

The
Five
O'Clock
Club

Avoiding Career Crises

The pure and simple truth is rarely pure and never simple.

Oscar Wilde

Getting the Impossible Job Done— and Getting Fired

Gloria had been fired from her job even though, by her own estimation, she was doing a superb job. She had accomplished a dramatic turn-around, growing a division that had floundered for 20 years into a billion-dollar business.

But to reach that level of success, she had stepped on a lot of toes. That was only part of the problem, however. She had not spoken to her boss for more than two years. As she ignored him and went about reaching her goals, he bided his time and eventually got rid of her.

Bosses may give you an impossible assignment. But if you have left too much destruction in your path as you reach your goals, they will hold it against you. Now Gloria had to learn to act differently or she would fail in her next job, too. In fact, her job search was not going well because hiring managers sensed something was wrong with her managerial style. Gloria was convinced there was something wrong with all of them. It took Gloria a year to accept that she had a style problem and needed to make changes in her attitude and behavior. When she changed her attitude, she was able to attract employers who valued her business skills.

George, on the other hand, had an excellent relationship with his boss and had learned to coach her tactfully. When he saw a situation that might prove dangerous to his boss, George would warn her, give her information, and make her look good. People like George tend to be valued and rarely get derailed.

The employee-vendor relationship to his or her customers is something like professional/client relationships in the past, but the difference lies in the pace of change. Traditional professional/client relationships were not change-driven. They developed slowly over time, and they settled into mutually satisfying patterns of complementary activity and reward. Today, however, change occurs so quickly and so constantly that customers, both inside and outside the organization, always need something they don't have.

William Bridges, *JobShift: How to Prosper in a Workplace without Jobs*

Peers: They Can Help You—or Not

Kari, an executive from another country, had a cultural problem. Of her 10 peers, she spoke only to two. According to Kari, the others were not smart and she considered them a waste of her time. In her old country, which had a strong class system, it was acceptable to pay attention to certain people and snub others.

"If I have to be at these boring meetings, I might as well get something out of it."

Kari's bosses had heard enough complaining from her peers and they resented having to deal with this ongoing problem.

When Kari realized her attitude was a cultural issue, the solution was clear. I explained to her that in this country you should at least appear to get along with everyone. You don't have to spend time with them or have brainy discussions, but you do have to say hello and be cordial. For your boss's sake as well, develop good relationships with your peers. Kari began to loosen up and smile. She even found that she liked a few of those she had formerly shunned.

Having gifts that differ according to the grace given to us, let us use them.

Romans 12:6

Look at Your Relationships from Your Boss's Point of View

Steve had a problem with his peers. He was brilliant, but as you have already learned, this alone is not enough. He was not about to lose his job, but he had hoped that his competence would be enough to warrant getting promoted to be head of his group. Instead, it was obvious to management that he and his peers did not get along and they announced that they were hiring an outsider to become head of the group. Now Steve wondered what he had done wrong and he faced a new problem: How should he act around his new boss and how could he protect his job, since a new boss often wants to select his own team?

I told Steve that he had indeed messed up in the past because he hadn't seen things from his boss's point of view. He bickered with his peers and complained to his boss about them. Even when Steve was *right,* he was deeply resented and his peers wasted energy trying to prove he was wrong. Obviously Steve was part of the problem, not part of the solution. His boss simply wanted people to cooperate. Steve had missed an opportunity to enhance his value as a leader by making a situation worse.

In general, managers want to promote someone who will be a popular choice with their peers. Management does not want to risk losing anyone because they promoted an unpopular person.

Look at situations from your manager's point of view. Cultivate relationships with your peers. You don't have to go overboard, but do be friendly, share articles or other information that may interest them—and ask how the weekend was!

If you are strong and smart in your own job, give credit to your peers when credit is due. Show respect for their efforts. In meetings, say, "I think Jane did a superb job on that project." And let them know some of the things *you're* working on. Then, if you become the boss, they'll know that you'll give them credit, share information, and respect what they do.

A study done by the Center for Creative Leadership showed that happier people tend to get ahead. The people at the top of a hierarchical organization are the happiest and the people further down the organization's ladder are less happy. The Center believes happy people rise to the top. Out of every group, from the lowest level in an organization to the highest, there are happy people and these are the ones who get promotions. They tend to get along better with others, volunteer above and beyond the call of duty, and simply put more energy and thought into their jobs. If a manager has a choice between promoting the person who is enthusiastic and pitches in or the person who walks around unhappy and complaining, she will certainly select the former.

A study of recent college graduates who got jobs—as opposed to ones who did not—showed that the ones who were most enthusiastic landed the jobs. Even at the most senior levels, that enthusiastic approach carries some weight with hiring managers. That is why it is important to find a job you enjoy doing and that you also do well. You are more likely to stand out among peers who are complaining and dissatisfied.

Even though Steve had a bad relationship with his peers for many years, it was not too late. He made a list of all of his peers, noted what his relationship with each one was and what he wanted it to be, and then took action. He quickly patched up every relationship—especially by acknowledging others' accomplishments. By the time the new boss came in, human resources was very involved and wanted to make sure each person accepted the new boss, as this was a major transition for the company. Steve had an opportunity to stand out. All of his peers told human resources that they resented an outsider coming in and they deserved the job. Steve, after having been coached, said positive things about the new boss and added, "I'm looking forward to working with him." Steve didn't get the boss's job, but he did make a good impression. He moved his career forward by being assigned to special task forces—and he had a more pleasant time at work.

You've got to get up every morning
with a smile on your face,
And show the world all the love in your heart,
Then people gonna treat you better.
You're gonna find, yes, you will,
That you're beautiful as you feel.

Carole King

The Quarterly Exercise

*Woe to him that is alone when he falleth,
for he hath not another to help him up.*

The Wisdom of Solomon—Apocrypha

Every three months, make a list of your bosses, peers, subordinates, and clients. As mentioned earlier, *Bosses* are people at higher levels who can influence your career. Don't go strictly by the organizational chart. *Bosses* would include your boss and your boss's boss, perhaps some of your boss's peers, and maybe even one or two people outside of your organization who are in the position of influencing your career. Remember: *Influencers* may even be in other geographic areas.

Most people have 6 to 8 bosses. Make a list of yours on the worksheet.

Each quarter, go through your list and ask yourself: "What does this person think of me and what *should* they think of me?" If your bosses forget that you had extensive marketing experience before you took this job, you can easily remind them of this. If they have not noticed that you have been working 70 hours a week on an important project, make sure they know.

Always know your Eight-Word Message so if you run into a boss in an elevator you can quickly slip it into the conversation, however brief it may be. You have many opportunities to communicate with people more senior than you, but you have to plan your communication. This is a way to manage informally the impression senior bosses

have about you. Don't let something build up until it's a major problem and you have to ask for a formal meeting. Instead, manage your internal public relations as you go along.

> • **For bosses, ask yourself, "What do these people think of me and what *should* they think of me?"**
> • **For peers, ask yourself, "What is my relationship with each of these people and what *should* it be?"**

Now, **make a list of your peers—usually 12 to 14 people who are at your level**. Here again, you are not simply plucking the names from your division's organization chart. Certain peers may work right up the hall; others may be in other cities, departments, or divisions. Review the list every quarter and ask yourself, "What is my relationship with each of them and what should it be?"

You don't have to take everyone to lunch or go out for drinks! Often, simply saying "hello" is all it takes to have a decent relationship. Or perhaps you want to ask certain people how they enjoyed the weekend or the status of a major project. With others, you may want to exchange information about the projects on which you are each working.

If your peers are out of town, you may have to pick up the phone for a brief chat. The relation-

117

ship you have with your peers is critical to your success. And having a good relationship usually takes very little effort.

In addition to reviewing your relationships with your bosses and peers, also make a list of your *subordinates* (those at a lower level than you in the organization). These may include your secretary or your boss's secretary, for example. Do you treat your subordinates well? Do they complain about you to their bosses?

Also make a list of your clients—those you service inside or outside your organization. Most people are conscious of focusing on their clients, so that may not be an issue for you. However, to be thorough, make a list of these as well and review your list at least quarterly.

Names of *Bosses*, Their Impression of Me, and My Plan for Each

1. _____
   _____
2. _____
   _____
3. _____
   _____
4. _____
   _____
5. _____
   _____
6. _____
   _____
7. _____
   _____
8. _____
   _____

Names of Peers and My Relationship with Each

1. _____
2. _____
3. _____
4. _____
5. _____
6. _____
7. _____
8. _____
9. _____
10. _____
11. _____
12. _____
13. _____
14. _____

My plan for developing relationships with my peers:

_____

_____

_____

Barbara Walters: And you think you will walk again?

Christopher Reeve: I think it's very possible I'll walk again.

Walters: And if you don't?

Reeve: Then I won't walk again.

Walters: As simple as that?

Reeve: Either you do or you don't. See, it's like a game of cards and if you think the game is worthwhile, then you just play the hand you're dealt. Sometimes you get a lot of face cards, sometimes you don't. But I think the game's worthwhile. I really do.

Christopher Reeve, former star of *Superman,* in an interview with Barbara Walters.

The Promotability Index

Will You Actually Get Promoted?
Or Are You Simply Promotable?

When Is It Time to Move On?

People say: "I've been at my current job six years. I'm killing myself, but I wonder when, if ever, I'll be promoted." How can a person tell? And in this job market, employees are sometimes deciding to move out in order to move up.

But before jumping blindly from one job to another, reassess your situation. What are your chances of getting promoted where you are?

Half the people who come to The Five O'Clock Club are employed and have decided it's time to move on. But before moving on, ask yourself: Are you learning new skills that increase your marketability and fit in with your Forty-Year Vision? If so, stay.

If not, try to improve your present position. If you want to change fields, can you do it within your present company? If you need new skills, get them on your own or get them where you are now. If you want to start your own business, keep your day job and start it at night. If there's no benefit in staying, then move on.

CASE STUDY *Jim*
Moved Too Much

Jim had an amazing career—moving up every year and a half or two by switching companies. He lost his most recent job because of a downsizing, but had no trouble getting interviews since all of his jobs had been with Fortune 100 firms.

Then his job hopping caught up with him. Because he'd had five jobs in eight years, prospective employers were wary. Why had he not been promoted?

After a lengthy search, Jim found a job in a city that was not to his liking. He could stay there awhile to offset the image of being a vagabond or consult there while continuing to search.

Sometimes Job Hopping Is Okay

In certain industries, job hopping is to be expected—many parts of the entertainment field, for example, or the Internet industry. But other industries want employees to be more stable.

Four Key Indicators That You Will Get a Promotion

There's a big difference between being *promotable* (valued highly as a right-hand person or team member but staying right where you are) and actually getting promoted. We all know people who have the qualifications to move up but who just never do. Ask yourself these questions:

1. **Are you READY?**
   - Are you considered a star? Have you developed a reputation in your field? Are you active in your industry? Do you help others in your department?

- Are you so known for your skills that people look to you for help?

- Is the next move an obvious career step? If the move doesn't make sense to you, it probably won't make sense to others either. Also remember that a lateral move may be the right one for you at this point

- Have you trained your replacement? You'd better do that or bosses will be reluctant to leave a hole in the organization.

If you don't like your boss, chances are your boss doesn't like you.

2. **Are you INCLUDED?**

- Are you the type who simply helps out while the choice assignments go to someone else? Or do you get good assignments so you're seen as a person on the leading edge?

- Are you asked to represent your department on important projects and task forces?

- Are you invited to meetings where your peers are excluded?

- Do you volunteer for critical responsibilities, including tasks for which your boss is responsible?

You work hard, are valued—even considered promotable—but maybe your boss would like to keep you right where you are. So ask yourself these questions:

3. **Are you ACCEPTABLE to others?**

- Do you get along well with your peers? Bosses want to make popular decisions. And if your peers do not like you, they might not support your promotion. Those who are disliked rarely become the boss because of the danger of having others resign.

- Do you get along well with your boss? Make sure your boss looks to you for input. If you don't like your boss, chances are your boss doesn't like you.

- Have you supported your boss and never undermined him or her? If not, you're doomed.

- Have you become part of the power center? Are you known to your boss's peers and others above you? (Use the *Eight-Word Message* for this.) If no one knows your talents or likes you, you won't be promoted. Few promotions are made without some involvement from the company power structure. Power structures don't like unknown quantities.

If no one else is moving, you're probably not either. Your company is stagnant.

4. **Are you in the RIGHT PLACE at the RIGHT TIME?**

- If you are doing everything right, but your company is not doing well, you're not going anywhere. You will stay as a valued employee, but you are unlikely to get promoted.

- Is your boss going somewhere? If not, he or she may be a roadblock.

When should you leave? Don't wait until you're so battered that you can barely think straight. Consider lateral moves into faster-growing companies. Big companies add credentials to your résumé; smaller companies add responsibility and experience.

Career Development Starts at Home

Think of ideas for changing your present job to move it in the direction you want to go. If you know where you are heading, you can be open to new assignments or projects that would give you experience in those areas. Assume responsibility for new areas. Move away from old areas no longer compatible with your long-term career goals. When special projects come up that would give you new skills or update your old skills, gradually start working on those projects—feeling them out—and then taking them over if they seem right.

Start out working in these areas informally. This will be nonthreatening to both you and the company. You are not asking your company to make a big decision about whether or not you *should* handle these areas—just slip into them. And if things don't seem to be working out, slip out early in the game.

If you slip in by *helping out* on a project, you can get more enmeshed in it and eventually become an expert in that area. At the same time, be sure not to ignore the work for which you are primarily responsible. If you spend time on the new area and your old job starts to slip, you are in trouble. You've got to do both for a while. When it gets to be too much of a burden for you, you will either have to ask for additional help while you continue to handle both areas or try to unload the area that no longer interests you. Just be sure the work that interests you is important to your employer.

If you are improving your skills and knowledge—and looking for opportunities—opportunities will present themselves.

Oh I could show my prowess, be a lion not a mou-esse, if I only had the nerve.

The Cowardly Lion in the movie
The Wizard of Oz

A Mindset of Strength

People are used to depending on their employers. They say, "My boss won't train me in this new area" or "Only those who went to Ivy League schools get into that program."

Make your own program. Don't let *them* stop you. You operate from greater strength when you do not feel completely dependent on your present employer and your employer is usually better off as well. If you are well versed in what is going on in your field or industry, you are more marketable and your employer benefits from your knowledge and contacts. Take better care of yourself professionally. If you are frustrated that your employer is not doing enough to help you, help yourself.

The earth is a place to live in, where we must put up with sights, with sounds, with smells, too, by Jove!— breathe dead hippo, so to speak, and not be contaminated. And there, don't you see? Your strength comes in, the faith in your ability for the digging of unostentatious holes to bury the stuff in—your power of devotion, not to yourself, but to an obscure, backbreaking business.

Joseph Conrad, *Heart of Darkness*

Ongoing Career Management and Career Exploration

People who are successful in their careers know that *job search* involves ongoing career management and career exploration: building relationships, researching areas inside and outside the company, and developing marketable skills. This approach is more work than simply responding to job postings, but it is a surer and faster way to get ahead in today's market.

All of this fits in with what we teach at The Five O'Clock Club: It is best for both the employee and the employer if *job hunting* is seen as a continual process—and not just something that happens when a person wants to change jobs. Job search means continually being aware of market conditions both inside and outside your present company and continually learning what you have to offer—to both markets.

With this approach, workers are safer because they are more likely to keep their present jobs longer: They learn to change and grow as the company and industry do. And if they have to go elsewhere, they will be more marketable. Companies are better off because employees who know what is going on outside their insular halls are smarter, more sophisticated, and more proactive—making the company more competitive.

The Five O'Clock Club

PART FIVE

Searching for a New Job within Your Present Firm

BUILD YOUR RÉSUMÉ, CONTACT PEOPLE, FOLLOW UP

The
Five
O'Clock
Club

How to Improve Your Position Where You Are

A man's work is in danger of deteriorating when he thinks he has found the one best formula for doing it. If he thinks that, he is likely to feel that all he needs is merely to go on repeating himself . . . so long as a person is searching for better ways of doing his work, he is fairly safe.

Eugene O'Neill

The techniques you use for job hunting inside your company are often the same as those you would use outside. You can look at ads for ideas, network, write proposals, even do some outside interviewing to learn more about how to position yourself and gain a realistic assessment of your value.

Job Hunters at The Five O'Clock Club Sometimes Stay with Their Present Employers—but in a Stronger Position

Half the people who attend The Five O'Clock Club are employed. Some think they are in danger in their present positions and want to start looking now; others are simply unhappy.

Although employed people come to The Five O'Clock Club because they want jobs elsewhere, a surprising number end up becoming more valued by their present companies. That's because these workers start exploring what is going on outside their companies, pick up new skills that make themselves marketable, and often take that information back to their present employers. Because they no longer feel dependent on one company, they develop greater self-esteem and become more assertive in developing ideas and programs for their present employers. Their employers start to treat them differently.

"Joe took the day off to go to the ball game. So I'll be sitting in for him until he gets back. Would you like me to fetch you something?"

Continuous Improvement

This process of staying aware and marketable is what employees of the future will have to do to keep their present jobs longer or to make career moves within their present companies.

With all of the changes occurring in most corporations, your firm may be one of the important places to look if you want to make a career change—or if you simply want to get ahead.

I can never be what I ought to be until you are what you ought to be. You can never be what you ought to be until I am what I ought to be.

Martin Luther King, Jr.,
The American Dream

"But I love what I'm doing right now and I want to keep on doing it."

The same thing happened to me. Twice. The first time, I was 21 years old and in the computer programming department of a large company. Programmers brought their computer *dumps* to us—the debugging team—and we told them where their programs went wrong. The debugging section was considered an elite group and I loved my job. But the technology changed and the computers began to tell the programmers where their programs had gone wrong. They didn't need us anymore.

The company gave me another job; I don't even remember what it was. I'm sure I didn't like it as much as the debugging job. Technology is often the cause of our jobs changing.

Ten years later, a similar thing happened. I was then a training manager in a large company (by then I had gotten my M.B.A. in behavioral science). I was in that job for three years and one day it was gone. The company had gone through five downsizings over a number of years and then decided to cut out the training program altogether. I had loved my job so much that I was oblivious to the larger changes taking place.

Doing a good job is not enough. Sometimes changes in your company affect your job.

Technology causes changes, companies change, and sometimes people change. Someday you may decide that your job is not as enjoyable for you as it once was. Maybe the job is the same, but something inside you has changed. Perhaps you now want to move to a more people-oriented job rather than an intensely technical one. As people get older, their values change. That is fine. But a problem occurs when people who have never given it another thought say they want a change and have no idea what kind of change they want.

Deciding where you want to go with your life is not an easy process. And it is not something to be taken too lightly. After all, it is your life that we're talking about. Start to get ready for your next change—whatever it may be. Even if you love what you are doing right now, figure out what you find so enjoyable about your present position. Then when you want a change, you will have some idea of the kind of change you want.

Making a Move in a Medium or Large Company

Many people think that job hunting internally in a large corporation consists of only two steps:

- responding to job postings, and then
- doing well in interviews.

Job postings are one path to a new job, but they are not the way most people move into new jobs within the same companies.

An Overview of How to Get a New Job in Your Present Company

Your first move, as already noted, is to gain new skills while staying in your present position. At the same time, you need to learn more about what is going on both inside and outside your company.

You've heard it said: "It's not what you know, but who you know." It's probably a lot of both. You can improve both your skills and your contacts. You can also conduct an organized internal search at the same time you carry out an organized external search. Here's an overview of how to look internally:

- Focus on three or more departments, divisions, or businesses of interest to you in the company where you are now employed.

- Research those departments, divisions, or businesses.

- Build relationships with 4 to 6 people in each area.

- Find out how those functions are performed in other companies.

- Perhaps take that information back to your present employer.

- Develop the skills you need to make yourself marketable in those departments, divisions, or businesses.

Moving internally takes work but is less frustrating than simply responding to job postings. Incidentally, an outsider who wanted to work for your company might follow exactly the same approach. Whether you are inside or outside, staying marketable and keeping in touch is how most people get jobs.

The heart and soul of competing is knowing how to appeal to your customers.

Don Peterson, chairman, Ford Motor Co.
Speech, San Francisco, July 1, 1987

The Details of How to Search for a New Job in Your Present Company

You are more likely to find a new job in your present company if you use an organized approach and if you do not put all of your eggs into one basket. Follow these steps:

1. Find out which departments or businesses at your present company are of interest to you. You can do a preliminary investigation by:

   - networking within the company to find out the best areas for you to explore, and
   - doing research through your annual report, other printed materials, and the company's website.

2. Using the Internal Job Search Worksheet, list two of your company's departments, divisions, or businesses you would like to explore. It's a good idea to make copies of this worksheet to research additional company areas. There may be many departments where you could find a new home.

3. Now you need to get to know people in each of those areas. For each one, list the names of 4 to 6 people you think you should get to know.

   If you don't yet know the names of the appropriate people in those areas, ask others for their advice, or study the organization charts for those businesses. Even people *outside* your company may be able to tell you who to see inside.

4. Figure out how you will get in to see each of these people. The three main techniques for getting in to see a person at your present company are listed below.

   a. **Networking directly to that person** through someone you already know (see the chapters on networking).

   b. **Building a network** in to that person or in to that general area. Even if the people you know do not work in the areas in which you are interested, they can refer you to people in those areas, who can then refer you on to other people in the department or division.

   If you don't know anyone outside your department, you can get to meet more people in your company by:

   - serving on committees,

- volunteering for internal programs such as United Way or the blood drive,
- joining task forces,
- meeting fellow employees at association meetings for the field you are targeting, or
- simply meeting people in elevators or the company cafeteria.

    You can tell them you are curious about their area and suggest the two of you have lunch sometime.

  c. **Contacting the person directly**, such as by writing an internal memo (see the chapter "Targeted Mailings: Just Like Networking").

    On the worksheet, list the methods you are likely to use to meet with each person.

5. Next, figure out what to say to each person. Handle these meetings the same way you would any networking meeting (see chapters on networking). However, you may also want to ask them:

- what they do there,
- plans for the area,
- the kinds of people they tend to look for, even though they may not be hiring at the moment,
- how you stack up against the kinds of people they tend to look for. You can ask, "If you had an opening right now, would you consider hiring someone like me? Why or why not?"
- skills and abilities you would need to move into that area someday, and
- how they think you might gain the skills and abilities you are now lacking.

As you establish relationships with people in specific business areas, get to know more about each business and understand what skills you need to make yourself more desirable. Your goal is to have people saying, "I sure wish I had an opening right now. I'd love to have someone like you on board." Then when a job opens up, you will be the one most likely to get it.

6. It is usually not enough to find out about an area inside your present company. To be strongly considered for a position, it is a good idea to also learn how that area functions outside of your company. You will be more knowledgeable and more marketable—inside and outside of your company at the same time.

    Many functional areas exist across industries: customer service, computers, purchasing, corporate sales, public relations—to name a few.

    Still other areas may *seem* to be related strictly to your industry yet actually are found in many industries. For example, banks are involved in *check transaction processing,* which may seem like a function related only to financial institutions. Yet many industries—hospitals, large fund-raising organizations, direct-mail houses—are engaged in heavy transaction processing. Broadly define the field you are in. It may well exist in other industries—but in a very different way. This will open up the industries where you can transfer your skills.

    Regardless of where you work inside your company, think of how your function is handled outside—especially in other industries.

    You can learn more by:

- joining professional associations,
- reading trade journals,
- taking courses, and
- networking to people outside of your company—including those outside your industry.

The more you know about the areas you are exploring, the more information you can share with people in the departments or businesses you are exploring. This will put you in a better position to figure out how you can help them.

Using the worksheet on the next page, list the methods you plan to use to investigate each area outside of your present company.

7. As you investigate, **you may find you lack certain skills that seem to be in demand**. Acquiring these new skills will make you more marketable, both inside and outside of your present company. Using that same worksheet, list the skills, experiences, and knowledge you need to develop and how you think you may go about acquiring them.

8. Keep in touch (about every two months) with 4 to 6 people in each department or business:

   • Find out what is happening in the department or business.

   • Let them know what is happening to you, such as new projects on which you are working and new information or skills you have picked up that would be of interest to them.

9. Continue to research (using the techniques listed in #6) those areas you have been exploring outside of your present company.

10. Continue to take that information back to those departments or businesses in which you are interested.

11. Keep responding to job postings for those departments or businesses.

Do Not Jeopardize Your Present Situation

At first, take the most cautious steps possible. Reading trade journals and joining trade organizations are usually among the safest options. You can join simply because you are interested in the subject and because "I thought it would help me do better in my present job if I were more knowledgeable about this area."

I chose, and my world was shaken—so what?
The choice may have been mistaken,
the choosing was not . . .

Stephen Sondheim, "Move On,"
Sunday in the Park with George

How to Conduct an Internal Job Search—Worksheet

I gave a lecture inside a major corporation to encourage employees to manage their own careers. Someone in the audience said, "I've answered six job postings for a certain department. They give the jobs only to people they know." "That's probably true," I said, "and how many people do you think you would have to know in a department to have a chance of getting a job there?" She replied, "Uh, six."

Six is a good estimate of how many people you would have to be in touch with **on an ongoing basis** before you would stand a chance of getting a job in a certain area—providing you had the skills and personality they were looking for. Make sure you are aiming at a number of departments and also be sure to build your network and base of support and information *outside* of your present company. That base will make you more marketable inside, and help you to hedge your bets in case things do not work out where you are employed at present.

Beyond that, follow the normal job-search approach used at The Five O'Clock Club.

For Target _____ :

Department, division, or business: _____

Position/function: _____

Geographic area: _____

People to Contact	Title	Method of Contact	Date of Last Contact	Target Date
1.				
2.				
3.				
4.				
5.				
6.				
7.				

For Target _____ :

Department, division, or business: _____

Position/function: _____

Geographic area: _____

People to Contact	Title	Method of Contact	Date of Last Contact	Target Date
1.				
2.				
3.				
4.				
5.				
6.				
7.				

CASE STUDY *Joe*
Making Himself More Marketable

Two years ago, Joe, a finance professional, found a new job in his present company. It was not easy. Hiring managers saw him as having essentially the same skills as hundreds of other finance professionals. Joe did not want to go through that again. To make himself more marketable, Joe decided to differentiate himself from his competitors by developing new skills.

Joe started to look—not for a new job—but for information to help him decide which new skills he should develop. He spoke with a number of people both inside and outside of his company and learned there would be a strong demand for those who knew Lotus Notes and had his particular background in finance.

When Joe investigated learning Lotus Notes, he found that it would take six months and thousands of dollars. It would be a big investment—even though he already had a computer at home. His department did not use Lotus Notes, so Joe knew he would not be able to convince his boss to pay for his certification. Joe decided to make an investment in himself.

Studying Lotus Notes in the evenings and on weekends, it took Joe a little longer than he had expected. As he got closer to becoming certified, Joe recontacted those people inside and outside his company who had advised him earlier to let them know of his progress.

Joe's department was downsized just as he was recontacting people. He received a number of offers outside, but one department inside offered Joe the opportunity to work on a Lotus Notes project for three months. Then he would have the hands-on experience he needed. It seemed like a perfect fit because Joe already knew a lot about the company, which would help him in this project. He jumped at the chance.

In addition, Joe kept up his contacts inside and outside the company. They were glad to hear about his new assignment, and urged him to continue to stay in touch. Joe felt more secure now with a lot of people knowing what he was doing. The new project could turn into a long-term assignment or even a permanent position. On the other hand, he knew better than to depend on that, and wanted to have other options in case he needed to line up another assignment.

To keep your present job longer . . .

. . . and help make your company stronger, think of yourself as an investigator on behalf of your organization. Read trade journals about your function and industry. Join associations. Find out what is happening internationally. Investigate the new technologies affeccting your area.

When you meet people from other companies and industries (and countries) who do what you do, compare what they are doing to the way your company does it. If the way they are doing it is better, take that information back to your company. Keep on investigating and learning. If you decide you need to pick up new skills, find some way to get them.

Joe was starting to feel more in control of his career. He knew that the next move would always be up to him and he wanted to be ready.

As he continued to develop contacts, he lined up two outside consulting assignments. He could have stayed with his present employer—even full-time—but he decided to become a consultant because it made him feel more secure and energized.

If you are interested in moving into a different area, you may have to reposition yourself to make yourself more marketable. It is relatively easy to move into the same job in a different department, but more difficult to move into a new job in another department. You may be seen as someone trying to break into the new area who does not have the experience others have in that area. Gain the experience you need to make yourself more marketable.

How to Research Those Areas
Outside of Your Present Company

It is not enough to keep in touch with people in various departments inside your present company. Chances are, you need to learn more about their work and their issues, and not only from them but by speaking to people on the outside. In addition, you may need to pick up a few new skills to make yourself desirable.

For each department, division, or business you are targeting, list how you plan to learn more about each area, the skills you need to develop, and how you plan to develop them.

Of course, you cannot become expert in every area you are targeting. Just as with an outside search, you will conduct a Preliminary Target Investigation to see which are worth your while and then you will concentrate on those in which you are sincerely interested and which you feel are worth it.

You may have to gain experience in the new field *outside* of your present company (see "How to Change Careers"). However, it is generally easier to change careers inside a company—where you already have a good reputation and knowledge of the company—rather than go outside.

For Target _____ :

Department, division, or business: _____

Position/function: _____

Geographic area:_____

How to learn about this new area	Skills, experiences, and knowledge needed	How I plan to develop myself
1.		
2.		
3.		
4.		
5.		
6.		
7.		

For Target _____ :

Department, division, or business: _____

Position/function: _____

Geographic area:_____

How to learn about this new area	Skills, experiences, and knowledge needed	How I plan to develop myself
1.		
2.		
3.		
4.		
5.		
6.		
7.		

132

Getting Offers Inside: Negotiating a New Job

If you have been following the system, you have been talking to people in several areas of your present company. You have also been talking to people outside. Now you are getting offers.

Because you have spent time gathering information both inside and outside of the company:

- You now have insight about your standing in the marketplace.
- You have information that will help you do better in your new job at your present company.
- You have developed contacts to whom you can turn when you have questions in your new job.
- You understand better what you can do for this new department, division, or business at your present company.

You have received an offer inside your present company and are in the negotiation stage. The hiring team has told you the work they need to have done. But consider negotiating for additional assignments and experience you want. Think of other work you can do for the department to make you even more valuable to them or give you an opportunity for growth. Define the duties you can undertake immediately so you can provide immediate value. This is the time to make sure the job will satisfy their needs as well as your own. Following are some examples:

CASE STUDY *Joan*
Negotiating the Job

Joan has a strong accounting background and the real estate area was interested in her because of that. However, Joan was interested in learning more about real estate and also wanted to have more people contact. She said to the hiring manager, "I know you need my accounting help and I am very interested in doing that for you. But one of the main reasons I'm interested in your department is that I want to learn about real estate and I also want to have more contact with people. Perhaps I could devote myself to solving your accounting problems, but also sit in on real estate deal meetings so I can learn that area of the business at the same time. After a few years, if I do well, perhaps I could move into that area completely and train someone new to do the accounting work."

CASE STUDY *Jacob*
Opportunity for Development

Jacob is interviewing in one division for a controller's position having to do with the Middle East and Africa, his areas of strength. However, he has always had an interest in Latin America and thinks this will be a huge growth market in the future. The Latin American market fits in with his long-term plan of being a business head in his company someday for a Latin American country.

He said to the hiring team: "I know you need my help in the Middle East and Africa and I love working on those countries. But I am also extremely interested in Latin America. I'm afraid that if I come in here, I'll get to work only on the Middle East and Africa. I'd like to also be assigned to one small Latin American country so I can learn more about that area. I happen to be fluent in Spanish and Portuguese so I can get up to speed fast."

Growing the Job

Instead of just listening to what they need to have done in this job, propose additional responsibilities, if you think that is appropriate.

"This job calls for someone to handle customer-service complaints, but I also have excellent writing skills. I could put together an internal newsletter to give other customer-service representatives information on how they could do their jobs better."

*Any time we think the problem is "out there,"
that thought is the problem. We empower
what's out there to control us.
The change paradigm is "outside-in"—what's out
there has to change before we can change.*

Stephen R. Covey, *The Seven Habits of Highly
Effective People*

Keeping Up in Your Field

Let the hiring team know the duties you could immediately undertake to make yourself valuable. And think of the additional training you may need, if appropriate, to do even better in this job and help you be even more valuable in the future.

"I've been working in computers for 13 years and certainly understand the systems you have in place and the need you have for upgrading your current systems. I'm afraid, however, that my skills will become obsolete if I spend the two years it will take to completely revamp your current system. I was wondering if I could be involved with the new technologies in a way that would not interfere with getting done what you need to have done. For example, I could sit in on new-technology task forces or be part of a team on a small new-technology project. That way, I would do the work you need to have done, but also feel that I am taking care of my own future."

Other Areas to Negotiate

In addition to job responsibilities and training, consider negotiating some of the following:

- start date,
- date of first review,
- additional resources (people, equipment, systems) you need to do the job well,
- work hours, if you have special needs, and
- travel.

For example, "I see that this job requires 70 percent fieldwork. I was wondering if there were any way the job could be restructured so my field-work time would be limited to 50 percent."

Salary Increases

In making a move within a company, salary increases are often *not* negotiable. This is because the company is allowing you to grow in your career and is therefore encouraging you to move to other areas when appropriate. However, the company does not want to be penalized for giving you this relative freedom to change jobs.

Understand the Political Situation

If you have any questions about company policy, **find people you trust who can advise you**. Observe what others have done. Ask others who have made moves how they did it. Every company is different. An internal search can be very sensitive. Find out the parameters in *your* company before you put yourself at risk.

Warning: Most companies still operate under the outmoded model: Employees who try to develop themselves or move elsewhere in the company may be seen as traitors to their immediate bosses and threats to their employers. Be cautious in planning your internal move.

However, you still must take care of yourself and remain marketable so you are not dependent on one employer. Proactively figure out what you bring to the party while finding out—and fitting into—the new direction your company and industry are taking.

A few enlightened companies are actually helping their employees manage their own careers—and become more marketable both inside and outside the company. Those companies hope to have the flexible, high-performing workforces they will need to support the company's ambitious—and changing—plans.

Yes, there is a risk that those highly marketable employees will leave the company. But the alternative is to keep employees strapped into tightly defined jobs, relatively ignorant about what is going on in the outside world. Smart, competitive companies know that it is better to encourage all employees to be flexible and knowledgeable—at the risk of losing a few—rather than encourage employees to stay stale and dependent on the firm.

All jobs in today's economy are temporary.

It is difficult for us today to appreciate how new and different the world of "holding a job" was for village-born people. They could no longer move about among a variety of tasks, in a variety of locations, on a schedule set by the sunlight and the weather and the particular demands of the season.

from William Bridges

. . . [T]he thought of losing my job didn't trouble me as much as it troubled lifers such as, say, Dash Riprock. That is not to say I did not care; I cared immensely. I thrived on praise more than most and thus sought to please. But I was willing to take greater risks than if I had felt deeply proprietary about my career. I was, for instance, willing to disobey my superiors, and that caused them to sit up and take notice far more quickly than if I had been a good soldier.

Michael Lewis, *Liar's Poker*

For all your ills, I give you laughter.

Rabelais

The
Five
O'Clock
Club

How to Change Careers

If an idea, I realized, were really a valuable one, there must be some way of realizing it.

Elizabeth Blackwell
(the first woman to earn a medical degree)

So you thought you would spend a few years trying out various fields and pick the one you liked the most. The problem is that once you landed your first accounting job, your résumé said "accountant." Now you're having a hard time being considered for a technology or sales job instead.

All things being equal, finding a job similar to your old one is quicker. A career change will probably take more time. What's more, the job-hunting techniques are different for both.

When a large American steel company began closing plants in the early 1980s, it offered to train the displaced steelworkers for new jobs. But the training never "took;" the workers drifted into unemployment and odd jobs instead. Psychologists came in to find out why, and found the steelworkers suffering from acute identity crises. "How could I do anything else?" asked the workers. "I am a lathe operator."

Peter Senge,
The Fifth Discipline

It's Not Easy to Categorize Job Hunters

The easier it is to categorize you, the easier it is for others to see where you fit in their organizations and for you to find a job. Search firms, for example, generally will not handle career changers. They can more easily market those who want to stay in the same function in the same industry.

I worked for one company for nine years, and made three major career changes—from computer programming and business systems analysis to training and development to advertising and promotion. Of course, I acquired skills in each area by doing volunteer work outside the company and thus gained some experience. However, my outside experience would not have been enough to give me credibility in those areas outside the company. So, as we always say at the Club, the best job hunt starts at home. If you want to make a major career change, first see what you can do within your present organization.

You Must Offer Proof of Your Interest and Competence

Many job changers essentially say to a prospective employer, "Give me a chance. You won't be sorry." They expect the employer to hire them on faith and that's unrealistic. The employer has a lot to lose. First, you may lose interest in the new area after you are hired. Second, you may know so little about the new area that it turns out not to be what you had imagined. Third, you may not bring enough knowledge and skill to the job and fail—even though your desire may be sincere.

The hiring manager should not have to take those risks. It is the job hunter's obligation to prove he or she is truly interested and capable.

Civility is not a sign of weakness, and sincerity is always subject to proof.

John F. Kennedy
Inaugural Address, January 20, 1961

How You as a Career Changer Can Prove Your Interest and Capability

- Read the industry's trade journals.
- Get to know the people in that industry or field.
- Join its organizations; attend the meetings.
- Be persistent.
- Show how your skills can be transferred.
- Write proposals.
- Be persistent.
- Take relevant courses, part-time jobs, or do volunteer work related to the new industry or skill area.
- Be persistent!

CASE STUDY *Ted*
Almost Gave Up Too Soon

Ted wanted to move from the cosmetics industry to the casino industry. As a career changer, he had to offer proof to make up for his lack of experience. One proof was that he had read the industry's trade newspapers for years. When he met people in his search, he could truthfully tell them that he had followed their careers. He could also say he had hope for himself because he knew that so many of them had come from outside the industry.

Another proof of his interest was that he had sought out so many casino management people at trade association meetings and by contacting them directly. After a while, he ran into people he had met on previous occasions. Employers want people who are sincerely interested in their industry, their company, and the function the new hire will fill. Sincerity and persistence count, but they are usually not enough.

Another proof Ted offered was that he figured out how to apply his experience to the casino industry and its problems. Writing proposals to show how you would handle the job is one way to prove you are knowledgeable and interested in an area new to you. Some people prove their interest by taking courses, finding part-time jobs, or doing volunteer work to learn the new area and build marketable skills.

Ted initially decided to *wing it* and took trips to Atlantic City and Las Vegas hoping someone would hire him on the spot. That didn't work and took two months and some money. Then he began a serious job hunt—following the system explained in the following pages. He felt he was doing fine, but the hunt was taking many months and he was not sure it would result in an offer.

After searching in the casino industry for six months, Ted began a campaign in his old field— the cosmetics industry. Predictably, he landed a job there quickly. Ted took this as a sign that he didn't have a chance in the new field. He lost sight of the fact that a career change is more difficult and takes longer.

Ted accepted the cosmetics position, but his friends encouraged him to continue his pursuit of a career in the casino industry—a small industry with relatively few openings compared with the larger cosmetics industry.

Shortly after he accepted the new position, someone from Las Vegas called him for an interview and he got the job of his dreams. His efforts paid off because he had done a thorough campaign in the casino industry. It just took time.

Ted was not unusual in giving up on a career change. It can take a long time and sometimes the pressure to get a paycheck will force people to take inappropriate jobs. That's life. Sometimes we have to do things we don't want to do. There's nothing wrong with that.

What *is* wrong is forgetting you had a dream. What *is* wrong is expecting people to hire you on faith and hope when what they deserve is proof that you're sincere and that hiring you has a good chance of working. *What is wrong is underestimating the effort it takes to make a career change.*

In the future, most people will have to change careers. Your future may hold an involuntary career change as new technologies make old skills obsolete. Those same new technologies open up new career fields for those who are pre-pared—and ready to change. Know what you're up against. Don't take shortcuts. And don't give up too early. Major career changes are normal today and may prove desirable or essential tomorrow.

Ruth made a great mistake when he gave up pitching. Working once a week, he might have lasted a long time and become a great star.

Tris Speaker, manager of the Cleveland Indians, commenting on Babe Ruth's plans to change from a pitcher to an outfielder, spring 1921

Getting the Most from Your Accomplishments

No modest man ever did or ever will make a fortune.

Lady Mary Wortley Montagu

For most of us, it is relatively easy to describe what we do on our jobs. What is more challenging is to describe the impact of what we have done, in terms of the benefits to ourselves, both personally and professionally, and the benefits to the organization.

Analyzing your accomplishments in depth can help you identify the impact you have had and the value you bring to the organization.

In the Assessment section, you began to think about your life and your work experience. You identified your satisfying accomplishments through the Seven Stories exercise.

Now it's time to review some of these accomplishments in depth, considering the personal/professional and organizational benefits of each accomplishment. It's a good idea to work with your Career Buddy on this. As you review each example, your Career Buddy can listen for skills you used to achieve that accomplishment.

He or she can also help you identify the benefits of the accomplishment to you both personally and professionally, as well as the skills that you enhanced through this accomplishment.

You can do the same for your Career Buddy. The following are some questions to help you think more specifically about each benefit category. But if skills come up that were not identified

as part of your initial self-assessment results, be sure to add them to your list.

"The horror of that moment," the King said,
"I shall never forget."
"You will, though," said the Queen,
"if you don't make a memorandum of it."

Lewis Carroll

"Congratulations, Michaels! You've been promoted. There's no extra pay or benefits, but there's plenty of over-time."

Personal/Professional Benefits

- How did you feel at the conclusion of the accomplishment?
- What were your rewards? Money? Promotion? More responsibilities? Job offer?
- What did you learn personally?
- What did this accomplishment do for your reputation in the organization? In the community?
- How did it affect your visibility to your organization? To your profession?
- Did you learn anything new?
- How did it affect your relationships with others in the organization?

Organizational Benefits

- What were the results of the accomplishment for the organization?
- How did the accomplishment impact sales, morale, turnover, productivity, communications, culture, training, public relations, image, profitability, market, products/services?
- Is there a way to quantify the results—add numbers or statistics along with descriptive terms such as *significantly increased* or *minimal cost*?

For the purposes of this exercise, focus on accomplishments from your work life in any job, (or from your personal life if they are relevant), starting with your greatest accomplishments. Work through as many as you can.

Accomplishment Example

Reorganized department's filing system.
Personal/Professional Benefit

- Viewed as valuable contributor (personal)
- Learned the important projects in the department (professional)

Organizational Benefit

- Improved department's efficiency

Skills Enhanced

- Building rapport and trust, coordinating, integrating, organizing, project management

Accomplishment Example:

Organized and trained sales force.
Personal/Professional Benefit

- Felt much more self-confident (personal)
- Developed ability to train other sales people (professional)

Organizational Benefit

- 60 percent increase in sales

Skills Enhanced

- Training, development, marketing, sales, team building

Accomplishment Statements

Statements of accomplishments are an essential part of a good résumé. They are a highly effective way to express yourself in job interviews and they are superb illustrative and supportive material for career-development discussions.

By using accomplishment statements rather than responsibility statements, you demonstrate that you made a difference for the organization and you had a positive impact. *You are selling yourself short if you merely state your responsibilities.* You risk being perceived as an average employee and average employees may have fewer opportunities.

An impressive listing of accomplishments can distinguish you. Accomplishments are the single most effective element in creating value.

Here are some guidelines for writing accomplishment statements:

- Start with action verbs
- Quantify results wherever possible
- Show how the organization benefited. This will avoid a "So what?" attitude on the part of the reader or listener.
- Write the accomplishment statement so it will impress your manager, so he or she will think: "Wow!" rather than "Ho-hum."

All accomplishment statements serve as examples or proof of several skills you have—basic skills transferable to other areas of the organization.

Another way of looking at accomplishments is as job goals in hindsight; they should meet the same criteria as job goals. These criteria include establishing a time frame, making sure the goal is measurable, and showing the anticipated benefit to the organization.

Security is mostly a superstition. It does not exist in nature, nor do the children of men as a whole experience it. Avoiding danger is no safer in the long run than outright exposure. Life is either a daring adventure or nothing.

Helen Keller

Ways to Use Accomplishment Statements

It will take some time to write well-thought-out accomplishment statements. But it is worth the time you spend because you will use these accomplishment statements over and over for many years. For example, you will use them in:

- performance reviews,
- career discussions,
- résumé writing,
- networking interviews, and
- job interviews.

Now spend more time working on your own accomplishment statements. Then review them with your Career Buddy or someone else whose perspective and feedback you value.

Sample Accomplishment Statements

- Organized and trained a sales force for selected marketing territories that resulted in a 60 percent increase in sales and profits.
- Initiated a membership update system for a major nonprofit organization that reduced return mail by 30 percent.
- Created and implemented an employee training film library to upgrade skills of 50 staff members. Results revealed that 100 percent of staff used services, thus increasing their training skills by 65 percent.
- Increased customer value by working with teams to continuously improve order-entry and -delivery systems.
- By establishing guidelines and procedures, stabilized monthly data-input flow at near-perfect levels for more than 1.5 years.
- Enhanced customer relationships by instituting targeted-selection system for selecting new employees in customer-contact positions.
- Planned and implemented an office filing system; reduced the time required for locating information by 50 percent.
- Set up a bookkeeping system that reduced the amount of time to prepare payroll by 50 hours.
- Retained 50 percent of customers through an innovative tracking system to assist sales representatives in customer follow-up.
- Led a team effort that cut substantial costs, enhanced customer value, and retained valuable employees in key strategic positions.
- Planned, developed, and managed execution of all direct-mail and telemarketing programs

for film-distribution business; increased penetration of base by 10 percent in 2002; exceeded Plan IBA by $700 million.

- Within highly competitive market, planned, developed, and managed execution of all print and direct-mail programs for national direct-mail business; increased revenue by 25 percent; achieved marketing expense ratio of 150+.

- Managed a small business team for retail customers that achieved 1,000 sales calls within a short time period; efforts resulted in $1 million in new business.

- Generated 5 or 6 referrals to other areas of the company per month, that resulted in significant new business.

- Worked with marketing-support areas to develop brochures and marketing materials by demonstrating initiative to complete the project on time and within budget. Brochure resulted in 100 additional applications.

- As a team member, designed and implemented a sales program that resulted in 500 calls and 400 referrals to produce larger market share and maintain existing customers.

People are always blaming their circumstances for what they are. I don't believe in circumstances. The people who get on in this world are the people who get up and look for the circumstances they want, and if they can't find them, make them.

George Bernard Shaw

Elliott's Résumé:
Making a Career Change

Think like a duchess, act like a duchess, talk like a duchess, and one day you will be a duchess!

Henry Higgins to Eliza Doolittle in
George Bernard Shaw's *Pygmalion*

Elliott had been in sports marketing years ago and had enjoyed it tremendously. However, he had spent the past four years in the mortgage industry and was having a hard time getting back into his old field. When a job hunter wants to change industries—or go back to an old industry—he cannot let his most recent position act as a handicap. For example, a person who has always been in pharmaceuticals marketing who now wants to get into marketing in another industry, should rewrite his or her résumé to emphasize generic marketing skills and remove most references to pharmaceuticals.

The sports people saw him as a career changer—and a mortgage man. Even when he explained that marketing mortgages is the same as marketing sports, people did not believe him. He was being positioned by his most recent experience, which was handicapping him.

In Elliott's case, the summary in his new résumé helped a great deal to bring his old work experience right to the top of the résumé. In addition, Elliott removed the word *mortgage* from the description of his most recent job; his title at the mortgage company now stands out more than the company name; and he got rid of company and industry jargon—such as the job title of segment director—not easily understood outside of his company.

Notice how Elliott's description of what he did for the mortgage business is now written generically—it can apply to the marketing of *any* product. With his new résumé, Elliott had no trouble speaking to people in the sports industry. They no longer saw his most recent experience as a handicap and he soon had a terrific job as head of marketing for a prestigious sporting-goods company.

If you want to move into a new industry or profession, state what you have done generically so people will not see you as tied to the old.

Bring Something to the Party

When it comes down to negotiating yourself into a new position, seemingly unrelated skills from former positions may actually help you get the job.

For example, some of my background had been in accounting and computers when I decided to go into career coaching. My CFO (chief financial officer) experience helped me ease into the career-coaching field. I applied to a 90-person career-coaching company and agreed to be its CFO for a while—provided I was also assigned clients to coach. They wanted a cost-accounting system, so my ability to create one for them was what I *brought to the party*. I was willing to give the company something they wanted (my business experience) in exchange for doing something I really wanted to do (coaching executives).

Combining the new with the old, rather than jumping feet first into something completely new, is often the best way to move your career in a different direction. You gain the experience you need in the new field without having to come in at the entry level. Equally important, it is less stressful because you are using some of your old strengths while you build new ones.

Coming from a background different from the field you are targeting can also give you a bargaining chip. If you are looking at an area where you have no experience, you will almost certainly be competing with people who do have experience. You can separate yourself from the competition by saying, "I'm different. I have the skills to do this job and I can also do other things these people can't do." It works!

Moving from One Division to Another in Your Company

Although Elliott's situation is certainly a more dramatic change than moving from one division of your company to another, his strategy still applies when you seek a similar job in another part of your company. This does not preclude your making a total change. The more diverse and larger your company, the greater the odds that moving from one division to another is not unlike Elliott's change. For example, your organization may have a cable TV division and another that publishes trade books. Using the proper methods and learning new skills may enable you to make the move from one of these divisions to the other.

"Before" Résumé

Elliott Jones

421 Morton Street

Chase Fortune, KY 23097

Sears Mortgage Company

2000–present

Vice President, Segment Director, Shelter Business

- Director of $4.6 billion residential mortgage business for the largest mortgage lender in the nation.
- Organized and established regional marketing division for the largest mortgage lender in nation, a business that included first and second mortgages and mortgage life insurance.

SportsLife Magazine

1998–2000

Publisher and Editor

- Published and edited the largest health/fitness magazine. Increased circulation 175%.

and so on. . . .

Elliott Jones

421 Morton Street

Chase Fortune, KY 23097

MARKETING EXECUTIVE
with 15-plus years in the leisure/sporting goods industry

Domestic and international experience; multibrand expertise specializing in marketing, new business development, strategic planning, and market research.

Proven record of identifying customer segments, developing differentiable product platforms, communication strategies, sales management, share growth, and profit generation.

Sears Mortgage Company   **2000–present**

VICE PRESIDENT, BUSINESS DIRECTOR
Residential Real Estate Business

- Business Director of $4.6 billion business. Managed strategic planning, marketing, product development, and compliance.
- Consolidated 4 regional business entities into 1; doubled product offerings. Grew market share 150 basis points and solidified #1 market position.
- Developed and executed nationally recognized consumer and trade advertising, public relations, and direct-response programs.
- Structured product-development process that integrated product introductions into the operations and sales segments of the business.
- Organized and established regional marketing division for largest mortgage lender in nation, a business that included first and second mortgages and mortgage life insurance.

SPORTSLIFE MAGAZINE   **1998–2000**
Publisher and Editor

- Published and edited the nation's largest consumer health and fitness magazine and increased circulation by 175%.

and so on. . . .

The
Five
O'Clock
Club

Jessie: Pulling Together Her Background to Move Up

There is at bottom only one problem in the world and this is its name. How does one break through? How does one get into the open? How does one burst the cocoon and become a butterfly?

Thomas Mann, *Doctor Faustus*

Jessie's background was in marketing, customer service, and training. She had also done a lot of work in database administration, but she didn't want to do *that* again.

When Jessie did her Forty-Year Vision, she discovered she wanted to have her own training company someday. She also thought she'd like to have four or five people working for her.

To head in that direction, it would be best if Jessie could work for the corporate training department and learn how training programs were developed, marketed internally, and administered. Jessie thought it would be best if she not only did stand-up training but also managed a few projects.

Jessie needed to decide what to write at the top of her résumé to position herself for the job she wanted next. You are most strongly positioned when you can say that you already *are* exactly what you want to do next. Since Jessie had already done training and project management,

she highlighted those two skills at the top of her résumé. This increased the chances that hiring managers would want her to do exactly those two things for them. Since Jessie was also willing to market training programs to other departments, she highlighted her marketing skills as well.

When Jessie made up her list of target divisions to contact in her search, she focused exclusively on training departments within those divisions. She called each one to find out the names of the people she should contact. She sent her résumé to each person with a cover letter and followed up with phone calls.

Jessie got a lot of meetings and landed three job offers. She got to see how three different departments in three different divisions operated! And she learned how to run her own business when she was ready.

---

*I fall, I stand still . . . I trudge on,
I gain a little . . . I get more eager
and climb higher and begin to see the
widening horizon. Every struggle is a victory.*

Helen Keller,
on her studies at Radcliffe College

JESSIE WOODWARD

3010 Norwood Lane
Mansfield, Texas 55222

(555) 826-3555 (home)
(555) 622-5800 (office)

Training Manager / Project Manager
- **Administration**   • **Product Marketing**

- **Coordinated 36 consultants and 200 executive seminars per year.**
  - In the course of four years, a class was never canceled due to mis-scheduling.
- Key player in design and implementation of a "Self-Directed Team," five-day training program.
- **Delivered a three-month training program. Designed curriculum.**
- Key player in $1 million renovation of a four-story training facility.
- **Marketed training programs and materials.**
- Regularly taught a 13-day training program.
  - **Trained 25 students on bank procedures and computer systems.**
  - **Managed computer setup, testing, and troubleshooting.**
- Created a training guide for instructors to utilize during a 13-day program.
- Content knowledge includes: Organization Vision & Values, Professional Image, Management Essentials, Customer Service / Sales Techniques, Retail/Wholesale Product Knowledge, Employee Benefits.

**Dynamic, goal-oriented, enthusiastic manager
with "outstanding interpersonal skills."**

InterFirst Bank, N.A.   1998–present

Operations / Customer Service Manager
Administration / Negotiation / Information Systems

Marketing / Customer Service
- **Managed a customer-service team of four direct reports.**
  - Conducted coaching sessions and performance reviews.
- Established goals and objectives.
- **Opened an average of 15 new accounts per quarter.**
- Maintained a standard of exceptional service for 200 middle-market business customers.
  - Praised by customers for anticipating their needs and communicating effectively.

Information Systems / Administration
- Maintained a database of credit facilities over $80 million.
  - **Provided ongoing training to the staff on system upgrades.**
- Maintained a tracking system for account activity.
- **Successfully negotiated past due loan payments in excess of $125,000.**
- Generated monthly document exception reports.
- Approved/processed money transfers, bankers' acceptances and letters of credit.

Training Officer / Project Manager
- Performed needs analyses and actions plans as the organization moved forward.
  - Met with division executives to determine training goals and objectives.
  - Developed training curriculum and calendar.
- Provided training and coaching in the area of branch operations and sales techniques.

Recognized as a seasoned trainer by top management.

InterFirst Bank, N.A. , cont'd.   1998–present
Training Officer / Project Manager, cont'd.
- Researched vendor services and negotiated contracts.
  - Managed a $250,000 expense budget.
- Facilitated "train-the-trainer" sessions.
- Interviewed and recruited retail bank staff.
- Managed the production of a training video.
- Maintained inventory of training material.

Training Manager / Administrator / Project Manager
- Managed an annual expense budget of $1 million.
- Coordinated multiple executive-level seminars. Consistently praised for quality.
- Negotiated contracts with vendors and outside training facilities.
- Interfaced with domestic and international consultants on program design.
- Purchased office equipment. Organized training sessions.
- Managed the reorganization of a training library.

Dean Witter Reynolds   1993–1998
Sales Assistant
- Communicated information on products to high-profile customers.
- Assisted senior vice president with daily sales. Opened new accounts.
- Researched companies, annual reports, Standard & Poor's ratings, etc.

Cashier Training Institute   1992–1993
Trainer
- Delivered multiple programs on daily basis to typical group size of 25 participants.
- Provided training on retail bank procedures, computer systems, and secretarial techniques.
- Monitored participants' performance over three-month time span.

Manufacturers Hanover Trust Company   1988–1991
Trainer / Operations Supervisor
- Supervised branch staff.
- Cross-sold products and opened accounts.
- Provided training in areas of:
  - Customer Service   – Computer Systems
  - Sales Techniques   – Branch Procedures

EDUCATION

University of Dallas—graduated 1996, School of Industrial and Labor Relations
University of Texas, Arlington—Business Administration Degree, June 2002

AFFILIATIONS

Texas State Mentoring Program

The
Five
O'Clock
Club

Résumé Checklist:
How Good Is Your Résumé?

1. **Positioning:**
   - If I spend just **10 seconds** glancing at my résumé, what ideas/words pop out? (specific job titles, degrees, specific company names):

   _____

   - This is how I am *positioned* by my résumé. Is this how I want to be positioned for this target area? Or is this positioning a handicap for the area I am targeting?

"I looked over your resume, and the good news is I like the paper it's typed on. Do you really want to know the bad news?"

2. **Level:**
   - What **level** do I appear to be? Is it easy for the reader to guess in 10 seconds what my level is? (For example, if I say I "install computer systems," I could be making anywhere from $15,000 to $200,000 a year.)

3. **Summary Statement:**
   - If I have no summary statement, I am being positioned by the most recent job on my résumé. Is that how I want to be positioned?
   - If I have a summary, does the very first line position me for the kind of job I want next?
   - Is this followed by a statement that elaborates on the first statement?
   - Is this followed by statements that prove how good I am or differentiate me from my likely competitors?
   - Have I included a statement or two that give the reader an indication of my personality or my approach to my job?

4. **Accomplishments:**
   - Within each job, did I merely list historically what I did, or did I state my accomplishments with an eye to what would interest the reader in my target area?
   - Are the accomplishments easy to read?
     - Bulleted rather than long paragraphs.
     - No extraneous words.
     - Action oriented.
     - Measurable and specific.

- Relevant. Would be of interest to the readers in my target area. Either the accomplishment is something they would want me to do for them or it shows the breadth of my experience.

5. **Overall Appearance:**

- Is there plenty of white space? Or is the information squeezed so I can fit it on one or two pages?

- Is it laid out nicely so it can serve as my marketing brochure?

6. **Miscellaneous:**

- Length: Is the résumé as short as it can be while still being readable?

- Writing style: Can the reader understand the point I am trying to make in each statement?

- Clarity: Am I just hoping the reader will draw the right conclusion from what I've said? Or do I take the trouble to state things so clearly that there is no doubt that the reader will come away with the right message?

- Completeness: Is all important information included? Have all dates been accounted for?

- Typos: Is my résumé free of errors?

Your Two-Minute Pitch: The Keystone of Your Search

The Five O'Clock Club

Fortune favors the brave.

Terence, *Phormio*

**If your pitch
(the way you position yourself)
is wrong, everything else
about your search is wrong.**

Your Two-Minute Pitch is the backbone of your search. You'll use it in job and networking interviews and in your cover letters. You'll be ready when someone calls and says, "So tell me about yourself."

Your résumé summary statement could serve as the starting point for your pitch. Keep in mind:

- to whom you are pitching,
- what they are interested in,
- who your likely competitors are, and
- what you bring to the party that your competitors do not.

In your pitch, you are *not* trying to tell your life story. Instead:

- Let this person know that you are competent and interested in the area in which he or she is interested.
- Say things that are relevant.
- Come across at the right level.

Think about your target audience and what you want to say to them. Examine your background to find things that fit.

What's Wrong with This Pitch?

Take a look at the beginning of another client's pitch and see if you can tell what's wrong.

I have five years' experience in education and training: in helping develop training programs, in administering training centers, etc.

What's wrong with this pitch? We can't know until we know to whom he is talking. It turns out that the pitch was wrong because the interviewer was not interested in training but in personal computers. How much did my client know about PCs? A lot. "Why, I can make PCs dance," he said. "The only problem is that the hiring manager would probably want someone who could network them together and I've never done that."

"*Can* you do that?" I asked.

"Of course I can do it," he replied.

"Then go *do* it," I said, "so you can tell her you have already done it. Network together the computers you have at home. And join a group that specializes in that. Ask one of the people if you can go along and help him or her network computers together."

Here's the pitch one week later:

I have five years' experience in computers, specializing in PCs. I have built PCs from scratch and I've done software and applications programming on PCs. I also understand how important networking is.

I've even networked together the PCs I have at home and I belong to a group of PC experts, so I always know to whom to talk when tricky things come up. I can do anything that needs to be done with PCs. I can make PCs dance!

I'm excited about talking to you because I know your shop relies on PCs.

Do you see how a pitch has to be tailored to each specific situation?

Know Something about Them

When you go for an interview and they immediately say: "Tell me about yourself," how will you know how to position yourself? You don't want to bound into a standard Two-Minute Pitch unless you feel that you know something about them.

If you don't know anything at all about them or the job, you may say: "I'd be happy to tell you about myself, but could you first tell me a little about the kind of job we're talking about?"

They Won't *Get It*, So Just Tell Them

Most job hunters think: I'll just tell them my background and they'll see how it fits in with their needs. But they probably won't see.

> **Don't expect the hiring team to figure out something about you. If you have a conclusion you'd like them to reach about you, *tell* them what it is.**

If you want them to see how all of your jobs have been involved in international, say, "All of my jobs have been involved in international." Isn't that easy?

If you want them to know you have done things finance people at your age rarely do, then tell them that.

Do you want them to know that FORTRAN is your favorite language? Then don't just say, "I

have three years of FORTRAN experience." That's not your point. Do you want them to know that you can make computers dance? Tell them. Don't make them figure it out for themselves.

Make your message so clear that if someone says to them, "Tell me about John," they will know what to tell the other person about you.

Communicating Your Pitch

Many job hunters try to cram everything they can into their Two-Minute Pitch, but then people can't hear it. Think about those who are considered great communicators.

Today, our standards are based on the medium of TV. The best communicators speak on a personal level—the way people talk on TV. Whether you are addressing a big audience or are on a job interview, cultivate a TV style—a friendly, one-on-one conversational style—not a *listing of what I've done* style.

The interviewer is assessing what it would be like to work with you. Make your pitch understandable. Before people go on TV, they decide the three major points they want to make—what they want the audience to remember.

What do you want your *audience* to remember about you? Polish both your Two-Minute Pitch and the two or three accomplishments that would interest this person. Prepare your pitch about each accomplishment the same way you prepared your Two-Minute Pitch. For example, don't say:

"I started out in this job in program support, where I traveled to x and y and worked on special projects, etc." if what you *really* want them to know is: "That was a great assignment. I helped arrange the details for nine speeches given by my department head. I organized the handouts, arranged for delivery, and sold our company's books at the meetings. I sold more books than any assistant they'd ever had and I enjoyed every minute of it. This has convinced me that sales is the field for me."

Use a conversational tone. Speak the way you would normally speak.

Two Minutes Is a Long Time; Show Enthusiasm.

In this TV society, people are used to 15-second sound bites on the news. As the communicator, you have to engage the listener. If you are a boring person, the very least you can do is sit forward in your chair. Reinforce your main points. Don't say too many things. Sound enthusiastic.

I once did a magazine article on who gets jobs and who gets to keep them. In my research, I talked to deans of business and engineering schools.

I learned that the person most likely to get the job is the one who sounds enthusiastic. And the one who gets to keep the job is the enthusiastic one—even over people who are more qualified. Employers keep people who are willing to pitch in and do anything to help the company.

Display enthusiasm. If you really want this job, act like it. It does not hurt your salary-negotiation prospects.

Summary of What I Have/Want to Offer
To Help Me Develop My Pitch

You must know:

- to whom you are pitching; you have to know something about them.
- what they ideally would want in a candidate.
- what their interests are.
- who your likely competitors are.
- what you bring to the party that your competitors do not.

For Target 1:

Geographic area: _____

Industry or company size: _____

Position/function: _____

1. What is the most important thing I want this target to know about me? (This is where you position yourself. If they know nothing else about you, this is what you want them to know.)
   _____

2. What is the second most important thing I want this target to know about me? (This could support and/or broaden your introductory statement.) _____
   _____
   _____
   _____

3. Key selling points: statements/accomplishments that support/**prove** the first two statements:
   a. _____
   b. _____
   c. _____
   d. _____
   e. _____

4. Statement of why they should be interested in me/what separates me from my competition:
   _____
   _____
   _____
   _____
   _____

5. Other key selling points applicable even indirectly to this industry or position:
   _____
   _____

6. Any objection I'm afraid the interviewer may bring up and how I will handle it:
   _____
   _____

The
Five
O'Clock
Club

How to Network Your Way In

I use not only all the brains I have,
but all I can borrow.

Woodrow Wilson

In the old days, networking was a great technique. We job hunters were appreciative of the help we got, and treated those we met with respect and courtesy. We targeted a field, and then used networking to meet people and form lifelong relationships with them, and to gather

"Your resume is quite impressive. However, I'm a little concerned about you biting your last 4 bosses."

information about the area. We called it "information gathering," but it also often led to jobs.

Today, stressed-out, aggressive, demanding job hunters want a job quickly, and expect their "contacts" to hire them, refer them to someone important (obviously not the person with whom they are speaking), or tell them where the jobs are. The old way worked; this new attitude does not. This chapter tells you how to network correctly.

Network informally by talking to acquaintances who may know something about your target area. **Network formally** by contacting people at their jobs to get information about their organization or industry. Networking is one way to find out what skills are needed where, what jobs may be opening up, and where you might be able to fit in. Talking to people because "they might know of something for me" rarely works. Use the networking—or information-gathering—process *to gather information and to build new relationships.*

Keep away from people who belittle your ambitions. Small people always do that, but the really great make you feel that you, too, can become great.

Mark Twain

Build Lifelong Relationships

You are also trying to build lifelong relationships. If a target area interests you, get to know the people in it and let them get to know you. It is unreasonable to expect them to have something

155

for you just because you decided to contact them right now. Some of the most important people in your search may provide you with information and no contacts—or jobs. Be sincerely grateful for the help you get, form a relationship that will last a lifetime, and plan to **recontact the people you meet regularly**.

Remember, you are not talking to people assuming they have heard of job openings. That approach rarely works. For example, if someone asked you if you happened to know of a position in the purchasing department in your old organization, your answer would be no. But if they said, "I'm really interested in your former organization. Do you happen to know *anyone* I could talk to there?" you could certainly give them the name of someone.

This is how people find jobs through networking. As time passes, the people you've met hear of things or develop needs themselves. If you keep in touch, they will tell you what's happening. It is a long-term process, but an effective one.

As you talk to more and more people, you will gather more and more information about business situations and careers in which you think you are interested. And the more people you meet and tell about your career search, the more people who are out there to consider you for a job or a referral to a job when they know of one. But remember—they have to know you first. Networking allows you to meet people without asking them for a job and putting them on the spot. And the fact is, **if they like you and happen to have an appropriate job for you, they will *tell* you about it—you will not have to ask**.

People *like* to talk to sincere, bright people, and send on those who impress them. People will not send you on if you are not skilled at presenting yourself or asking good questions.

> *Life is a series of collisions with the future;*
> *it is not a sum of what we have been*
> *but what we yearn to be.*
>
> José Ortega y Gasset

CASE STUDY *Monica*

Networking When You Don't Know Anyone

Monica wanted to work in publishing. She was in a temporary job in an accounting area and told everyone she had always wanted to work in publishing and would like to meet with people who worked in those divisions of her present organization. She read the trade magazines to find out more about those industries. She also joined an association of people in the publishing industry so she could learn more about the industry.

Then she contacted some people directly who were in the publishing divisions of her organization. Monica found that one of the best contacts she made during her search was a man close to retirement who was on a special assignment with no staff. There was no possibility of her ever working for him, but he gave her great insights into the industry and told her the best people to work for within the organization. He saved her from wasting many hours of her time and she felt free to call him to ask about specific people she was meeting.

Over time, lots of people got to know Monica and Monica got to know the publishing industry. She eventually heard of a number of openings, and was able to tell which ones were better than others. Monica is off to a good start in her new profession because she made lifelong friends she can contact *after* she is in her new job.

Using the networking technique correctly takes:

- time (because setting up meetings, going on them, and following up takes time),
- a sincere desire for information and building long-term relationships, and
- preparation.

You Are the Interviewer

In an information-gathering meeting, *you* are conducting the meeting. The worst thing you can do is to sit, expecting to be interviewed.

The manager, thinking you honestly wanted information, agreed to see you. Have your questions ready. After all, you called the meeting.

It is better to die on one's feet than to live on one's knees, but some individuals appear actually to believe that it is better to crawl around on one's bare belly.

Nathan Hare, in *The Black Scholar,* November 1969

The Information-Gathering or Networking Process

1. **Determine your purpose.** Decide what information you want or what contacts you want to build. Early on in your job search, networking with people at your own level helps you research the field you have targeted. At this point in your search, you are not trying to get hired. Later, meet with more senior people. *They* are in a position to hire you someday.

2. **Make a list of people you know.** In the research phase, you made a list of the departments and divisions you thought you should contact. You need lists of appropriate important people or organizations you want to contact. Then, when you meet someone who tends to know people, you can ask if that person
knows anyone on your list.

   Now make a list of all the people you already know (people with whom you work, human resources, etc.). Don't say you do not know enough appropriate people. If you know one person, that's enough for a start.

   Don't discard the names of potential contacts because they are not in a position to hire you. Remember, you are not going to meet people to ask for a job, but to ask for information. These contacts can be helpful, provide information, and most likely have other friends or contacts who will move you closer and closer to your targets.

People to Contact in Each Target Area

Now you want to get in to see people in your targeted departments and divisions. Whether you contact them by using someone else's name ("John Doe suggested I contact you") or by writing to them directly ("I have always been interested in publishing and have followed your career for some time"), the meetings will all be networking meetings.

   You will not be idly chatting with these people. Instead, you will have your pitch ready (see the section on the Two-Minute Pitch), and will tell them the kind of job you have in mind. For example:

   "I'm interested in the editorial process. I have a degree in English and three years in administrative work where a lot of writing was required. Can you suggest the names of people who might have contact with those divisions in our organization or do you know anyone who works in those divisions?" Tell *everyone* the target you are going after. You never know who knows somebody.

No matter what accomplishments you make, somebody helps you.

Althea Gibson, in *Time,* August 26, 1957

3. **Contact the people you want to meet.** In the beginning of your search, practice on people who know you well. If you say a few things wrong, it won't matter. You can see them again later.

   But as you progress in your search, most of the people you meet should not be people you know well. Extend your network beyond those people with whom you are comfortable. As you build your network of contacts (people you know refer you to people you don't know and they refer you to others), you will get further away from those people with whom you originally began. But as you go further out, you are generally getting closer to where the jobs are. Be willing to go to even further networking levels. Many people report they got their jobs through someone six or seven levels removed from where they started.

You will probably want to contact the people you do not know personally by letter or E-mail. Force yourself to write that letter and then follow up. People who are busy are more likely to spend time with you if you have put some effort into your attempt to see them. Busy people can read your message when they want rather than having to be dragged away from their jobs to receive your phone call. Often, people who receive your message will schedule an appointment for you through their secretary and you will get in to see them without ever having spoken to them. (On the other hand, some job hunters are in fields where people are used to picking up the phone. *Cold calling* can work for them.)

- Identify the link between you and the person you wish to meet; state why you are interested in talking to that person.

- Give your summary and two short examples of achievements that would interest the reader.

- Indicate that you will call in a few days to see when you can meet briefly.

Enclose your résumé if it supports your case. Do not enclose it if your letter is enough or if your résumé hurts your case.

4. **Call to set up the appointment** (first, build up your courage). When you call, you will probably have to start at the beginning. Do not expect a person to remember anything in your e-mail or letter. Don't even expect him or her to remember that you wrote. Say, for example, "I sent you an E-mail recently. Did you receive it?"

Remind him or her of the reason you wrote. Have your message in front of you—to serve as your script—because you may again have to summarize your background and state some of your accomplishments.

If the person says the organization has no openings at this time, that is okay with you—

A Sample Note for Information Gathering

Dear Mr. Brown:

Penny Webb suggested I contact you because she thought you could give me the information I need.

I'm interested in heading my career in a different direction. I have been with the cable division of Entertainment Corporation for two years and I could stay here forever, but I have always wanted to work in the publishing industry. Penny thought you could tell me something about your division.

My two years' experience includes editing 40-page corporate proposals and drafting various internal documents. In addition, I have excellent interpersonal skills, having served as a liaison with other departments in my division regarding our computer system. Finally, I have a degree in English.

I'd like some solid information from you on the job possibilities for someone like me. I'd greatly appreciate a half hour of your time and insight. I'll call you in a few days to see when you can spare the time.

Sincerely,

---

you were not necessarily looking for a job; you were looking for information or advice about the job possibilities for someone like yourself, or you wanted to know what is happening in the profession, division, or industry.

If the person says he or she is busy, say, "I'd like to accommodate your schedule. If you like, I could meet you in the early morning or late evening." If he or she is still too busy, say, "Is it okay if we set something up for a month from now? I would call you to confirm so you could reschedule our meeting if it's still not a good time for you. And I assure you I won't take up more than 20 minutes of your time." Do your best to get on her or his calendar—even if the date is a month away. (Remember: You are trying to form lifelong relationships. Don't force yourself on people, but do get in to see them.)

Don't let the manager interview you over the phone. You want to meet in person. You need face-to-face contact to build the relationship and to have her or him remember you.

Rather than leave a message, keep calling back to maintain control. If no one returns your call, you will feel rejected. But be friendly with the secretary; apologize for calling so often. An example: "Hello, Joan. This is Louise DiSclafani again. I'm sorry to bother you, but is Mr. Johnson free now?"

"No, Ms. DiSclafani, he hasn't returned yet. May I have him call you?"

"Thanks, Joan, but that will be difficult. I'll be in and out a lot, so I'll have to call him back. When is a good time to call?"

Expect to call seven or eight times. Accept it as normal business. It is not personal.

God does not die on the day when we cease to believe in a personal deity, but we die on the day when our lives cease to be illuminated by the steady radiance, renewed daily, of a wonder, the source of which is beyond all reason.

Dag Hammarskjold

5. **Prepare for the meeting.** Plan for a networking meeting as thoroughly as you would for any other business meeting. Follow the agenda listed in step 6.

   Remember that it is *your* meeting. You are the one running it. Beforehand:

   - Set goals for yourself (information and contacts).

   - Jot down the questions you want answered.

   - Find out all you can about the person and the person's responsibilities and areas of operations.

   - Rehearse your Two-Minute Pitch and accomplishments.

   Develop good questions, tailoring them to get the information you need. Make sure what you ask is appropriate for the person with whom you are meeting. You wouldn't, for example, ask a senior vice president of marketing, "How does marketing work?" That question is too general. Instead, do your research—both in the library and by talking with more junior people.

Decide what information you want or what contacts you want to build. Early on in your job search, networking with people at your own level helps you research the field you have targeted. At this point in your search, you are not trying to get hired. Later, meet with more senior people—the ones who are in a position to hire you someday.

Then when you meet the senior vice president, ask questions more appropriate for someone of that level. You may want to ask about the rewards of that particular business, the frustrations, the type of people who succeed there, the group values, the long-range plans for the business. Prepare three to five open-ended questions about the business or organization for the person to answer.

If you find you are asking each person the same questions, think harder about the information you need or do more library research. The quality of your questions should change over time as you become more knowledgeable, more of an insider—and more desirable as a prospective employee. In addition, you should be giving information back. If you are truly an insider, you must have information to give.

If you have always done it that way, it is probably wrong.

Charles Kettering

6. **Conduct the meeting.** If this is important to you, you will continually do better. Sometimes people network forever. They talk to people, but there is no flame inside them. Then one day something happens: They get angry or just fed up with all of this talking to people. They interview better because they have grown

more serious. Their time seems more important to them. They stop going through the motions and get the information they need. They interview harder. They feel as though their future is at stake. They don't want to chat with people. They are hungrier. They truly want to work in a certain industry or organization. And the manager with whom they are talking can sense their seriousness and react accordingly.

Format of an Information-Gathering Meeting

Prepare for each meeting. The questions you want to ask and the way you want to pitch, or position, yourself, will vary from one meeting to another. Think it all through. **Review the chapter "Format of a Networking Meeting" (presented later on) before *every* networking meeting. If you use it, you will have a good meeting.**

- Exchange pleasantries—to settle down. This is a chance to size up the other person and allow the other person to size you up. It helps the person to make a transition from whatever he or she was doing before you came in. One or two sentences of small talk: "Your offices are very handsome" or "Your receptionist was very professional" or "You must be thrilled about your promotion."

- Why am I here? The nature of your networking should change over time. In the beginning, you don't know much and are asking basic questions. But you can't keep asking the same questions. Presumably, you have learned something in your earlier meetings. As you move along, you should be asking different, higher-level questions—and you should also be in a position to give some information back to people with whom you are meeting. That's what makes you an insider—someone who knows a lot about the field.

  This is a basic example of "Why I am here":

Thanks so much for agreeing to meet with me. David Madison thought you could give me the advice I need. I'm meeting with publishing managers in the organization. I want to move my career into the publishing area.

If the meeting is in response to a targeted mailing, you may say something like:

I'm so glad you agreed to meet with me. I've been following your division's growth in the international area and thought it would be great to meet with you.

Remind the person of how you got his or her name and why you are there. He or she may have forgotten the contents of your letter or who referred you.

Here are additional suggestions on *why I am here* (notice how there is a progression from early to later in the search process):

- I'm trying to decide what my career path should be. I have these qualifications and I'm trying to decide how to use them. For example, I'm good at ___ and ___. I think they add up to ___. What do you think?

- I want to get into publishing and I'm meeting people in the field. Jamie Horowitz, a colleague of mine, met you at the United Way meeting a few weeks ago and thought you would be a good person for me to meet.

- I've researched the publishing industry and think the operations area would be a good fit for me. I was especially interested in learning more about your organization's operations area and I was thrilled when Charles Conlin at the Publishing Association mentioned your name as a guru in the industry.

- I have met with a number of people in our various publishing units and I think some meetings may turn into job offers. I'd like your insight about which units might be the best fit for me. I wrote to you because I know I'll be in publishing soon and I know you are one of the most important players in our company.

- I've worked in the publishing industry for five years, three years within our company, and have also learned sophisticated computer programming at night. I am looking for a situation that would combine both areas because the growth opportunities are limited in my present division. Richard Bayer thought I should speak with you, since your division is so highly computerized.

- Establish credibility with your Two-Minute Pitch. (For more information about this important part of the meeting, see that chapter.) After you say why you are there, they are likely to say something like: "How can I help you?" You respond: "I wanted to ask you a few things, but first let me give you an idea of who I am." There are a number of reasons for doing this:

1. The person will be in a better position to help you if he or she knows something about you.
2. It's impolite to ask a lot of questions without telling the person who you are.
3. You are trying to form a relationship with this person—to get to know each other a bit.

- Ask questions appropriate for this person. Really think through what you want to ask. You might even have your list of questions in front of you; this will make you look serious and help keep you on track.

- As he or she answers your questions, talk more about yourself *if appropriate*. "That's interesting. The fact is I've had a lot of pubic relations experience in the jobs I've held." By the time you leave the meeting, you should know something about each other.

- Ask for referrals if appropriate. This is an opportunity to extend your network. "I've made a list of people in the various divisions in which I'm interested. What do you think of these divisions?" "Are there other divisions or departments you would suggest?" "Who do you think I should contact at each of the good areas on this list?" "Could you tell me something about the person you suggested in that area?" "May I use your name?"

As you probe, they may respond that they do not know of any job openings. That's okay with you. You simply need to meet with more people in your target areas, whether or not they have positions available: "I'm just trying to get as much information as possible."

Some job hunters get annoyed when they go away without contacts. They are thinking short term and are not trying to build long-term relationships. But you were not *entitled* to a meeting with the manager. He or she was kind to meet with you at all.

If you get no contacts, be very grateful for what you do get. It may be he or she has no names to give. On the other hand, so many people network incorrectly (aggressively and abrasively), that managers are often reluctant to give out names until the job hunter has kept in touch for a number of months and proved his or her sincere interest. Many managers feel used by job hunters who simply want names and are not interested in *them*.

- Gather more information about the referrals (for instance, "What is Harvey Kaplan like?")

- Formal expression of gratitude. Thank the person for the time he or she spent with you.

- Offer to stay in touch. Constantly making new contacts is not as effective as keeping in touch with old ones. "May I keep in touch with you to let you know how I'm doing?" You might call later for future contacts, information, etc.

- Write a follow-up note and be sure to follow up again later. This is most important and a powerful tool. State how the meeting helped you or how you used the information. Be sincere. If appropriate, offer to keep the manager informed of your progress.

- Recontact your network every two to three months. Even after you get a job, these people will be your contacts to help you in your new job—and maybe you can even help them! After all, you are building lifelong relationships, aren't you? See the section, "Following Up When There Is No Immediate Job."

Remember:

- You are *not* there simply to get names. You may often get excellent information but no names of others to contact. That's fine.

- Be grateful for whatever help people give you and assume they are doing their best.

- Remember, too, that this is *your* meeting and you must try to get all you can out of it.

- This is not a job interview. In a job interview, you are being interviewed. In a networking meeting, you are *conducting* the meeting.

Follow precisely the chapter *Format of a Networking Meeting*. If you use it, you will have a good meeting.

Our plans miscarry because they have no aim. When a man does not know what harbor he is making for, no wind is the right wind.

Seneca the Younger, Roman statesman

Our dignity is not in what we do but in what we understand. The whole world is doing things.

George Santayana, *Winds of Doctrine*

Many things are lost for want of asking.

George Herbert, *Jacula Prudentum*

Format of a Networking Meeting

Prepare for each meeting. The questions you want to ask and the way you *pitch* or position yourself will vary from one meeting to another. Think it all through.

The Format of the Meeting

- **Pleasantries.** This is a chance to size up the other person and allow the other person to size you up. It's a chance to settle down. Just two or three sentences of small talk are enough.
- **Why am I here?** For example: "Thanks so much for agreeing to meet with me. Ruth Robbins thought you could give me the advice I need. I'm meeting with publishing managers in the organization. I want to move my career into the publishing area." Remind the person of how you got his or her name and why you are there.
- **Establish credibility with your Two-Minute Pitch.** After you tell the person why you are there, they are likely to say something like: "Well, how can I help you?" Then you respond, for example: "I wanted to ask you a few things, but first let me give you an idea of who I am." There are a number of reasons for doing this:
  1. The person will be in a better position to help you if he or she knows something about you.
  2. It's impolite to ask a lot of questions without telling the person who you are.
  3. You are trying to form a relationship with this person—to get to know each other a bit.
- **Ask questions** appropriate for this person. Really think through what you want to ask. For example, you wouldn't ask the marketing manager: "What's it like to be in marketing?" You would ask that of a more junior person. Consider having your list of questions in front of you so you will look serious and keep on track.
- As the person is answering your questions, **tell him or her more about yourself if appropriate**. For example, you might say: "That's interesting. When I was at XYZ Company, we handled a similar problem in an unusual way. In fact, I worked on the project . . ."
- **Ask for referrals if appropriate.** For example: "I'm trying to get in to see people in the departments and divisions on this list. Do you happen to know anyone in these areas? . . . May I use your name?"
- **Gather more information about the referrals** (such as: "What is Ellis Chase like?").
- **Formal time of gratitude.** Thank person for the time he or she spent with you.
- **Offer to stay in touch.** Remember: Making a lot of new contacts is not as effective as making not quite so many contacts but then *recontacting* those people later (see the chapter "Following Up after a Networking Meeting").
- **Write a follow-up note and be sure to follow up again later.**

Remember:

- You are *not* there simply to get names. You may often get excellent information but no names of others to contact. That's fine.
- Be grateful for whatever help people give you and assume they are doing their best.
- Remember: This is *your* meeting and you must try to get all you can out of it.
- This is not a job interview. In a job interview, you are being interviewed. In a networking meeting, *you* are conducting the meeting.

Business is a game, the greatest game in the world if you know how to play it.

Thomas J. Watson, Jr., former CEO of IBM

Other Meeting Pointers

- The heart of the meeting is relating your good points in the best way possible. Be concise and to the point. Don't be embarrassed about appearing competent. Be able to recite your Two-Minute Pitch and key accomplishments without hesitation.

- Keep control of the meeting. Don't let the person with whom you're meeting talk too much or too little. If he goes on about something inappropriate, jump in when you can and relate it to something you want to say. Remember, this is *your* meeting.

- Find out which of your achievements she is really impressed with. This is her hot button, so keep referring to those achievements.

- Be self-critical as you go along with this process. Don't become so enamored with the process that you become inflexible. Don't become a professional information gatherer or job hunter.

- Interview hard. *Probe.* Be prepared to answer hard questions in return.

- Take notes when you are getting what you want. This lets the manager know that the meeting is going well and encourages more of the same. The person to whom you are talking is just like everyone else who is interviewed—everyone wants to do well.

- Show enthusiasm and interest. Lean forward in your chair when appropriate. Ask questions that sincerely interest you, and sincerely try to get the answers.

- Don't be soppy and agree with everything. It's better to disagree mildly and then come to some agreement than to agree with everything 100 percent.

- Remember your goals. Don't go away from any meeting empty-handed. Get information or the names of other contacts.

- Don't overstay your welcome. Fifteen minutes or half an hour may be all a busy person can give you. Never take more than one-and-a-half to two hours.

- If you are meeting over lunch, go someplace simple so you are not constantly interrupted by waiters.

- If you are looking for a job, don't conceal that fact.

- **If the person with whom you are meeting suggests passing on your résumé to someone else, that is usually not helpful**—unless you know who the person is and can follow up yourself. Say, "I hate to put you to that trouble. Would you mind if I called her myself and used your name?" If the manager does not agree to this, then you must accept his or her wishes.

- **If the person you are meeting tells you of a job opening**, say, "I'd like to know more about it, but I also had a few questions I'd like to ask you." Continue to get your questions answered. If you follow up only on the job lead, you will probably wind up with no job and no information.

- **These are only suggestions.** You must adopt your own style, your own techniques. You'll find the more you meet with people, the better you'll get at it. Start out with friends or in low-risk situations. You do not want to meet with your most promising prospects until you are highly skilled at networking meetings. The more you practice, the better you will become.

Nothing great was ever achieved without enthusiasm.

Ralph Waldo Emerson, *Circles*

Who Is a Good Contact?

A contact is any connection between you and the person with whom you are hoping to meet. Most often the contact is someone you've met in another information-gathering meeting, but think a little and you will find other, creative ways to establish links with people. Here are a few real-life examples:

Example 1: "I worked on the blood drive the year you headed it up."

Example 2: "You taught the 'Making It Happen' course three years ago and I was in the group."

Example 3: "I have seen you in the halls at headquarters for the past six months . . ."

Example 4: "A friend of mine, Clara Jones, was in your 'Getting Promoted' class and talked about you endlessly. Since then, I have wanted to speak with you to get your advice."

. . . [W]e know that suffering produces perseverance; perseverance character; and character hope.

Romans 5: 3–4

Other Sources of Contacts

In addition, you can consider:

- Contacting acquaintances—even more than friends. Friends may be reluctant to act as contacts for you. You reflect more on them than you would on an acquaintance. And if things don't work out, they could lose your friendship—but acquaintances don't have as much to lose.

- Network every chance you get—at company picnics and in the cafeteria. Don't be like those job hunters who don't tell anyone they are looking for a job. You never know who knows someone who can help you. Everyone you meet knows a lot of people.

Summary

Networking is a powerful job-hunting tool—if it is used properly, which most often it is not. It is also a life skill you can and should use throughout your career. Become expert at it and do not abuse people. Give them something back.

If you think education is expensive, try ignorance.

Derek Bok, attributed

The
Five
O'Clock
Club

Targeted Mailings:
Just Like Networking

*There's nothing to writing. All you do is
sit down at a typewriter and open a vein.*
Walter ("Red") Smith, in *Reader's Digest,* July 1982

Networking is not the only way to job hunt. Consider targeted mailings when you want to see a particular person but have no formal contact. You must think of how you can create some tie-in to that person and contact him or her directly.

For the departments or divisions you have chosen, research the appropriate people to contact in each one. Ask each for a meeting—whether or not they have a job for you. You want to get in to see them *all* because your target is very small.

The Letter

- **Paragraph 1:** The opening paragraph for a targeted mailing should follow the format of a networking letter: State the reason you are writing and **establish the contact** you have with the reader.

> Congratulations on your new position! I know you are extremely busy (I've heard about it from others). After you are settled in, I would be interested in meeting with you. I think it would be mutually beneficial for us to meet, although I have no fixed idea of what could come of it.

After you have found something out about the person or the organization, pretend you are sitting with that person right now. What would you *say* to him or her? Your opening should reflect whatever you know about the organization or the person:

> Whenever people talk about divisions with excellent sales departments, your division's name always comes up. In fact, the people who run the Amalgamated Center, where I am now assigned, speak often of the quality of your department's work. I am interested in moving more directly into sales and I would like to meet with you.

- **Paragraph 2:**
  Give a **summary about yourself**.

- **Paragraph 3:**
  Note a few **key accomplishments that should be of interest to this target**.

- **Paragraph 4:**
  Ask for **half an hour** of their time and say you will **call them in a few days**. For example:

> I hope you will allow me half an hour of your time and insight to explore this area. I will call you in a few days to set up a mutually agreeable time.

> If you plan to follow up with a phone call, say so. (But if you say so, do it—or you may get no response while they wait for your call.)

Out-of-Town Search

For an *out-of-town search* (perhaps placed next to the last paragraph):

> As a result of many years' residence in Seattle, I would prefer to live and work in that area. In fact, I am in Seattle frequently visiting family and can arrange to meet with you at your office.

---

*There is no way of writing
well and also of writing easily.*

Anthony Trollope, *Barchester Towers*

Scannable Letters

As we have seen, other variations include the use of **underlining key points**, which can increase your response rate. This helps the busy reader scan the letter, be drawn in, and want to read the rest. Underlining makes certain key points pop out at the reader—anywhere in your text. Underline parts of sentences in no more than five places. Read the underlined parts to make sure they sound sensible when read together, have a flow, and make your point.

Even when I look at my own letters, I sometimes don't want to read them before I make them scannable. I rephrase my letters, underlining in a way that will make sense to the reader. People will read the salutation, then the first few words of your letter, and then the parts you have underlined. If they find these things compelling, they'll go back and read the rest of your letter.

Underlining should make sense. Don't underline the word *developed*, for instance, which doesn't make sense. Underline the word following it, which is *what* you developed, because that's probably the compelling part.

---

*Life is like playing a violin
solo in public and learning
the instrument as one goes on.*

Samuel Butler

Do What Is Appropriate

Strange as it may seem, **sometimes it can be very effective to ignore all of this**. Do what works in your organization and for you personally. It is sometimes better to follow your instincts rather than listen to the experts. You're smart. Think it through. Then make up your own mind.

The Follow-Up Call (after a Targeted Mailing)

When you call, you will probably have to **start again from the beginning**. Do not expect them to remember anything in your letter. Do not even expect them to remember you wrote to them. For example, when you phone:

- Say, "I sent you a letter recently. Did you receive it?"
- Remind them of the reason you wrote. You may again have to summarize your background and state some of your accomplishments.
- If they say they have no job openings at this time, that is okay with you—you were not necessarily looking for a job *with them*; you were looking for information or advice about the job possibilities for someone like you or perhaps you wanted to know what is happening in the profession, organization, or industry.

Leave messages that you called, but do not ask to have them call you back. Chances are, they won't, and you will feel rejected. However, be friendly with the assistant, and apologize for calling so often. If their assistants offer to have their bosses call you back, thank them but say you will be in and out and impossible to reach. You will have to call again. After the first call, try not to leave your name again. **Expect to call seven or eight times.** Do not become discouraged. It is not personal.

---

*Who has begun has half done.
Have the courage to be wise. Begin!*

Horace, Epistles

The Meeting

When you go in for your meeting, **handle it as you would a networking meeting** (unless the manager turns it into a job interview):

- Exchange pleasantries.
- State the reason you are there and why you wanted to see this particular person.
- Give your Two-Minute Pitch.
- Tell the manager how he or she can help you. Get the information you want, as well as names of a few other people with whom you should be talking.

As we have said, **be grateful for whatever help people give you**. They are helping you the best they can. If they do not give you the names of others to contact, perhaps they cannot because of a feeling of insecurity in their own jobs. Appreciate whatever they do give you.

Form a Relationship

Take notes during your meeting. Your follow-up notes will be more appropriate and then you will feel free to contact this person later. Keep in touch with people on a regular basis. Those who know you well will be more likely to help you.

A targeted mailing is a very powerful technique for hitting *every* department or division. Both can dramatically move your job hunt along. Try them!

Follow Up

Follow up with a customized note specifically acknowledging the help you received. These notes follow the same concept as follow-ups to networking meetings.

Final Thoughts

You will strike sparks with certain people you meet. They will develop a true interest in you and will surprise you with their help. I have had people invite me to luncheons to introduce me to important people or call me when they heard news they thought would interest me. I have even made new friends this way.

Of course, I have done my part, too, by keeping in touch to let them know how my campaign was going. If you are sincere about your search, you will find that the people you meet will also be sincere and will help. It can be a very heartwarming experience.

Take calculated risks. That is quite different from being rash.

Gen. George S. Patton, letter to his son, June 6, 1944

Targeted Mailings Require Research and Excellent Writing Skills

Targeted mailings work only if you've done your research (know which divisions and departments you want to contact) and if you're a good writer. Furthermore, you must target the right person and have something interesting to say to each person you are contacting. That's why targeted mailings work best for job hunters who clearly understand their target markets and the issues important in them.

Are You Sincere?

It's not enough to write to people and expect to get in to see them. They are probably busy with their own jobs and may be contacted by quite a few people.

Unless you sincerely want to see a person, you won't develop strategies to figure out how to get in to see him or her. You won't do your research. You won't do the follow-up phone calls that are required to prove your sincerity. You won't prevail when someone doesn't return your phone calls.

If you really want to see this person, you'll persevere. And you won't mind asking for an appointment one month from now if he or she is too busy to see you now. You may even say, "I know you're busy now. How about if we schedule something for a month from now and I'll call you in advance to confirm?"

> *The way to get good ideas is to get lots of ideas and throw the bad ones away.*
>
> Linus Pauling, American chemist

To Enclose Your Résumé or Not?

A cover story in *Time* magazine was titled "Junk Mail." People said, "Why do junk-mail companies enclose so many things in these envelopes that we get? They're wasting paper." In the Letters to the Editor, the junk-mail companies said they had no choice because the response rate increased so dramatically with the number of additional enclosures with the same message. If they have fewer enclosures, their response rate decreases dramatically.

The same is true for the mailings you are sending. Some people say, "If they see my résumé, they'll know I'm job hunting." But they'll probably know it anyway from your letter. People are very sophisticated today.

My rule of thumb is this: If it supports your case and it has a message that complements your cover letter, then enclose your résumé. You can say, "I've enclosed my résumé to let you know something more about me." If you have a brilliant résumé, why not enclose it?

On the other hand, if you want to make a career change, you probably do not want to enclose your résumé, because you can probably make a stronger case without it.

Do what is appropriate for you. Try it both ways and see which works better for you and your situation.

Stating Your Accomplishments in Your Cover Letter

Think of which of your accomplishments are of interest to your target market. You may want to list different accomplishments for the different industries to which you are writing.

Rank your bulleted accomplishments generally in order of importance to the reader, as opposed to chronologically or alphabetically. It may be that some other logic would be more appropriate in your case. Then do that.

On the following page is the letter of someone who has been successful with targeted mailings. Rather than simply copying this letter, **think of *one* actual individual on your list to whom you are writing and think of the compelling things you should say to make that person want to meet with you**. Even if you write exactly that same kind of letter to 20 people, it will sound more sincere and have more life if you write that first letter with a particular person in mind.

This letter was sent after a cold call to Ms. Rosenberg about the possibility of a stockbrokering position.

James J. Borland, III

140 West 81st Street
New York, New York 10000
jborland678@landmine.net

July 17, 20XX

Ms. Renée Rosenberg
Merrill Lynch
Liberty Place
165 Broadway
New York, New York 10000

Dear Renée:

I appreciate your offer to review and forward my résumé. I think you'll see how I've used my skills of persuasion throughout the years. For example, while working on the "Friends of Bill Thomas" Mayoral Campaign, I was on the phone all day long convincing politicians across a broad spectrum to either publicly commit to my candidate or, as was the case at the outset when resistance was strong and reactions negative, to cooperate behind the scenes. The continual give and take involved a lot of listening as people wanted to state their case, vent frustrations with personalities, and so on. One had to cajole and "massage" the local political types in an effort to have them deliver us an audience at events we staged in their communities. These same techniques—reasoning with people, getting my message across, listening, possessing a desire to please—all would be assets in a job where rejection is the norm.

On the other hand, I find I enjoy analyzing business. For example, in my current job I monitor revenue and other statistics daily to determine trends and affect policy. I coordinate 22 city marshals who participate in the street impoundment program and also deal directly with three garage towing operations under contract to us.

I enjoy working in an atmosphere where there is a lot of activity, where I'm measured by my results, where compensation is directly related to my ability to produce, and where the job is what I make it. I want to be with interesting people, people who matter, people who can have an impact. I feel that the securities business and the opportunity to train and grow the best at Merrill would be a challenge and an education. In this situation, I feel the most severe limitations and constraints would be my own and I like that.

I would be pleased to meet with someone in your organization to further discuss how my qualifications may lead to a career with Merrill.

Sincerely,

Enclosure

The
Five
O'Clock
Club

Following Up after a Networking Meeting

Opportunities are usually disguised as hard work, so most people don't recognize them.

Ann Landers, syndicated advice columnist, Rowes, *The Book of Quotes*

The follow-up after a networking meeting—or a meeting resulting from having contacted someone directly—is very different from the way you follow up after a job interview.

Analyze the meeting. In your letter, thank the interviewer. State the *specific* advice and leads you were given. Be personable. Say you will keep in touch. *Do* keep in touch.

Follow up every few months with a *status report* on how your search is going, an article, or news of interest to the manager.

Make sure people are thinking about you. You may contact the manager just as he or she has heard of something of importance to you.

Recontact those you met earlier in your search. Otherwise, you're like a salesman who works to get new leads while ignoring his old relationships. Get new leads but also keep in touch with people you've already met.

It's never too late to follow up. For example: "I met you three years ago and am still impressed by ___. Since then I have ___ and would be interested in getting together with you again to discuss these new developments." Make new contacts. Recontact old ones. It's never too late.

If you know anything that will make a brother's heart glad, run quick and tell it; and if it is something that will only cause a sigh, bottle it up, bottle it up.

Old Farmer's Almanac, 1854

*If (a man) is brusque in his manner, others will not cooperate.
If he is agitated in his words, they will awaken no echo in others.
If he asks for something without having first established a (proper) relationship, it will not be given to him.*

I Ching: *Book of Changes*
China, c. 600 B.C.

In differentiation, not in uniformity, lies the path of progress.

Louis Brandeis, U.S. Supreme Court Justice
Business—A Profession

**Trouble getting started?
What would you say to the person if he or she were sitting across from you right now? Consider that as the opening of your follow-up letter.**

Job hunters make a mistake when they fail to *recontact* people with whom they have formed relationships earlier in their search. Keep in touch on a regular basis so you increase your chances of contacting them just at a time when they have heard of something that may interest you—or may have a new need themselves.

Follow up with a customized note specifically acknowledging the help you received.

John Weiting

163 York Avenue – 12B
New York, New York 10000
(212) 555-2231 (day)
(212) 555-1674 (message)
jweiting@attnet.net

June 25, 20XX

Ms. Rachel Tepfer
Director of Training
Time Subsidiary Communications
8 Pine Street
New York, NY 10001

Dear Ms. Tepfer:

Thanks so much for seeing me. Your center is very impressive and seems very well run. But of course, that's what I had heard before I met you.

As you suggested, I sent for information on ASTD and was pleasantly surprised to see your name in there! It sounds like a great organization and I can't wait until they start to have meetings again in the fall.

I will definitely follow up with both Ann Brody and Jack Kaufman and appreciate your giving me their names. I've called them each a few times, but they are very busy people.

After I left your place, I wished I had asked you more about your own career. It was only at the very end that you brought up the interesting way you got your job. I had wrongly assumed that you came up through the ranks at Time Subsidiary Communications. Perhaps some other time I can hear the rest of the story.

I will keep you posted regarding my activities and perhaps I'll even run into you at ASTD meetings.

Thanks again for your time and insight. Till we meet again.

Cordially,

John Weiting

Sylvan Von Burg

To: Judy Acord

I enjoyed our conversation, which I found most helpful.

I will meet with Betsy Austin when she returns from overseas and will talk to Jim about seeing Susan Geisenheimer. I'll also contact Bob Potvin and Clive Murray, per your suggestion.

Again, thanks for your help. I'll let you know how things develop.

Sylvan

Follow-up letters don't have to be long, but they *do* have to be personal. Make sure the letters you write could not be sent to anyone else on your list.

Mr. Miguel Villarin
President
Commerce and Industry Association
Street Address
City, State

Dear Miguel:

Thank you for the time from your busy schedule. I enjoyed our discussion and appreciated your suggestions toward marketing myself. Your idea on using the Big 8 firms as pivot points in networking is an excellent one. As you requested, I have enclosed copies of my résumé. I plan to call you next week so I can obtain the names of the firms where my résumé was sent.

I have been thinking about using Robert Dobbs (Dobbs & Firth) in my networking efforts. Since he is a past president of Commerce and Industry I would be foolish not to tap such a source. Thanks again, Miguel.

Sincerely,

Janet Vitalis

Enclosures

Following Up When There Is No Immediate Job

Contrary to the cliché, genuinely nice guys most often finish first, or very near it.

Malcolm Forbes

During each meeting, you have taken up the time of someone who sincerely tried to help you. Writing a note is the only polite thing to do. Since the person has gone to some effort for you, go to some effort in return. A phone call to thank a person can be an intrusion and shows little effort on your part.

In addition to being polite, there are good business reasons for writing notes and otherwise keeping in touch with people who have helped you. For one thing, few people keep in touch, so you will stand out. Second, it gives you a chance to sell yourself again and to overcome any misunderstandings that may have occurred. Third, this is a promotional campaign and any good promoter knows that a message reinforced soon after a first message results in added recall.

If you meet someone through a networking meeting, for example, he or she will almost certainly forget about you the minute you leave and just go back to business. Sorry, but you were an interruption.

If you write to people almost immediately after your meeting, this will dramatically increase the chance they will remember you. If you wait two weeks before writing, they may remember meeting someone, but not remember you specifically. If you wait longer than two weeks, they

probably won't remember meeting anyone—let alone you.

So promptly follow the meeting with a note. Remind those to whom you write who you are and when they talked to you. Give some highlight of the meeting. Contact them again within a month or two. It is just like an advertising campaign. Advertisers will often place their ads at least every four weeks in the same publication. If they advertised less often, few people would remember the ad.

I was taught that the way of progress is neither swift nor easy.

Marie Curie

What Michael Did

This is a classic—and it worked on me. I wanted to hire one junior accountant for a very important project and had the search narrowed down to two people. I asked my boss for his input. We made up a list of what we were looking for and we each rated the candidates on 20 criteria. The final scores came in very close, but I hired Judy instead of Michael.

In response to my rejection, Michael wrote me a note telling me how much he still wanted to work for our organization and how he hoped I would keep him in mind if something else should come up. He turned the rejection into a positive contact. Notes are so unusual and this one was so personable that I showed it to my boss.

A few months later, Michael wrote again saying that he had taken a position with another firm. He was still very much interested in us and hoped to work for us someday. He promised to keep in touch, which he did. Each time he wrote, I showed the note to my boss. Each time, we were sorry we couldn't hire him.

After about seven months, I needed another helping hand. Whom do you think I called? Do you think I interviewed other people? Do you think I had to sell Michael to my boss? Michael came to work for us and we never regretted it. Persistence pays off.

As a splendid palace deserted by its inmates looks like a ruin, so does a man without character, all his material belongings notwithstanding.

Mohandas Gandhi

What to Say in Your Follow-Up Note

Depending on the content of your note, you may type or write it. Generally use standard business-size stationery, but sometimes Monarch or other note-size stationery, ivory or white, will do. A *job* interview follow-up should almost always be typed on standard business-size ivory or white stationery. However, if the organization seems to do a lot by E-mail, you may write follow-up notes via E-mail.

After an information-gathering meeting, play back some of the advice you received, any you intend to follow, and so on. Simply be sincere. What did you appreciate about the time the person spent with you? Did you get good advice you intend to follow? Say so. Were you inspired? Encouraged? Awakened? Say so.

If you think there were sparks between you and the person with whom you met, be sure to say you will keep in touch. Then do it. Follow-up letters don't have to be long, but they do have to be personal. Make sure the letters you write could not be sent to someone else on your list.

Sample Follow-Up to a Networking Meeting

PETER SCHAEFER

To: Alexandra Duran

Thanks again for contacting Brendan for me and for providing all those excellent contact names.

There's such a wealth of good ideas in the list that it will take me a while to follow up on all of them, but I'm getting to it and will let you know what develops.

Again, thanks for your extraordinary effort.

Cordially,

Peter

To keep in touch, simply let interviewers/network contacts know how you are doing. Tell them who you are seeing and what your plans are. Some people, seeing your sincerity, will keep sending you leads or other information.

Make new contacts. Recontact old ones by writing a *status report* every two months telling how well you are doing in your search. **Keeping up with old networking contacts is as important as making new ones.**

Some job hunters use this as an opportunity to write a proposal. During the meeting, you may have learned something about the organization's problems. Writing a proposal to solve them may create a job for you.

Alan had met with the head of a senior citizen's center, where he learned they needed new programs to keep the residents active. He visited a number of senior centers to see what their programs were, selected the ones he knew he could lead, and gathered the newsletters each center had. He then developed a *proposal* of programs he could run, such as bingo games and ballroom dance lessons.

In his follow-up note, he said he had visited a number of centers, come up with some ideas that he listed, and also gathered sample newsletters so he could put together a newsletter for the center. Equally important, he said he would like to visit with her again to discuss his proposal.

She went over the proposal with Alan and they created a position for him.

However, you are not trying to turn every networking meeting into a job possibility. You *are* trying to form lifelong relationships with people. Experts say that most successful employees form solid relationships with a lot of people with whom they keep in touch regularly throughout their careers. These people will keep you up to date in a changing economy, tell you about changes or openings in your field, and generally be your long-term allies. And you will do the same for them.

Has a man gained anything who has received a hundred favors and rendered none? He is great who confers the most benefits.

Ralph Waldo Emerson, "Essay on Compensation"

The
Five
O'Clock
Club

Basic Job-Interview Techniques

Just know your lines and don't bump into the furniture.

Spencer Tracy's advice on acting

An interview is not simply a conversation; it's showtime, folks. You will be competing against people who are well rehearsed and know their lines.

Develop Your Lines

In an interview, being unable to express yourself clearly is worse than lacking experience. Refine your sales pitch by listing on a 3×5 card:

- the main reason the employer should want to hire you
- what you have to offer in the way of experience, credentials, and personality;
- two key accomplishments to support your interest in this position;
- an answer to what you think might be the employer's main objection to you, if any; and
- a statement of why you would want to work for this company.

Keep this card in your pocket or purse and review it just before going in for the interview so you will know your lines.

The world is moving so fast these days that the man who says it can't be done is generally interrupted by someone doing it.

Harry Emerson Fosdick

Look and Act the Part

Remember, this is show biz. Even if you don't feel self-confident, act as if you do. If you come in looking defeated, like a loser, why would anyone want to hire you? *Act* as if you are successful and feel good about yourself and you will increase your chances of actually *feeling* that way. Enthusiasm counts. Every manager is receptive to someone who is sincerely interested in the company and the position.

"He came in for an interview 3 hours ago, and I made the mistake of telling him to make himself comfortable."

Make yourself necessary to someone.

Ralph Waldo Emerson

During the Interview—Play the Part of a Consultant

Pretend for a minute that you own a small consulting company. When you first meet a prospective client, you probe to better understand the problems this person is facing. If the client has no problems, or if you cannot solve them, there is no place for you.

You are also there to sell your company. Therefore, as the manager talks about company problems, you reveal your own company's experience and credentials by asking questions or by telling how you have handled similar situations. You want to see how your company fits in with this company.

If the conversation goes astray, lead it back to the topics on your 3×5 card—the work you would do for them and your abilities. That way, you can make your points in context.

It is your responsibility to reassure the hiring manager that everything will work out. The manager does not want to be embarrassed later by discovering he's made a hiring mistake. It is almost as if you are patting the manager on the arm and saying, "There, there. Everything will be just fine. You can count on me."

If you are asked how you would handle a situation, reassure the manager that even though you do not know specifically what you would do (because, after all, you are not on the job yet), you know you can figure it out because:

- It won't be a problem. I'm good at these things.
- I'm very resourceful. Here's what I did as company controller. . . .
- I've been in that situation before. I can handle your situation even though I don't know the specifics.

Let the manager air his or her doubts about you. If you are told what these reservations are, you can reassure the manager right then or you can mull it over later and reassure the manager in writing.

Do not appear to be *shopping around*. Be sincerely interested in this particular division—at least during the interview.

Follow up on your meetings. Address the important issues, stress your interest and enthusiasm for the job, and state your major selling points—especially since you now know what is of interest to the interviewer.

Follow-up will dramatically increase the number of job offers you get. It is one of the most powerful tools you have to influence the situation.

If the interviewer has no problems, or if you cannot solve them, there is no place for you.

We're a society that's not about perfection, but about rectifying mistakes. We're about second chances.

Harry Edwards, in "Hardline," *Detroit Free Press,* May 1988

You must display self-confidence in your ability to handle the position. If you are not confident, why should the hiring manager take a chance on you? If you want the job, take a stand and say that you believe it will work.

I have always tried to be true to myself, to pick those battles I felt were important.

Arthur Ashe

Do Your Homework

Before the interview, research the division and the industry. If you're asked why you are interested in them, you will have your answer. Do library research. Call the public relations department and ask for literature or an annual report. Ask others about the part of the company that interests you. Also, check out the company's website. Show up early and read literature in the reception area, talk to the receptionist, and observe the people. Get a feel for the place.

Whensoever a man desires anything inordinately, he is presently disquieted within himself.

Thomas À Kempis

Questions You Might Ask in an Interview

You are there not only to answer the interviewer's questions, but also to make sure you get the information you need. Ask appropriate questions. What do you really want to know? Here are a few to get you thinking in the right direction:

QUESTIONS TO ASK HUMAN RESOURCES

- Can you tell me more about the responsibilities of the job?
- What skills do you think would be most critical for this job?
- Is there a current organization chart available for this area?
- What happened to the person who held this job before?
- What kinds of people are most successful in this area?
- What do you see as the department's strengths and weaknesses?

QUESTIONS TO ASK MANAGERS (AND PERHAPS PEERS)

- What are the key responsibilities of the job?
- What is the most important part of the job?
- What is the first problem needing the attention of the person you hire?
- What other problems need attention now? Over the next six months?
- How has this job been performed in the past?
- Are there other things you would like someone to do that are not a formal part of the job?
- What would you like to be able to say about the new hire one year from now?
- What significant changes do you see in the future?
- May I ask what your background is?
- What do you find most satisfying about working here? Most frustrating?
- How would you describe your management style?
- How is the department organized?
- May I meet the other people who work in the area?
- How is performance evaluated? By whom? How often?
- What skills are in short supply here?

The Rehearsal

*It may sound like a contradiction, but you achieve
spontaneity on the set through preparation
of the dialogue at home. As you prepare,
find ways of making your responses seem newly
minted, not preprogrammed.*

Michael Caine, *Acting in Film*

Even experienced job hunters need practice.
Each interview smooths out your presentation
and responses. As you get better, your self-confidence grows.

By now, you've had networking or information-gathering interviews. You will have practiced
talking about yourself and will have information
about your area of interest and the possibilities
for someone like you.

When I was unemployed, I had lots of interviews, but I was not doing well in them. I was
under so much stress I kept talking about what *I*
wanted to do rather than what I could do *for the
company*. I knew better, but I could not think
straight. An old friend who belongs to The Five
O'Clock Club helped me develop my *lines* for my
3×5 card. Then we practiced. After that, my interviews went well.

**Be sure to record every networking and
job interview on the Interview Record.**

Get a Job Offer

Sincerely intend to turn each interview into a
solid job offer. Do your best to make the position
into something acceptable. Make the most of
each interview. Negotiate changes in the job
itself. Suggest additional things you can do for the
company—jobs often can be upgraded a level or
two. Or perhaps the manager could refer you to
another area of the company. You should make
every effort to turn an interview into a reasonable
job offer.

- This is an opportunity to practice your negotiation skills and increase the number of interviews you turn into offers. You can always turn
the job down later.

- Getting job offers helps your self-esteem. You
can say you received a number of offers but
they didn't seem right for you. This puts you in
a stronger negotiating position.

- Even if you turn down an offer, stay friendly
with the hiring manager. This may lead to
another more appropriate offer later.

- When you get an offer you are not sure about,
say that you have a few other things you must
attend to, but will get back to them in a week.

- You may be surprised: Perhaps what you originally found objectionable can be changed to
your liking. If you end the process too early,
you lose the possibility of changing the situation to suit you. Having a job created especially
for you is the best outcome.

*To take what there is and use it, without waiting
forever in vain for the preconceived—to dig deep into
the actual and get something out of that
—this doubtless is the right way to live.*

Henry James

Aiming for the Second Job Out

Sometimes the job you really want is too big a step
for you right now. Instead of trying to get it in one
move, go for it in two moves. Make your next job
one that will qualify you for the job you really want.

What Do You Really Want?

*I am proud of the fact that I
never invented weapons to kill.*

Thomas A. Edison

If I had known, I should have become a watchmaker.

Albert Einstein,
on his role in making the atomic bomb possible

To get ahead, many people compromise what they want. A lot of compromising can result in material success but also feelings of self-betrayal and not knowing who you really are.

It can be difficult to hold on to your values and live the kind of life that is right for you. You may feel there is no hope for change. If you are really honest, you may discover that you have tried very little to make changes. Ask yourself what you have done to improve your situation.

Deciding where you want to work is a complex problem. Many unhappy professionals, managers, and executives admit they made a mistake in deciding to work for their present companies. They think they should have done more research and thinking before they took the job.

The stress of job hunting can impair your judgment. You may make a decision without enough information simply because you want to *move on*. Ego can also be involved: You want to get an offer quickly so you can tell others and yourself that you are worth something. Or you may deceive yourself into thinking you have enough information. Even if you are normally a good decision maker, you can short-circuit the decision-making process when it comes to your own career.

You will make better decisions when you are not deciding under pressure. Start now to see what your options are. Then you already will have thought them through in case you have to make a move quickly later.

A man should always consider how much he has more than he wants, and how much more unhappy he might be than he really is.

Joseph Addison

Objectively evaluate the information you come up with and develop contingency plans. Decide whether to leave your present position and evaluate new opportunities. List the pros and cons of each possibility for you and those close to you.

You may decide, for example, that a certain position is higher level, higher paying, and more prestigious, but you will have less time for your personal life, and the job will make demands on your income because you will have to take on a more expensive lifestyle. You may even decide you don't like the kind of work, the conditions, or the people, or that your lack of leisure time will push you farther away from the way you want to live.

Depending on your values, the job may be worth it or not. If you list the pros and cons, you are more likely to adhere to your decision and have fewer regrets. You are more likely to weigh the trade-offs and perhaps think of other alternatives. You will decide what is important to you. You will have fewer negative surprises later and will be warned of areas where you may need more information. You will make better decisions and have more realistic expectations about the future.

What If Your Interviews Are Not Turning into Job Offers?

If one man says to thee,
"Thou art a donkey," pay no heed.
If two speak thus, purchase a saddle.

The Talmud

Listen to gather better information. You may find that your target area is declining or you don't have the required background, or whatever. One of my clients kept saying that managers insulted her. If you have the same experiences again and again, find out what you are doing wrong.

Perhaps you are unconsciously turning people down. A job hunter may make unreasonable demands because, deep inside, he or she knows there are things dramatically wrong with a situation. The requests for more money or a better title are really to make up for the unacceptable working conditions. Then the company rejects the applicant. One job hunter thought he was turned down for the job. In reality, *he* turned down the job. He did not let an offer happen because he knew the job was not right and he made it fall through. There is nothing wrong with this—as long as he knows he could have had a job offer if he had wanted one.

Make sure you are addressing the company's problems—not your own. A major mistake I have made myself is focusing on what I wanted rather than on what the company or the manager needed.

Perhaps you are not talking to the right people. Are you interviewing with people two levels higher than you are—those in a position to hire you? If you are spending a lot of time talking to people at your own level, you can learn about the field, but this is unlikely to result in job offers.

If you don't know why, ask them. If appropriate, you may want to call a few of the people with whom you interviewed to find out why you did not get the job. If you are really stuck and feel you are not interviewing well, this can be very valuable feedback for you. You may even be able to turn a negative situation around.

Do Your Best, Then Let It Go

> *. . . you ought to say, "If it is the Lord's will."*
>
> James 4:15

You are trying to find a match between yourself and a company. You are not going to click with everyone, any more than everyone is going to click with you. Don't expect every interview to turn into a job offer. The more interviews you have, the better you will do at each one.

And don't punish yourself later. Do your best and then do your best again.

Hang in there. Get a lot of interviews. Know your lines. And don't bump into the furniture. You will find the right job. As M. H. Anderson said: "If at first you don't succeed, you are running about average."

> *So to avoid all that horror, prepare. Apart from anything else, preparation uses up a lot of the nervous energy that otherwise might rise up to betray you. Channel that energy; focus it into areas that you control.*
> *The first step in preparation is to learn your lines until saying them becomes a predictable reflex. And don't mouth them silently; say them aloud until they become totally your property. Hear yourself say them, because the last thing you want is the sound of your own voice taking you by surprise or not striking you as completely convincing.*
>
> Michael Caine, *Acting in Film*

How to Use the Interview Record

The
Five
O'Clock
Club

Obviously the way you move will be affected by the character you are playing; but natural movement comes from your "center," from the same place as a natural voice. When you walk from your center, you will project a solid perspective of yourself. Walk with that certainty and ease, and your path becomes a center of gravity. Your force pulls all eyes to you. Slouch or poke your head forward, or pull your shoulders back uncomfortably, and that power seeps away. Only a relaxed, centered walk creates a sense of strength. A centered walk can be very menacing, too. Even if you don't get film work on the basis of this advice, follow it and you'll never get mugged, either. Mind you, if you look like I do you'll never get mugged anyway because people generally think I have just been mugged.

Michael Caine, *Acting in Film*

O n the next page is a very important worksheet: the Interview Record. Make a lot of copies of this page for your own personal search. Every time you have a meeting—**whether a networking meeting or a job interview**—fill it out. Make note of with whom you met, to whom they referred you, and what happened in the meeting. Attach to the Interview Record a copy of your notes from the meeting, the follow-up letter you sent, and perhaps the letter that led to the meeting.

Two weeks after the meeting, you may not remember what you discussed. If you are having a productive search and you are meeting with 10 to 15 people each week, you will not be able to remember what each person said, let alone how you met each person. To keep track of your meetings, maintain a record of each one.

Some job hunters use a three-ring binder and arrange all of the Interview Records alphabetically, by industry or in some other logical order.

Some job hunters methodically cross-reference the names by noting who referred whom.

At the beginning of your search, you may think you will be searching for a short time. But part of a good search is to follow up with your contacts at least every two months. You can have a more intelligent follow-up if you have an Interview Record to refer to.

What convinces is conviction. Believe in the argument you're advancing. If you don't, you're as good as dead. The other person will sense that something isn't there, and no chain of reasoning, no matter how logical or brilliant, will win your case for you.

Lyndon Baines Johnson

Until you value yourself, you will not value your time. Until you value your time, you will not do anything with it.

Dr. M. Scott Peck

Interview Record

Name: _____

Position:_____

Company: _____

Address: _____

_____

_____

Phone: Business:_____

        Home:_____

E-mail: _____

Referred by: _____

Link to referral: _____

People spoken to (may require separate sheets.):

_____

_____

_____

Issues (advice, problems, plans, etc.):

_____

_____

_____

Key points to remember:

_____

_____

_____

Referrals (write additional names on back.):

Name:_____

Position: _____

Company:_____

Address: _____

_____

_____

Phone: Business:_____

        Home:_____

Date of initial contact: _____

Method used: _____
           (if letter, copy and attach to this sheet.)

Planned date of follow-up call to set up
appointment: _____
         (also record date on job-hunting calendar.)

Actual dates of calls to set up appointment:

_____

_____

_____

Appointment:_____

Follow-up note mailed:

       (Copy attached)

Follow-up 2:_____

Follow-up 3:_____

Follow-up 4:_____

Follow-up 5:_____

Follow-up 6:_____

       (Copies attached)

Other comments:
- tone of the meeting
- objections to you
- logical next steps
- feelings about job
- positives about you
- key issues to address
- influencers

The
Five
O'Clock
Club

Follow-Up after a Job Interview:
Consider Your Competition

Bullock shrugged. He'd been thinking about Bill that afternoon, trying to decide how to fit him into Deadwood Brickworks, Inc. It wasn't a question he could be useful. Anybody could be useful when you decided where they fit. That was what business was.

Pete Dexter, *Deadwood*

So far in the interview process, we have considered you and the hiring manager. By acting like a consultant, you can negotiate a job that's right for both you and him or her. But there are other players and other complexities in this drama. First, there are all the other people you meet during the hiring process. They are influencers and, in fact, may influence the hiring decision more than the hiring manager does. These are people the hiring manager trusts and on whose opinions he relies. In addition, there are complexities such as outside influencers, the timing of the hiring decision, and salary considerations. Finally, you have competitors. They may be other people the interviewer is seeing or an ideal candidate in the interviewer's mind.

This section contains case studies of how some people considered and dealt with their competition. In the next one, we'll give you the guidelines they followed, which helped them decide what they could do to win the job. Remember, the job hunt really starts after the interview. What can you do to turn the interview into an offer? This is the part of the process that requires the most analysis and strategic thinking.

Think *objectively* about the needs of the organization and of everyone you met and think about what you can do to influence *each* person.

If you're in a seller's market, however, you may not need to follow up: You'll be brought back for more meetings before you have a chance to breathe. *If you're in a buyer's market,* you will probably have to do some thoughtful follow-up to get the job.

Because effective follow-up is a lot of work, your first decision should be: Do I want to get an offer for this job? Do I want to *go for it*? If you are ambivalent, and are in a competitive market, you will probably *not* get the job. Someone else will do what he or she needs to do to get it.

Follow-ups will not guarantee you a specific job, but extensive follow-ups on a number of possibilities increase the number and quality of your offers. If you focus too much on one specific situation and how you can *make* them hire you, that won't work. You need both breadth and depth in your job hunt: You have both when you are in contact on a regular basis with 6 to 10 people who are in a position to hire you or recommend that you be hired. You must have 6 to 10 of these contacts in the works, *each* of which you are trying to move along.

Ideally, you will get to a point where you are moving them along together, slowing certain ones down and speeding others up, so you wind up with three concurrent job offers. Then you can select the one that is best for you. This will usually be the job that positions you best for the long run—the one that fits best into your Fifteen- or Forty-Year Vision. It will rarely be sensible to make a decision based on money alone.

Therefore, if one situation is taking all of your energy, stop right now for 10 minutes and think of how you can quickly contact other people in your target area (through networking, targeted mailings, job postings, or the help of human resources). It will take the pressure off and prevent you from trying to close too soon on this one possibility.

CASE STUDY *The Artist*
Status Checks Rarely Work

Most people think follow-up means calling for the status of the search. This is not the case:

At Citibank, a project I managed needed an artist. I interviewed 20 and came up with two piles: one of 17 rejects, and another of the 3 I would present to my boss and my boss's boss. A few people called to *follow up*. Here's one:

Artist: "I'm calling to find out the procedure and the status. Do you mind?"
Me: "Not at all. I interviewed 20 people. I'll select 3 and present them to my boss and my boss's boss."
Artist: "Thanks a lot. Do you mind if I call back later?"
Me: "No, I don't mind."

The artist called every couple of weeks for three months, asked the same thing, and stayed in the reject pile. To move out, he could have said things like:

- Is there more information I can give you?
- I've been giving a lot of thought to your project and have some new ideas. I'd like to show them to you.
- Where do I stand? How does my work compare with the work others presented?

If all you're doing is finding out where you are in the process, that's rarely enough. *The ball is always in your court.* It is your responsibility to figure out what the next step should be. Job hunters view the whole process as if it were a tennis game where—*thwack*—the ball is in the hiring manager's court. Wrong.

Me to job hunter: "How's it going?"
Job hunter to Kate: (*Thwack!*) "The ball's in their court now. They're going to call me."

When they call, it will probably be to say, "You are not included." If you wait, not many of your interviews will turn into offers.

A man is not finished when he's defeated; he's finished when he quits.

Richard Milhous Nixon

CASE STUDY *Rachel*
Trust Me

Rachel had been unemployed for nine months. This was her first Five O'Clock Club meeting. She was disgusted. "I had an interview," she said. "I know what will happen: I'll be a finalist and they'll hire the other person."

Rachel was nice, enthusiastic, and smart: She was always a finalist. Yet the more experienced person was always hired.

Here's the story. Rachel, a lobbyist, was interviewing at a law firm. The firm liked her background, but it needed some public relations help and perhaps an internal newsletter. Rachel did not have experience in either of those areas, although she knew she could do those things. She wrote a typical thank-you note playing up her strengths and playing down her weaknesses, but essentially ignoring the firm's objections. She highlighted the lobbying, and said that public relations and a newsletter would not be a problem. She could do it. She was asking the firm to *trust her.*

Lots of Job Hunters Take the *Trust Me* Approach

The following occurred during a group meeting at The Five O'Clock Club:

Me: "Do you want this job? Are you willing to go through a brick wall to get it?"
Rachel: "Yes. I am. I really want this job."
Me: "Let's think about overcoming their objections. If you can write a public relations plan after you get hired, why not do it now? Why ask them to trust you?"

Two people in the group had old public relations plans they lent her. Remember: The proposals or ideas you write will probably be wrong. That's okay. You're showing the company you can think the problem through and actually come up with solutions.

Rachel's lack of experience with newsletters was also an objection. We suggested Rachel call law firms in other cities and get their newsletters.

After doing research, Rachel sent a very different note. In this one she said she had been giving it more thought and was very excited about working for the firm. She had put together a public relations plan, *which she would like to review with them,* and had gotten copies of newsletters from other law firms, which gave her ideas of what she could do in a newsletter for them. Of course, she got the job.

Mediocrity obtains more with application than superiority without it.

Baltasar Gracian, *Oraculo Manual*

Uncovering Their Objections

Rachel got the job because she overcame the objections of the hiring committee. Start thinking about how you can overcome objections. This will change the way you interview and you will become more attuned to picking up on valid objections rather than quashing them. Then you can even solicit negatives. For example, you can ask:

- Who else is being considered?
- What do they have to offer?
- How do I stand in comparison with them?
- What kind of person would be considered an ideal candidate?
- What would you like to say about a new hire one year from now?

Get good at interviewing so you can solicit valid objections to hiring you.

He said, however, that the real secret of his fortune was that none of his mules worked as hard and with so much determination as he did himself.

Gabriel Garcia Marquez, *Love in the Time of Cholera*

Act Like a Consultant

Since most jobs are created for people, find out what the manager needs. Hiring managers often decide to structure the job differently depending on who they hire. Why not influence the hiring manager to structure the job for you?

Probe—and don't expect anything to happen in the first meeting. If you were a consultant trying to sell a $30,000 or $70,000 project (your salary), you wouldn't expect someone to immediately say, "Fine. Start working." Yet job hunters often expect to get an offer during the first meeting.

Forget about job hunting. This is regular business. You're selling an expensive package. Do what a consultant or a salesperson does: Ask about the organization's problems and its situation; think about how you could get back to the interviewer later. Get enough information so you can follow up and give the interviewer enough information so he or she will want to see you again. Move the process along: Suggest you meet with more people there. Do research. Have someone influence the interviewer on your behalf. Then get back to him or her again. That's what a consultant does. Remember to move the process along; outshine and outlast your competition.

The Other Decision Makers/Influencers

Many job hunters assume the hiring manager is the only person who matters. Big mistake. Others are not only influencers; in some cases, they may actually be the decision makers.

I'm a good example. I make terrible hiring decisions: Everyone I interview seems fine to me. So I have others meet with the candidates. Their opinions weigh more than mine. Any applicant who ignores them is ignoring the decision-makers—or at least the serious influencers.

Take every person you meet seriously. Don't be rude to the receptionist. He or she may say to the boss, "If you hire him, I'm quitting." The receptionist is definitely an influencer.

The people you want to reach . . . should be viewed as distinct target audiences that require different approaches and strategies.

Jeffrey P. Davidson, marketing consultant
Management World, September/October 1987

What Happens as Time Passes

He had made a fortune in business and owed it to being able to see the truth in any situation.

Ethan Canin, *Emperor of the Air*

Most jobs are *created* for people: Most interviewers don't know clearly what they will want the new person to do. Yet job hunters expect the hiring manager to tell them exactly what the job will be like and get annoyed when the manager can't tell them.

Generally the job description depends on who will be in the job. Therefore, help the hiring manager figure out what the new person should do. If you don't help him, another job hunter will. This is called *negotiating the job*. You are trying to remove all of the company's objections to hiring you, as well as all of *your* objections to working for them. Try to make it work for both of you. But time is your enemy. Imagine what happens in the hiring process as time passes:

You have an interview. When I, your coach, ask how it went, you tell me how great it was: The two of you hit it off and you are sure you will be called back. You see this interview as something frozen in time and you wait for the magical phone call.

But after you left, the manager met with someone else who brought up new issues. Now his criteria for what he wants have changed somewhat and consequently, his impression of you has also changed. He was honest when he said he liked you, but things look different to him now. Perhaps you have what he needs to meet his new criteria or perhaps you could convince him that his new direction is wrong, but you don't know what is now on his mind.

You call to find out *how things are going*. He says he is still interviewing and will call you later when he has decided. Actually, then it will probably be too late for you. His thinking is constantly evolving as he meets with people. You were already out of the running. *Your call did nothing to influence his thinking*: You did not address his new concerns. You asked for a status report of where he was in the hiring process and that's what you got. You did nothing to get back in the loop of people he might consider or find out the new issues now on his mind.

The manager meets more people, and further defines the position. Interviewing helps him decide what he wants. You are getting further and further away from his new requirements.

You are not aware of this. You remember the great meeting you two had. You remind me that he said he really liked you. You insist on freezing the moment in time. You don't want to do anything to rock the boat or appear desperate. You hope it works out. "The ball is in his court," you say. "I gave it my best. There's nothing I can do but wait." So you decide to give it more time . . . time to go wrong.

Annie: . . . *you want to give it time—*
Henry: *Yes—*
Annie: . . . *time to go wrong, change, spoil. Then you'll know it wasn't the real thing.*

Tom Stoppard, *The Real Thing*

You have to imagine what is going on as time passes. Perhaps the hiring manager is simply very busy and is not working on this at all. Or perhaps things are moving along without you. Statistics prove that the person who is interviewed last has the best chance of being hired. That's because the last person benefits from all the thinking the manager has done. The manager is able to discuss all of the issues of concern with this final applicant.

What You Can Do During the Interview

Boone smiled and nodded. The muscles in his jaw hurt. "What I meant was did you ever shoot anybody but your own self. Not that that don't count."

Pete Dexter, *Deadwood*

If you go into an interview with the goal of getting a job, you are putting too much pressure on yourself to come to closure. When you walk away without an offer, you feel discouraged. When you walk away without even knowing what the job is, you feel confused and lost.

Instead of criticizing managers who do not know what they want, try to understand them: "I can understand that there are a number of ways you can structure this position. Let's talk about your problems and your needs. Perhaps I can help."

Your goal in the interview is not to get an offer, but to build a relationship with the manager. This means you are on the manager's side—assessing the situation and figuring out how to move the process along so you can continue to help define the job.

Pay Attention to Your Competition

Most job hunters think only about themselves and the hiring manager. They don't think about the others being considered for the position. But you are different. You are acutely aware at all times that you have competition. Your goal is to get rid of them.

As you move the process along, you can see your competitors dropping away because you are doing a better job of addressing the hiring manager's needs, coming up with solutions to his problems and showing more interest and more competence than they do.

You are in a problem-solving mode. Here's the way you think: "My goal isn't to get a job immediately but to build a relationship. How can I build a relationship so someday when this person decides what he or she wants, it'll be me?" You have hung in there. You have eliminated your competition. You have helped define the job in a way that suits both you and the hiring manager. You have the option of saying, "Do I want this job or don't I?"

Without competitors there would be no need for strategy.

Kenichi Ohmae, *The Mind of the Strategist*

The
Five
O'Clock
Club

Starting Out on the Right Foot in Your New Job

It is not the critic who counts; not the man who points out how the strong man stumbled or where the doer of deeds could have done better.
The credit belongs to the man who is actually in the arena, whose face is marred by dust and sweat and blood; who strives valiantly; who errs and comes short again and again; who knows the great enthusiasms, the great devotions; who spends himself in a worthy cause; who, at best, knows in the end the triumph of achievement, and who, at worst, if he fails, at least fails while daring greatly, so that his place shall never be with those timid souls who knew neither victory nor defeat.

Theodore Roosevelt

Starting out can be tricky: You are *on board* but *the jury is still out* on you. It is a time of trial. You are often being watched to see if you will work out. Here are some things you need to do to start out on the right foot and keep moving in the right direction.

Before You Start

- Say thank you. Contact all the people who helped you get the new position. Often people don't make this effort because they feel they'll be in the new job for a long time. But today, when the average American changes jobs every four years, the odds are you're going to change jobs again soon. You need to keep up those contacts.

Then think about ways to keep in touch with these contacts—if you read something that someone on your list would appreciate, clip it and send it.

Right Away

- Don't fix things or do anything *big* for the first three months. That is one of the biggest mistakes people make. Take time to learn the system, the people, and the culture.

  You cannot possibly understand, in those first months, the implications of certain decisions you may make. You may be criticizing a project done by someone really important. Or you could be changing something that will affect someone on the staff in ways of which you aren't aware.

- Make yourself productive immediately. This does not contradict the point I just made. Do things that are safe. For example, install a new system where there has been none. This is "safe" because you aren't getting rid of some other system. What isn't safe? Firing half your staff the first week!

- Introduce yourself to everybody. Be visible— walk around and meet people as soon as possible, including those who work for you. Meet everybody. Too many managers meet only the *important* people while ignoring those who will actually do the day-to-day work.

- Don't make friends too fast. Someone who befriends you right away could also be on the way out. That doesn't mean you shouldn't be friendly, however. Go to lunch with several people rather than becoming known as someone who associates only with so-and-so. Get to know everybody and then decide with whom to get closer.

> **Try not to do anything too daring for the first three months. Take time to learn the system.**

In the First Three Months

- Learn the corporate culture. People new to jobs often lose those jobs because of personality conflicts rather than a lack of competence.

  Keep your head low until you learn how the company operates. Some companies have certain writing styles. Some expect you to speak a certain way. In certain companies, it's the way they hold parties. Do people work with their doors open or their doors shut?

  All those things are part of the culture, and they are unwritten. To learn them, you have to pay attention.

  Pay your dues before doing things at a variance with the corporate culture. After you build up some credits, you have more leeway. Let your personality emerge when you understand the company and after you have made some contributions.

- Learn the organizational structure—the real structure, not the one drawn on the charts. Ask your secretary to tell you who relates how with whom, who knows what, who thought of this project, who is important. You could be surprised.

- Find out what is important in your job. For example, when I coach people for a corpora-

tion, coaching is not the only important thing in my job. The people who come to me are sent by human resources so I must manage my relationship with human resources. It doesn't matter how good a coach I am if I don't maintain a good relationship with human resources.

- Pay attention to your peers. Your peers can prove as valuable to you as your boss and your subordinates. Do not try to impress them with your brilliance. That would be the kiss of death because you might cause envy and have a very large reputation to live up to. Instead, encourage them to talk to you. They know more than you do. They also know your boss. Look to them to teach you and in some cases protect you.

- Don't set up competition. Everyone brings something to the party and should be respected for his or her talent, no matter what their level. Find ways to show your respect by asking for their input on projects that require their expertise.

- Set precedents you want to keep. If you start out working 12-hour days, people will come to expect it of you—even if no one else is doing it. Then if you stop, people will wonder what's wrong.

> **Pay attention to your peers. Look to them to teach you and in some cases protect you.**

Three Months and Beyond

- Continue to develop contacts outside the company. If you need information for your job, sometimes the worst people to ask are your boss and the people around you. A network is also a tremendous resource to fall back on when your boss is busy—and you will seem resourceful, smart, and connected.

You'll be busy in your new job and may not keep up your outside contacts. In today's economy, that's a big mistake.

- Keep a hero file for yourself, a hanging file where you place written descriptions of all your successes. If you have to job hunt in a hurry, you'll be able to recall what you've done.

  You will also use it if you stay. If you want anything, whether it be a raise, a promotion, or responsibility for a particular project, you can use the file to build a case for yourself.

- Keep managing your career. Don't think, "I'll just take this job and do what they tell me,"

because you might get off on some tangent. Remember where you were heading and make sure your career keeps going that way.

Be proactive in moving toward your goal. Take on lots of assignments. If a project comes up that fits into your long-term plan, do it. If one doesn't fit into your plan, you can do it or you can say, "Oh, I'd love to do that, but I'm really busy." Make those kinds of choices all the time.

Know how to ask. There is nothing more difficult for some people. Nor for others, easier.

Baltasar Gracian, *The Art of Worldly Wisdom*

The
Five
O'Clock
Club

Thank-You Note
after Getting a Job

Someday soon you'll be able to write one of these too!

Vivian Belen
400 First Avenue
Dayton, Ohio 22090

May 8, 20XX

Mr. Ellis Chase
3450 Garden Place
Des Moines, Iowa 44466

Dear Ellis:

The happy news is that I have accepted a position in the Trustees Division. I'll be responsible for financial reporting and analysis, budgeting, and planning. I think it's a great match that will make good use of both my management skills and accounting experience and the environment is congenial and professional.

I really appreciated your interest in my job search. I very much enjoyed speaking with you about your career and I appreciated your advice and encouragement. The fact that you so willingly gave of your time meant a great deal to me and certainly was beneficial.

If I can reciprocate in some way, please feel free to be in touch with me. I will also be in contact with you in the months ahead. My new office is at 75 Rockfast Corner, Dayton, OH 22091. You can reach me at 200-555-1212.

Sincerely,

Vivian Belen

The
Five
O'Clock
Club

Epilogue

. . . the country demands bold, persistent experimentation. It is common sense to take a method and try it. If it fails, admit it frankly and try another. But above all, try something.

Franklin Delano Roosevelt,
speech, Atlanta, 1932

There is no one way to manage your career; one neat solution to career management cannot answer it all. There are many ways.

The results of what you do are neither good nor bad; they are simply results to be observed and thought about. They are indicators of the correctness of the direction you are pursuing; they are not indictments. They are not personal; they are the world's feedback on what you are doing. These results can keep you on track and if you look at them objectively, they should not throw you off track.

Information is not good or bad; it is simply information. Things are changing so fast that we each need all the relevant information we can get. We may tend to block out information we find threatening—but that is precisely the information we need. Knowing the truth of what is happening around us may help us decide how to take care of ourselves. The information is not out to harm us—it is simply there.

There is a path for you and you must look for it. Do not be stopped when others seem as though they are moving ahead. You, too, have a lot to offer: Just think about yourself and not them. You are on your own track. Put your energy into discovering what is special about you and then hold onto it.

You will be knocked down enough during your career. Don't knock yourself; push back. Push past the people who offer you discouragement. Find those nurturing souls who recognize your worth and encourage you.

To view your life as blessed does not require you to deny your pain. It simply demands a more complicated vision, one in which a condition or event is not either good or bad but is, rather, both good and bad, not sequentially but simultaneously.

Nancy Mairs (who has multiple sclerosis),
Carnal Acts

To be what we are, and to become what we are capable of becoming is the only end of life.

Robert Louis Stevenson

. . . [T]here are days when the result is so bad that no fewer than five revisions are required. In contrast, when I'm greatly inspired, only four revisions are needed.

John Kenneth Galbraith

Don't tell me the facts about yourself; tell me who you really are. When you are writing to someone, ask yourself, What am I really trying to say to this person? What would I say if this person were right here? You are writing to a real person and when your personality comes through and you say what you mean to say, your note is unique.

Read your work out loud. It will give you a sense of the timing, the flow. You will find out if it is readable. You will notice where it stumbles. Have someone else read it, too. Most people need an editor.

Take a few risks, but do so with some restraint. Don't be self-indulgent, but do let your personality seep through. You are not simply a *marketing professional with major banking experience.* You are *energetic with excellent training and a sense of stability.*

Pare down your writing. Get rid of the lines that have no energy. Think about getting rid of your first paragraph completely. Perhaps you wrote it just to warm up.

Write to make an impact, to influence the reader.

It is impossible to enjoy idling thoroughly unless one has plenty of work to do.

Jerome K. Jerome

Continue to manage your career or look for another job internally, but be easy on yourself. I worked on this book whenever I could, but some days I didn't feel like thinking, so I researched quotes or made a chart or organized my material. All these things made my writing easier—so I was always making progress.

The same can be applied to your internal career development. Some days you may research an industry or a number of companies or you may write a proposal or a follow-up note. But you have to spend most of your time out with people—just as I had to spend most of my time writing.

Career development takes practice, just as writing takes practice. I am not a professional writer and you are not a professional politician or internal job hunter. Neither of us, you or I, is per-fect. But we are each trying to understand the process. This understanding will make us each less anxious, and more patient, about what we are doing.

Develop tricks to nudge yourself along. Find someone to whom you can report your progress. Meet with a friend. Talking gives you perspective and the energy to keep on going.

Set goals for yourself. For example, aim at all times to be in contact, either in person or in writing, with six people who are in a position to influence your career. Keep in touch with these six people. Strive to add more people to your list, because others will drop off. Plan to continue to network even after you feel secure in a job. Make networking a part of your life.

Keep pushing even when you get afraid—especially when you get afraid. On the other hand, if you have been pushing nonstop for a while, take a break completely, relax, and then push again.

Get together with a friend and talk about your dreams. Talking about them makes them seem possible. And hearing yourself say them out loud tests how you really feel about them. Then you can discover the central dream—the one that will drive you.

Where I was born and how I have lived is unimportant.
It is what I have done with where I have been that should be of interest.

Georgia O'Keeffe

You will find endless resources inside yourself. Get inside yourself and find out what the dream is and then do it. Stir yourself up. Go for it.

The fact is: If you don't try, no one will care anyway. The only reason to do it is for yourself—so you can take your rightful place in the universe. The only reason to do it is that we each have our place and it seems a shame to be born and then to die without doing our part.

We are all controlled by the world
in which we live . . .
The question is this: are we to be controlled
by accidents, by tyrants, or by ourselves?

B. F. Skinner

The world is big. There are many options; some people try to investigate them all. Instead, begin with yourself. Understand that part. Then look at some options and test them against what you are. You can hold on to that as a sure thing. You can depend on what you are for stability.

I am larger, better than I thought,
I did not know I held so much goodness.

Walt Whitman

A former client called me today. When I first met him, he had been out of work for a year. Now he was calling, a few years later, to say he had received a big promotion at his company. He has found his niche and has never been happier. Everyone notices it. And he keeps on networking—keeps on enjoying the process. He's working hard to stay where he is.

The world keeps changing. It won't stop. We must change, too. We are the dreamers of dreams.

We are the music-makers,
And we are the dreamers of dreams . . .
Yet we are the movers and shakers
of the world for ever, it seems.

Arthur O'Shaughnessy,
"Music and Moonlight"

Far better it is to dare mighty things, to win glorious triumphs, even though checkered by failure, than to take rank with those poor spirits who neither enjoy much nor suffer much, because they live in the gray twilight that knows not victory nor defeat.

Theodore Roosevelt

The
Five
O'Clock
Club

PART SIX

What Is The Five O'Clock Club?

AMERICA'S PREMIER CAREER-COACHING NETWORK

How to Join the Club

The Five O'Clock Club:
America's Premier
Career-Coaching
and
Outplacement Service

"One organization with a long record of success in helping people find jobs is The Five O'Clock Club."

Fortune

- Job-Search Strategy Groups
- Private Coaching
- Books and Audio CDs
- Membership Information
- When Your Employer Pays

THERE *IS* A FIVE O'CLOCK CLUB NEAR YOU!

For more information on becoming a member, please fill out the Membership Application Form in this book, sign up on the web at: www.fiveoclockclub.com, or call: **1-800-575-3587** (or **212-286-4500** in New York)

The Five O'Clock Club Search Process

The Five O'Clock Club process, as outlined in *The Five O'Clock Club* books, is a targeted, strategic approach to career development and job search. Five O'Clock Club members become proficient at skills that prove invaluable during their *entire working lives.*

Career Management

We train our members to *manage their careers* and always look ahead to their next job search. Research shows that an average worker spends only four years in a job—and will have 12 jobs in as many as 5 career fields—during his or her working life.

Getting Jobs . . . Faster

Five O'Clock Club members find *better jobs, faster.* The average professional, manager, or executive Five O'Clock Club member who regularly attends weekly sessions finds a job by his or her 10th session. Even the discouraged, long-term job searcher can find immediate help.

The keystone to The Five O'Clock Club process is teaching our members an understanding of the entire hiring process. A first interview is primarily a time for exchanging critical information. The real work starts *after* the interview. We teach our members *how to turn job interviews into offers* and to negotiate the best possible employment package.

Setting Targets

The Five O'Clock Club is action oriented. *We'll help you decide what you should do this very next week to move your search along.* By their third session, our members have set definite job targets by industry or company size, position, and geographic area, and are out in the field gathering information and making contacts that will lead to interviews with hiring managers.

Our approach evolves with the changing job market. We're able to synthesize information from hundreds of Five O'Clock Club members and come up with new approaches for our members. For example, we now discuss temporary placement for executives, how to use voice mail and the Internet, and how to network when doors are slamming shut all over town.

The Five O'Clock Club Strategy Program

The Five O'Clock Club meeting is a carefully planned *job-search strategy program*. We provide members with the tools and tricks necessary to get a good job fast—even in a tight market. Networking and emotional support are also included in the meeting.

Participate in 10 *consecutive* small-group strategy sessions to enable your group and career coach to get to know you and to develop momentum in your search.

Weekly Presentations via Audio CDs

Prior to each week's teleconference, listen to the assigned audio presentation covering part of The Five O'Clock Club methodology. These are scheduled on a rotating basis so you may join the Club at any time. (In selected cities, presentations are given in person rather than via audio CDs.)

Small-Group Strategy Sessions

During the first few minutes of the teleconference, your small group discusses the topic of the week and hears from people who have landed jobs. Then you have the chance to get feedback and advice on your own search strategy, listen to and learn from others, and build your network. All groups are led by trained career coaches with years of experience. The small group is generally no more than six to eight people, so everyone gets the chance to speak up.

Let us consider how we may spur one another on toward love and good deeds. Let us not give up meeting together, as some are in the habit of doing, but let us encourage one another.

Hebrews 10:24–25

Private Coaching

You may meet with your small-group coach—or another coach—for private coaching by phone or in person. A coach helps you develop a career path, solve current job problems, prepare your résumé, or guide your search.

Many members develop long-term relationships with their coaches to get advice throughout their careers. If you are paying for the coaching yourself (as opposed to having your employer pay), please pay the coach directly (charges vary from $100 to $175 per hour). **Private coaching is *not* included in The Five O'Clock Club seminar or membership fee.** For coach matching, see our website or call **1-800-575-3587** (or **212-286-4500** in New York).

From the Club History, Written in the 1890s

At The Five O'Clock Club, [people] of all shades of political belief—as might be said of all trades and creeds—have met together. . . . The variety continues almost to a monotony. . . . [The Club's] good fellowship and geniality—not to say hospitality—has reached them all.

It has been remarked of clubs that they serve to level rank. If that were possible in this country, it would probably be true, if leveling rank means the appreciation of people of equal abilities as equals; but in The Five O'Clock Club it has been a most gratifying and noteworthy fact that no lines have ever been drawn save those which are essential to the honor and good name of any association. Strangers are invited by the club or by any members, [as gentlepeople], irrespective of aristocracy, plutocracy or occupation, and are so treated always. Nor does the thought of a [person's] social position ever enter into the meetings. People of wealth and people of moderate means sit side by side, finding in each other much to praise and admire and little to justify snarlishness or adverse criticism. People meet as people—not as the representatives of a set—and having so met, dwell not in worlds of envy or distrust, but in union and collegiality, forming kindly thoughts of each other in their heart of hearts.

In its methods, The Five O'Clock Club is plain, easy-going and unconventional. It has its "isms" and some peculiarities of procedure, but simplicity characterizes them all. The sense of propriety, rather than rules of order, governs its meetings, and that informality which carries with it sincerity of motive and spontaneity of effort, prevails within it. Its very name indicates informality, and, indeed, one of the reasons said to have induced its adoption was the fact that members or guests need not don their dress suits to attend the meetings, if they so desired. This informality, however, must be distinguished from the informality of Bohemianism. For The Five O'Clock Club, informality, above convenience, means sobriety, refinement of thought and speech, good breeding and good order. To this sort of informality much of its success is due.

Fortune, The New York Times, Black Enterprise, Business Week, NPR, CNBC and ABC-TV are some of the places you've seen, heard, or read about us.

The Schedule

See our website for the specific dates for each topic. All groups use a similar schedule in each time zone.

Fee: $49 annual membership (includes Beginners Kit, subscription to *The Five O'Clock News,* and access to the Members Only section of our website), **plus** session fees based on member's income (price for the Insider Program includes audio-CD lectures, which retails for $150).

Reservations required for first session. Unused sessions are transferable to anyone you choose or can be donated to members attending more than 16 sessions who are having financial difficulty.

The Five O'Clock Club's programs are geared to recent graduates, professionals, managers, and executives from a wide variety of industries and professions. Most earn from $30,000 to $400,000 per year. Half the members are employed; half are unemployed. *You will be in a group of your peers.*

To register, please fill out form on the web (at www.fiveoclockclub.com) or call 1-800-575-3587 (or 212-286-4500 in New York).

Lecture Presentation Schedule

- History of The 5OCC
- The 5OCC Approach to Job Search
- Developing New Targets for Your Search

- Two-Minute Pitch: Keystone of Your Search
- Using Research and the Internet for Your Search
- The Keys to Effective Networking
- Getting the Most Out of Your Contacts
- Getting Interviews: Direct/Targeted Mail
- Beat the Odds When Using Search Firms and Ads
- Developing New Momentum in Your Search
- The 5OCC Approach to Interviewing
- Advanced Interviewing Techniques
- How to Handle Difficult Interview Questions
- How to Turn Job Interviews into Offers
- Successful Job Hunter's Report

- Four-Step Salary-Negotiation Method

All groups run continuously. Dates are posted on our website. The textbooks used by all members of The Five O'Clock Club may be ordered on our website or purchased at major bookstores.

The original Five O'Clock Club was formed in Philadelphia in 1883. It was made up of the leaders of the day who shared their experiences "in a spirit of fellowship and good humor."

The Five O'Clock Club

Questions You May Have about the Weekly Job-Search Strategy Group

Job hunters are not always the best judges of what they need during a search. For example, most are interested in lectures on answering ads on the Internet or working with search firms. We cover those topics, but strategically they are relatively unimportant in an effective job search.

At The Five O'Clock Club, you get the information you really need in your search—*such as how to target more effectively, how to get more interviews, and how to turn job interviews into offers.*

What's more, you will work in a small group with the best coaches in the business. In these strategy sessions, your group will help you decide what to do, this week and every week, to move your search along. You will learn by being coached and by coaching others in your group.

We find ourselves not independently of other people and institutions but through them. We never get to the bottom of our selves on our own. We discover who we are face to face and side by side with others in work, love, and learning.

Robert N. Bellah, et al., *Habits of the Heart*

Here are a few other points:

- For best results, attend on a regular basis. Your group gets to know you and will coach you to eliminate whatever you may be doing wrong— or refine what you are doing right.

- The Five O'Clock Club is a members-only organization. To get started in the small-group teleconference sessions, you must purchase a minimum of 10 sessions.

- The teleconference sessions include the set of 16 audio-CD presentations on Five O'Clock Club methodology. In-person groups do not include CDs.

- After that, you may purchase blocks of 5 or 10 sessions.

- We sell multiple sessions to make administration easier.

- If you miss a session, you may make it up any time. You may even transfer unused time to a friend.

- Although many people find jobs quickly (even people who have been unemployed a long time), others have more difficult searches. Plan to be in it for the long haul and you'll do better.

Carefully read all of the material in this section. It will help you decide whether or not to attend.

- The first week, pay attention to the strategies used by the others in your group. Soak up all the information you can.

- Read the books before you come in the second week. They will help you move your search along.

To register:

1. Read this section and fill out the application.

2. After you become a member and get your Beginners Kit, call to reserve a space for the first time you attend.

To assign you to a career coach, we need to know:

- your current (or last) field or industry
- the kind of job you would like next (if you know)
- your desired salary range in general terms

For private coaching, we suggest you attend the small group and ask to see your group leader, to give you continuity.

The Five O'Clock Club is plain, easy-going and unconventional. . . . Members or guests need not don their dress suits to attend the meetings.

(From the Club History, written in the 1890s)

What Happens at the Meetings?

Each week, job searchers from various industries and professions meet in small groups. The groups specialize in professionals, managers, executives, or recent college graduates. Usually, half are employed and half are unemployed.

The weekly program is in two parts. First, there is a lecture on some aspect of The Five O'Clock Club methodology. Then, job hunters meet in small groups headed by senior full-time professional career coaches.

The first week, get the textbooks, listen to the lecture, and get assigned to your small group. During your first session, *listen* to the others in your group. You learn a lot by listening to how your peers are strategizing *their* searches.

By the second week, you will have read the materials. Now we can start to work on *your* search strategy and help *you* decide what to do next to move your search along. For example, we'll help you figure out how to get more interviews in your target area or how to turn interviews into job offers.

In the third week, you will see major progress made by other members of your group and you may notice major progress in your own search as well.

By the third or fourth week, most members are conducting full and effective searches. Over the remaining weeks, you will tend to keep up a full search rather than go after only one or two leads. You will regularly aim to have 6 to 10 things *in the works* at all times. These will generally be in specific target areas you have identified, will keep your search on target, and will increase your chances of getting multiple job offers from which to choose.

Those who stick with the process find it works.

Some people prefer to just listen for a few weeks before they start their job search and that's okay, too.

How Much Does It Cost?

It is against the policy of The Five O'Clock Club to charge individuals heavy up-front fees. Our competitors charge $4,000 to $6,000 or more, up front. Our average fee is $360 for 10 sessions (which includes audio CDs of 16 presentations for those in the teleconference program). Those in the $100,000+ range pay an average of $540 for 10 sessions. For administrative reasons, we charge for 5 or 10 additional sessions at a time.

You must have the books so you can begin studying them before the second session. (You can purchase them on our website or at major bookstores.) If you don't do the homework, you will tend to waste the time of others in the group by asking questions covered in the texts.

Is the Small Group Right for Me?

The Five O'Clock Club process is for you if:

- You are truly interested in job hunting.
- You have *some* idea of the kind of job you want.
- You are a professional, manager, or executive—or want to be.
- You want to participate in a group process on a regular basis.

- You realize that finding or changing jobs and careers is hard work, but you are absolutely willing and able to do it.

If you have no idea about the kind of job you want next, you may attend one or two group sessions to start. *Then* see a *coach privately* for one or two sessions, develop tentative job targets, and return to the group. You may work with your small-group coach or contact us through our website or by calling **1-800-575-3587** (or **212-286-4500** in New York) for referral to another coach.

How Long Will It Take Me to Get a Job?

Although our members tend to be from fields or industries where they expect to have difficult searches, *the average person who attends regularly finds a new position within 10 sessions.* Some take less time and others take more.

One thing we know for sure: **Research shows that those who get *regular* coaching during their searches get jobs faster and at higher rates of pay than those who search on their own or simply take a course.** This makes sense. If a person comes only when they think they have a problem, they are usually wrong. They probably had a problem a few weeks ago but didn't realize it. Or the problem may be different from the one they thought they had. Those who come regularly benefit from the observations others make about their searches. Problems are solved before they become severe or are prevented altogether.

Those who attend regularly also learn a lot by paying attention and helping others in the group. This *secondhand* learning can shorten your search by weeks. When you hear the problems of others who are ahead of you in the search, you can avoid them completely. People in your group will come to know you and will point out subtleties you may not have noticed that interviewers will never tell you.

Will I Be with Others from My Field/Industry?

Probably, but it's not that important. If you are a salesperson, for example, would you want to be with seven other salespeople? Probably not. You will learn a lot and have a much more creative search if you are in a group of people who are in your general salary range but not exactly like you. Our clients are from virtually every field and industry. The *process* is what will help you.

We've been doing this since 1978 and understand your needs. That's why the mix we provide is the best you can get.

Career Coaching Firms Charge $4,000–$6,000 Up Front. How Can You Charge Such a Small Fee?

1. We have no advertising costs, because 90 percent of those who attend have been referred by other members.

   A hefty up-front fee would bind you to us, but we have been more successful by treating people ethically and having them pretty much *pay as they go.*

   We need a certain number of people to cover expenses. When lots of people get jobs quickly and leave us, we could go into the red. But as long as members refer others, we will continue to provide this service at a fair price.

2. We focus strictly on *job-search strategy,* and encourage our clients to attend free support groups if they need emotional support. We focus on getting *jobs,* which reduces the time clients spend with us and the amount they pay.

3. We attract the best coaches, and our clients make more progress per session than they would elsewhere, which also reduces their costs.

4. We have expert administrators and a sophisticated computer system that reduces our overhead and increases our ability to track your progress.

May I Change Coaches?

Yes. Great care is taken in assigning you to your initial coach. However, if you want to change once for any reason, you may do it. We don't encourage group hopping: It is better for you to stick with a group so that everyone gets to know you. On the other hand, we want you to feel comfortable. So if you tell us you prefer a different group, you will be transferred immediately.

What If I Have a Quick Question Outside of the Group Session?

Some people prefer to see their group coach privately. Others prefer to meet with a different coach to get another point of view. Whatever you decide, remember that the group fee does *not* cover coaching time outside the group session. Therefore, if you wanted to speak with a coach between sessions—even for *quick questions*—you would normally meet with the coach first for a private session so he or she can get to know you better. *Easy, quick questions* are usually more complicated than they appear. After your first private session, some coaches will allow you to pay in advance for one hour of coaching time, which you can then use for quick questions by phone (usually a 15-minute minimum is charged). Since each coach has an individual way of operating, find out how the coach arranges these things.

What If I Want to Start My Own Business?

The process of becoming a consultant is essentially the same as job hunting and lots of consultants attend Five O'Clock Club meetings. However, if you want to buy a franchise or existing business or start a growth business, you should see a private coach.

How Can I Be Sure That The Five O'Clock Club Small-Group Sessions Will Be Right for Me?

Before you actually participate in any of the small-group sessions, you can get an idea of the quality of our service by listening to all 16 audio CDs that you purchased. If you are dissatisfied with the CDs for any reason, return the package within 30 days for a full refund.

Whatever you decide, just remember: *It has been proven that those who receive regular help during their searches get jobs faster and at higher rates of pay than those who search on their own or simply attend a course.* If you get a job just one or two weeks faster because of this program, it will have more than paid for itself. And you may *transfer unused sessions to anyone you choose.* However, the person you choose must be or become a member.

The
Five
O'Clock
Club

When Your Employer Pays

*D*oes your employer care about you and others *whom they ask to leave the organization?* If so, ask them to consider The Five O'Clock Club for your outplacement help. The Five O'Clock Club puts you and your job search first, offering a career-coaching program of the highest quality at the lowest possible price to your employer.

Over 25 Years of Research

The Five O'Clock Club was started in 1978 as a research-based organization. Job hunters tried various techniques and reported their results back to the group. We developed a variety of guidelines so job hunters could choose the techniques best for them.

The methodology was tested and refined on professionals, managers, and executives (and those aspiring to be) from all occupations. Annual salaries ranged from $30,000 to $400,000; 50 percent were employed and 50 percent were unemployed.

Since its beginning, The Five O'Clock Club has tracked trends. Over time, our advice has changed as the job market has changed. What worked in the past is insufficient for today's job market. Today's Five O'Clock Club promotes all our relevant original strategies—and so much more.

As an employee-advocacy organization, The Five O'Clock Club focuses on providing the services and information that the job hunter needs most.

Get the Help You Need Most: 100 Percent Coaching

There's a myth in outplacement circles that a terminated employee just needs a desk, a phone, and minimal career coaching. **Our experience clearly shows that downsized workers need qualified, reliable coaching more than anything else.**

Most traditional outplacement packages last only 3 months. The average executive gets office space and only 5 hours of career coaching during this time. Yet the service job hunters need most is the career coaching itself—not a desk and a phone.

Most professionals, managers, and executives are right in the thick of negotiations with prospective employers at the 3-month mark. Yet that is precisely when traditional outplacement ends, leaving job hunters stranded and sometimes ruining deals.

It is astonishing how often job hunters and employers alike are impressed by the databases of *job postings* claimed by outplacement firms. Yet only 10 percent of all jobs are filled through ads and another 10 percent are filled through search firms. Instead, direct contact and networking—done The Five O'Clock Club way—are more effective for most searches.

You Get a Safety Net

Imagine getting a package that protects you for a full year. Imagine knowing you can come back if your new job doesn't work out—even months later. Imagine trying consulting work if you like. If you later decide it's not for you, you can come back to The Five O'Clock Club.

We can offer you a safety net of one full year's career coaching because our method is so effective that few people actually need more than 10 weeks in our proven program. But you're protected for a year.

You'll Job Search with Those Who Are Employed—How Novel!

Let's face it. It can be depressing to spend your days at an outplacement firm where everyone is unemployed. At The Five O'Clock Club, half the attendees are working, and this makes the atmosphere cheerier and helps to move your search along.

What's more, you'll be in a small group of your peers, all of whom are using The Five O'Clock Club method. Our research proves that those who attend the small group regularly and use The Five O'Clock Club methods get jobs faster and at higher rates of pay than those who only work privately with a career coach throughout their searches.

So Many Poor Attempts

Nothing is sadder than meeting someone who has already been getting job-search *help*, but the wrong kind. They've learned the traditional techniques that are no longer effective. Most have poor résumés and inappropriate targets and don't know how to turn job interviews into offers.

You'll Get Quite a Package

You'll get up to 14 hours of private coaching—well in excess of what you would get at a traditional outplacement firm. You may even want to use a few hours after you start your new job.

And you get up to one full year of small-group career coaching. In addition, you get books, audio CDs, and other helpful materials.

To Get Started

The day your human resources manager calls us authorizing Five O'Clock Club outplacement, we will immediately ship you the books, CDs, and other materials and assign you to a private coach and a small group.

Then we'll monitor your search. Frankly, we care about you more than we care about your employer. And since your employer cares about you, they're glad we feel this way—because they know we'll take care of you.

What They Say about Us

The Five O'Clock Club product is much better, far more useful than my outplacement package.

Senior executive and Five O'Clock Club member

The Club kept the juices flowing. You're told what to do, what not to do. There were fresh ideas. I went through an outplacement service that, frankly, did not help. If they had done as much as the Five O'Clock Club did, I would have landed sooner.

Another member

When Your *Employer* Pays for The Five O'Clock Club, *You* Get:

- **Up to 14 hours of guaranteed private career coaching** to determine a career direction, develop a résumé, plan salary negotiations, etc. In fact, if you need a second opinion during your search, we can arrange that too.

- Up to **ONE YEAR of small-group teleconference coaching** (average about 5 or 6 participants in a group) headed by a senior Five O'Clock Club career consultant. That way, if you lose your next job, you can come back. Or if you want to try consulting work and then decide you **don't like it, you can come back**.

- **Two-year membership** in The Five O'Clock Club: Beginners Kit and two-year subscription to *The Five O'Clock News*.

- **The complete set of our four books** for professionals, managers, and executives who are in job search.

- **A boxed set of 16 audio CDs** of Five O'Clock Club presentations.

COMPARISON OF EMPLOYER-PAID PACKAGES

Typical Package	Traditional Outplacement	The Five O'Clock Club
Who is the client?	The organization	Job hunters. We are employee advocates. We always do what is in the best interest of job hunters.
The clientele	All are unemployed	Half of our attendees are unemployed; half are employed. There is an upbeat atmosphere; networking is enhanced.
Length/type of service	3 months, primarily office space	1 year, exclusively career coaching
Service ends	After 3 months—or *before* if the client lands a job or consulting assignment	After 1 full year, no matter what. You can return if you lose your next job, if your assignment ends, or if you need advice after starting your new job.
Small-group coaching	Sporadic for 3 months Coach varies	Every week for up to 1 year; same coach
Private coaching	5 hours on average	Up to 14 hours guaranteed (depending on level of service purchased)
Support materials	Generic manual	• 4 textbooks based on over 25 years of job-search research • 16 40-minute lectures on audio CDs • Beginners Kit of search information • 2-year subscription to the Five O'Clock Club magazine, devoted to career-management articles
Facilities	Cubicle, phone, computer access	None; use home phone and computer

The
Five
O'Clock
Club

The Way We Are

The Five O'Clock Club means sobriety, refinement of thought and speech, good breeding and good order. To this, much of its success is due. The Five O'Clock Club is easy-going and unconventional. A sense of propriety, rather than rules of order, governs its meetings.

J. Hampton Moore, *History of The Five O'Clock Club*
(written in the 1890s)

Just like the members of the original Five O'Clock Club, today's members want an ongoing relationship. George Vaillant, in his seminal work on successful people, found that "what makes or breaks our luck seems to be . . . our sustained relationships with other people." (George E. Vaillant, *Adaptation to Life,* Harvard University Press, 1995)

Five O'Clock Club members know that much of the program's benefit comes from simply showing up. Showing up will encourage you to do what you need to do when you are not here. And over the course of several weeks, certain things will become evident that are not evident now.

Five O'Clock Club members learn from each other: The group leader is not the only one with answers. The leader brings factual information to the meetings and keeps the discussion in line. But the answers to some problems may lie within you or with others in the group.

Five O'Clock Club members encourage each other. They listen, see similarities with their own situations, and learn from that. And they listen to see how they may help others. You may come across information or a contact that could help someone else in the group. Passing on that information is what we're all about.

If you are a new member here, listen to others to learn the process. And read the books so you will know the basics that others already know. When everyone understands the basics, this keeps the meetings on a high level, interesting, and helpful to everyone.

Five O'Clock Club members are in this together, but they know that ultimately they are each responsible for solving their own problems with God's help. Take the time to learn the process, and you will become better at analyzing your own situation, as well as the situations of others. You will be learning a method that will serve you the rest of your life, and in areas of your life apart from your career.

Five O'Clock Club members are kind to each other. They control their frustrations—because venting helps no one. Because many may be stressed, be kind and go the extra length to keep this place calm and happy. It is your respite from the world outside and a place for you to find comfort and FUN. Relax and enjoy yourself, learn what you can, and help where you can. And have a ball doing it.

There arises from the hearts of busy [people] a love of variety, a yearning for relaxation of thought as well as of body, and a craving for a generous and spontaneous fraternity.

J. Hampton Moore *History of The Five O'Clock Club*

The Five O'Clock Club

Lexicon Used at The Five O'Clock Club

Use The Five O'Clock Club lexicon as a shorthand to express where you are in your job search. It will focus you and those in your group.

I. Overview and Assessment

How many hours a week are you spending on your search?
Spend 35 hours on a full-time search, 15 hours on a part-time search.

What are your job targets?
Tell the group. A target includes industry or company size, position, and geographic area.

The group can help assess how good your targets are. Take a look at *Measuring Your Targets*.

How does your résumé position you?
The summary and body should make you look appropriate to your target.

What are your backup targets?
Decide at the beginning of the search before the first campaign. Then you won't get stuck.

Have you done the Assessment?
If your targets are wrong, everything is wrong. (Do the Assessment in *Targeting a Great Career*.) Or a counselor can help you privately to determine possible job targets.

II. Getting Interviews

How large is your target (e.g., 30 companies)? How many of them have you contacted?
Contact them all.

How can you get (more) leads?
You will not get a job through search firms, ads, networking, or direct contact. Those are techniques for getting interviews—job leads. Use the right terminology, especially after a person gets a job. Do not say, "How did you get the job?" if you really want to know "Where did you get the lead for that job?"

Do you have 6 to 10 things in the works?
You may want the group to help you land one job. After they help you with your strategy, they should ask, "How many other things do you have in the works?" If *none*, the group can brainstorm how you can get more things going: through search firms, ads, networking, or direct contact. Then you are more likely to turn the job you want into an offer because you will seem more valuable. What's more, 5 will fall away through no fault of your own. Don't go after only 1 job.

How's your Two-Minute Pitch?
Practice a *tailored* Two-Minute Pitch. Tell the group the job title and industry of the hiring manager they should pretend they are for a role-playing exercise. You will be surprised how good

the group is at critiquing pitches. (Practice a few weeks in a row.) Use your pitch to separate you from your competition.

You seem to be in Stage One (or Stage Two or Stage Three) of your search.

Know where you are. This is the key measure of your search.

Are you seen as an insider or an outsider?

See *How to Change Careers* for becoming an insider. If people are saying, "I wish I had an opening for someone like you," you are doing well in meetings. If the industry is strong, then it's only a matter of time before you get a job.

III. Turning Interviews into Offers

Do you want this job?

If you do not want the job, perhaps you want an offer, if only for practice. If you are not willing to go for it, the group's suggestions will not work.

Who are your likely competitors and how can you outshine and outlast them?

You will not get a job simply because "they liked me." The issues are deeper. Ask the interviewer: "Where are you in the hiring process? What kind of person would be your ideal candidate? How do I stack up?"

What are your next steps?

What are *you* planning to do if the hiring manager doesn't call by a certain date or what are you planning to do to assure that the hiring manager *does* call you?

Can you prove you can do the job?

Don't just take the *trust me* approach. Consider your competition.

Which job positions you best for the long run? Which job is the best fit?

Don't decide only on the basis of salary. You will most likely have another job after this. See which

job looks best on your résumé and will make you stronger for the next time. In addition, find a fit for your personality. If you don't *fit*, it is unlikely you will do well there. The group can help you turn interviews into offers and give you feedback on which job is best for you.

"Believe me, with self-examination and a lot of hard work with our coaches, you can find the job . . . you can have the career . . . you can live the life you've always wanted!"

Sincerely,
Kate Wendleton

Membership

As a member of The Five O'Clock Club, you get:

- A year's subscription to *The Five O'Clock News*—10 issues filled with information on career development and job-search techniques, focusing on the experiences of real people.

- Access to *reasonably priced* weekly seminars featuring individualized attention to your specific needs in small groups supervised by our senior coaches.

- Access to one-on-one coaching to help you answer specific questions, solve current job problems, prepare your résumé, or take an in-depth look at your career path. You choose the coach and pay the coach directly.

- An attractive Beginners Kit containing information based on over 25 years of research on who gets jobs . . . and why . . . that will enable you to improve your job-search techniques—immediately!

- The opportunity to exchange ideas and experiences with other job searchers and career changers.

All that access, all that information, all that expertise for the annual membership fee of only $49, plus seminar fees.

How to become a member—by mail or E-mail:

Send your name, address, phone number, how you heard about us, and your check for $49 (made payable to "The Five O'Clock Club") to The Five O'Clock Club, 300 East 40th Street - Suite 6L, New York, NY 10016, or sign up at www.fiveoclockclub.com.

We will immediately mail you a Five O'Clock Club Membership Card, the Beginners Kit, and information on our seminars followed by our magazine. Then, call **1-800-575-3587** (or **212-286-4500** in New York) or e-mail us (at info@fiveoclockclub.com) to:

- reserve a space for the first time you plan to attend, or
- be matched with a Five O'Clock Club coach.

Membership Application

The Five O'Clock Club

☐ **Yes! I want to become a member!**

I want access to the most effective methods for finding jobs, as well as for developing and managing my career.

I enclose my check for $49 for 1 year; $75 for 2 years, payable to *The Five O'Clock Club*. I will receive a Beginners Kit, a subscription to *The Five O'Clock News,* access to the Members' Only area on our website, and a network of career coaches. Reasonably priced seminars are held across the country.

Name: _____

Street Address: _____

City: _____ State: _____ Zip Code: _____

Work phone: (_____) _____

Home phone: (_____) _____

E-mail: _____

Date: _____

How I heard about the Club: _____

Navigating Your Career: Developing Your Plan, Manage Your Boss, Get Another Job Inside

The following *optional* information is for statistical purposes. Thanks for your help.

Salary range:

☐ under $30,000   ☐ $30,000–$49,999   ☐ $50,000–$74,999

☐ $75,000–$99,999   ☐ $100,000–$125,000   ☐ over $125,000

Age: ☐ 20–29   ☐ 30–39   ☐ 40–49   ☐ 50+

Gender: ☐ Male   ☐ Female

Current or most recent position/title: _____

Please send to:
Membership Director, The Five O'Clock Club,
300 East 40th St.-Suite 6L, New York, NY 10016

The original Five O'Clock Club® was formed in Philadelphia in 1893. It was made up of the leaders of the day who shared their experiences "in a setting of fellowship and good humor."

Index

About the Author

Kate Wendleton is a nationally syndicated columnist and a respected authority and speaker on career development, having appeared on the *Today Show,* CNN, CNBC, *The Larry King Show,* National Public Radio, and CBS, and in *The Economist, The New York Times, The Chicago Tribune, The Wall Street Journal, Fortune* magazine, *Business Week,* and other national media.

She has been a career coach since 1978, when she founded The Five O'Clock Club and developed its methodology to help job hunters and career changers of all levels in job-search strategy groups. This methodology is now used by branches of The Five O'Clock Club that meet weekly in the United States and Canada.

Kate also founded Workforce America, a not-for-profit affiliate of The Five O'Clock Club that ran for 10 years. It served adults in Harlem who were not yet in the professional or managerial ranks. Workforce America helped adults in Harlem move into better-paying, higher-level positions as they improved their educational level and work experience.

Kate founded, and directed for seven years, The Career Center at The New School for Social Research in New York. She also advises major corporations about employee career-development programs and coaches senior executives.

A former CFO of two small companies, she has 20 years of business-management experience in both manufacturing and service businesses.

Kate attended Chestnut Hill College in Philadelphia and received her MBA from Drexel University. She is a popular speaker for associations, corporations, and colleges.

When she lived in Philadelphia, Kate did long-term volunteer work for the Philadelphia Museum of Art, the Walnut Street Theatre Art Gallery, United Way, and the YMCA. Kate currently lives in Manhattan with her husband.

Kate Wendleton is the author of The Five O'Clock Club's four-part career-development and job-hunting series, among other books.

About The Five O'Clock Club and the "Fruytagie" Canvas

Five O'Clock Club members are special. We attract upbeat, ambitious, dynamic, intelligent people—and that makes it fun for all of us. Most of our members are professionals, managers, executives, consultants, and freelancers. We also include recent college graduates and those aiming to get into the professional ranks, as well as people in their 40s, 50s, and even 60s. Most members' salaries range from $25,000 to $400,000 (one-third of our members earn in excess of $100,000 a year). For those who cannot attend a Club, *The Five O'Clock Club Book Series* contains all of our methodologies—and our spirit.

The Philosophy of The Five O'Clock Club

The "Fruytagie" Canvas by Patricia Kelly, depicted here, symbolizes our philosophy. The original, which is actually 52.5" by 69" inches, hangs in the offices of The Five O'Clock Club in Manhattan. It is reminiscent of popular 16th century Dutch "fruytagie," or fruit tapestries, which depicted abundance and prosperity.

I was attracted to this piece because it seemed to fit the spirit of our people at The Five O'Clock Club. This was confirmed when the artist, who was not aware of what I did for a living, added these words to the canvas: "The garden is abundant, prosperous and magical." Later, it took me only 10 minutes to write the blank verse "The Garden of Life," because it came from my heart. The verse reflects our philosophy and describes the kind of people who are members of the Club.

I'm always inspired by Five O'Clock Clubbers. They show others the way through their quiet behavior . . . their kindness . . . their generosity . . . their hard work . . . under God's care.

We share what we have with others. We are in this lush, exciting place together—with our brothers and sisters—and reach out for harmony. The garden is abundant. The job market is exciting. And Five O'Clock Clubbers believe that there is enough for everyone.

About the Artist's Method

To create her tapestry-like art, Kelly developed a unique style of stenciling. She hand-draws and hand-cuts each stencil, both in the negative and positive for each image. Her elaborate technique also includes a lengthy multilayering process incorporating Dutch metal leaves and gilding, numerous transparent glazes, paints, and wax pencils.

Kelly also paints the back side of the canvas using multiple washes of reds, violets, and golds. She uses this technique to create a heavy vibration of color, which in turn reflects the color onto the surface of the wall against which the canvas hangs.

The canvas is suspended by a heavy braided silk cord threaded into large brass grommets inserted along the top. Like a tapestry, the hemmed canvas is attached to a gold-gilded dowel with finials. The entire work is hung from a sculpted wall ornament.

Our staff is inspired every day by the tapestry and by the members of The Five O'Clock Club. We all work hard—and have FUN! The garden *is* abundant—with enough for everyone.

We wish you lots of success in your career. We—and your fellow members of The Five O'Clock Club—will work with you on it.

—Kate Wendleton, President

The original Five O'Clock Club was formed in Philadelphia in 1883.
It was made up of the leaders of the day, who shared their experiences
"in a spirit of fellowship and good humor."

 **THE GARDEN OF LIFE IS abundant, prosperous and magical. ❦ In this garden, there is enough for everyone. ❦ Share the fruit and the knowledge ❦ Our brothers and we are in this lush, exciting place together. ❦ Let's show others the way. ❦ Kindness. Generosity. ❦ Hard work. ❦ God's care.**

Art: Fruytagie Wall Canvas © 1995 Patricia Kelly. Text: © 1995 Kate Wendleton, The Five O'Clock Club®
The Five O'Clock Club is a registered trademark.

The Five O'Clock Club Job-Search Series
for Professionals, Managers and Executives

THOMSON

DELMAR LEARNING

We'll take you through your entire career. 1. Start by understanding yourself and what you want in **Targeting a Great Career**. 2. *Package Yourself with a Targeted Résumé* done The Five O'Clock Club Way. 3. Then *Shortcut Your Job Search* by following our techniques for getting meetings. 4. Turn those interviews into offers with *Mastering the Job Interview* and *Winning the Money Game*. 5. Finally, do well in your new job with *Navigating Your Career*.

- Figure out what to do with your life and your career
- Develop a résumé that separates you from your competitors
- Shortcut your search by using the Internet and other techniques properly
- Learn how to turn those job interviews into job offers
- Use our Four-Step Salary Negotiation Method to get what you deserve

The Five O'Clock Club's Book Series has enabled thousands of professionals, managers, and executives to correct their job-search mistakes. Most who attend regularly and read our books–even those unemployed up to two years—have a new job within only ten weekly sessions.

Most people conduct a passive job search. Their approach is ordinary, non-directed, fragmented, and ineffective.

The Five O'Clock Club was started in 1978 as a research-based organization. The methodology was tested and refined on professionals, managers, and executives (and those aspiring to be)–from all occupations and economic levels.

Launching the Right Career

Now, students, recent grads, and those who want a career instead of a job can use the same techniques used by thousands of professionals, managers and executives. Get that internship, develop a resume that gets you interviews, and learn how to interview well.

Ever since the beginning, The Five O'Clock Club has tracked trends at every meeting at every at every location. Over time, our advice has changed as the job market has changed. What worked in the past is not always sufficient for today's job market. Today's Five O'Clock Club Book Series contains all the relevant old strategies–and so much more. The Five O'Clock Clubbers who do best read and re-read the books, marking them up and taking notes. Do the same and you will do better in your search.

Targeting a Great Career
ISBN: 1-4180-1504-0

Packaging Yourself: The Targeted Résumé
ISBN: 1-4180-1503-2

Shortcut Your Job Search: The Best Way to Get Meetings
ISBN: 1-4180-1502-4

Mastering the Job Interview and Winning the Money Game
ISBN: 1-4180-1500-8

Navigating Your Career: Develop Your Plan, Manage Your Boss, Get Another Job Inside
ISBN: 1-4180-1501-6

Launching the Right Career
ISBN: 1-4180-1505-9

258 pp., 7 3/8" x 9 1/4", softcover

About the Author:

Kate Wendleton is a nationally syndicated careers columnist and recognized authority on career development, having appeared on *The Today Show*, CNN, CNBC, *Larry King Live*, National Public Radio, CBS, and in the *New York Times, Chicago Tribune, Wall Street Journal, Fortune, Business Week,* and other national media. She has been a career coach since 1978 when she founded The Five O' Clock Club and developed its methodology to help job hunters and career changers at all levels. A former CFO of two small companies, Kate has twenty years of business experience, as well as an MBA.

www.delmarlearning.com

To place an order please call: (800) 347-7707 or fax: (859) 647-5963
Mailing Address: Thomson Distribution Center, Attn: Order Fulfillment, 10650 Toebben Dr., Independence, KY 41051